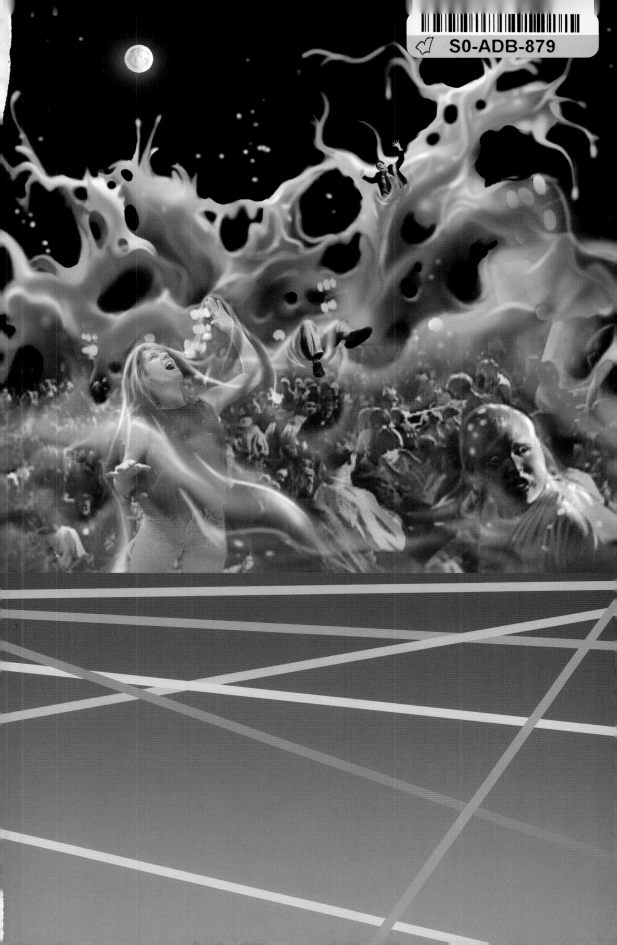

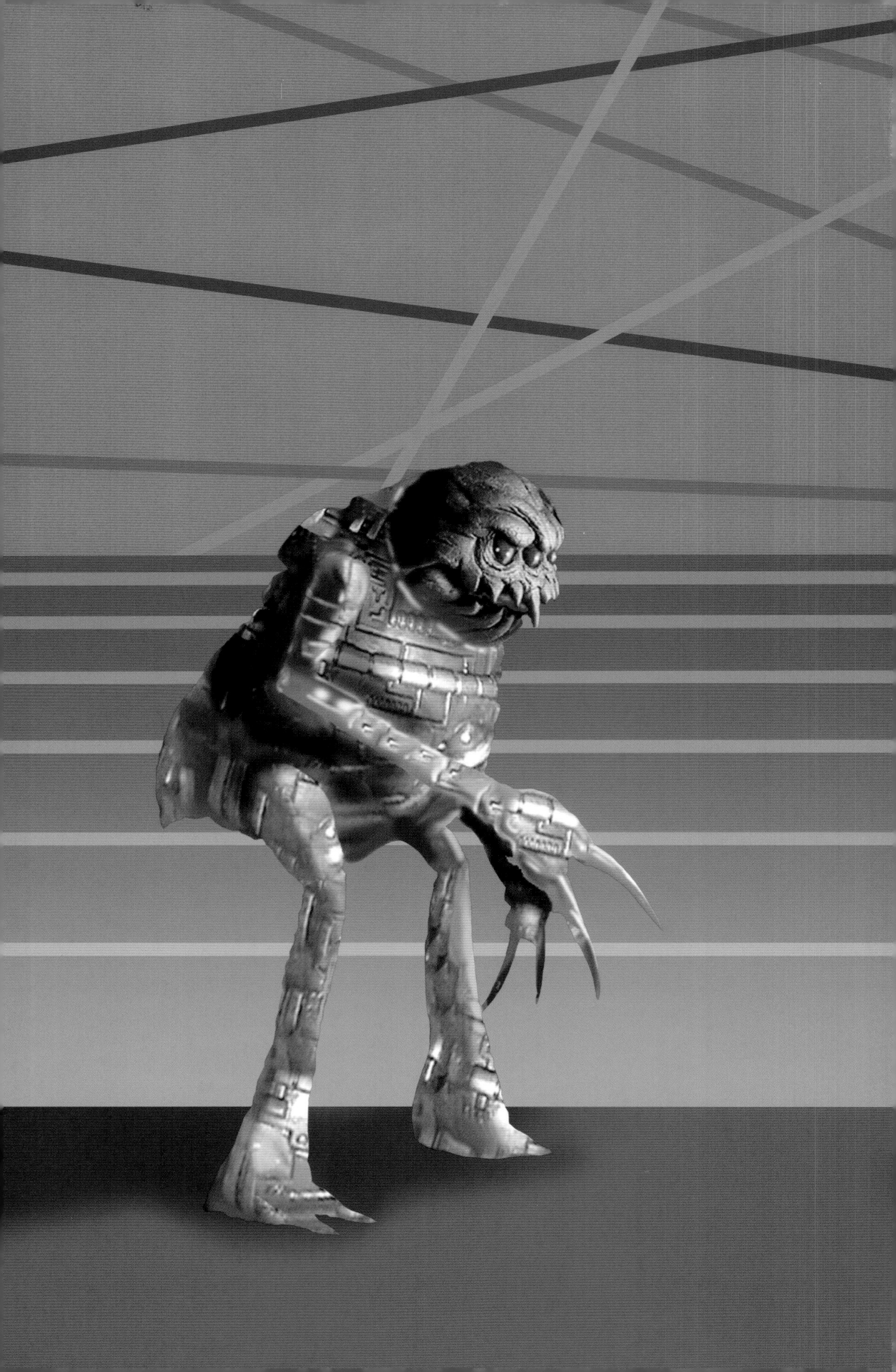

# PETE VON SHOLLY'S
# MORBID™
## 2
## DEAD BUT NOT OUT!

## by Pete Von Sholly

DARK HORSE BOOKS™

Publisher: Mike Richardson

Editor: Dave Land

Assistant Editor: Katie Moody

Designer: Amy Arendts

Art Director: Lia Ribacchi

**PETE VON SHOLLY'S MORBID 2 — DEAD BUT NOT OUT!**

Published by Dark Horse Books
A division of
Dark Horse Comics, Inc.
10956 SE Main Street
Milwaukie, OR 97222

www.darkhorse.com

To find a comics shop in your area call the Comic Shop Locator Service toll-free at (888) 266-4226

First edition: February 2005
ISBN: 1-59307-289-9

1 3 5 7 9 10 8 6 4 2
Printed in China

# OPERATING TABLE OF CONTENTS

# MORBID

**Welcome to the birth of another MORBID thing!**

**Please see the first MORBID for a normal introduction. I like to get a little artwork in once in a while along with all the photo stuff! Hope that's okay.  Yrs as always, PVS**

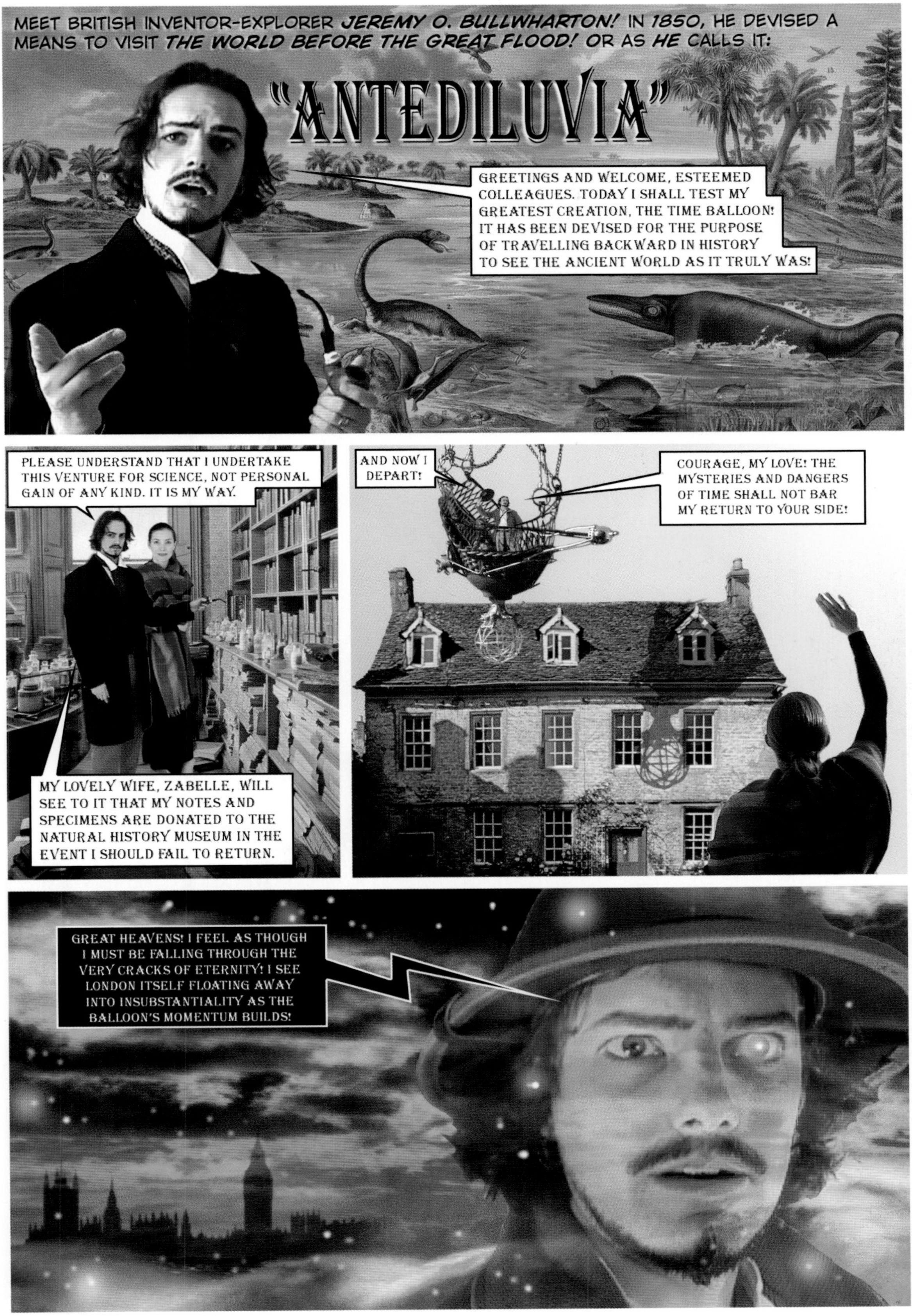
MEET BRITISH INVENTOR-EXPLORER JEREMY O. BULLWHARTON! IN 1850, HE DEVISED A MEANS TO VISIT THE WORLD BEFORE THE GREAT FLOOD! OR AS HE CALLS IT:
"ANTEDILUVIA"
GREETINGS AND WELCOME, ESTEEMED COLLEAGUES. TODAY I SHALL TEST MY GREATEST CREATION, THE TIME BALLOON! IT HAS BEEN DEVISED FOR THE PURPOSE OF TRAVELLING BACKWARD IN HISTORY TO SEE THE ANCIENT WORLD AS IT TRULY WAS!
PLEASE UNDERSTAND THAT I UNDERTAKE THIS VENTURE FOR SCIENCE, NOT PERSONAL GAIN OF ANY KIND. IT IS MY WAY.
MY LOVELY WIFE, ZABELLE, WILL SEE TO IT THAT MY NOTES AND SPECIMENS ARE DONATED TO THE NATURAL HISTORY MUSEUM IN THE EVENT I SHOULD FAIL TO RETURN.
AND NOW I DEPART!
COURAGE, MY LOVE! THE MYSTERIES AND DANGERS OF TIME SHALL NOT BAR MY RETURN TO YOUR SIDE!
GREAT HEAVENS! I FEEL AS THOUGH I MUST BE FALLING THROUGH THE VERY CRACKS OF ETERNITY! I SEE LONDON ITSELF FLOATING AWAY INTO INSUBSTANTIALITY AS THE BALLOON'S MOMENTUM BUILDS!

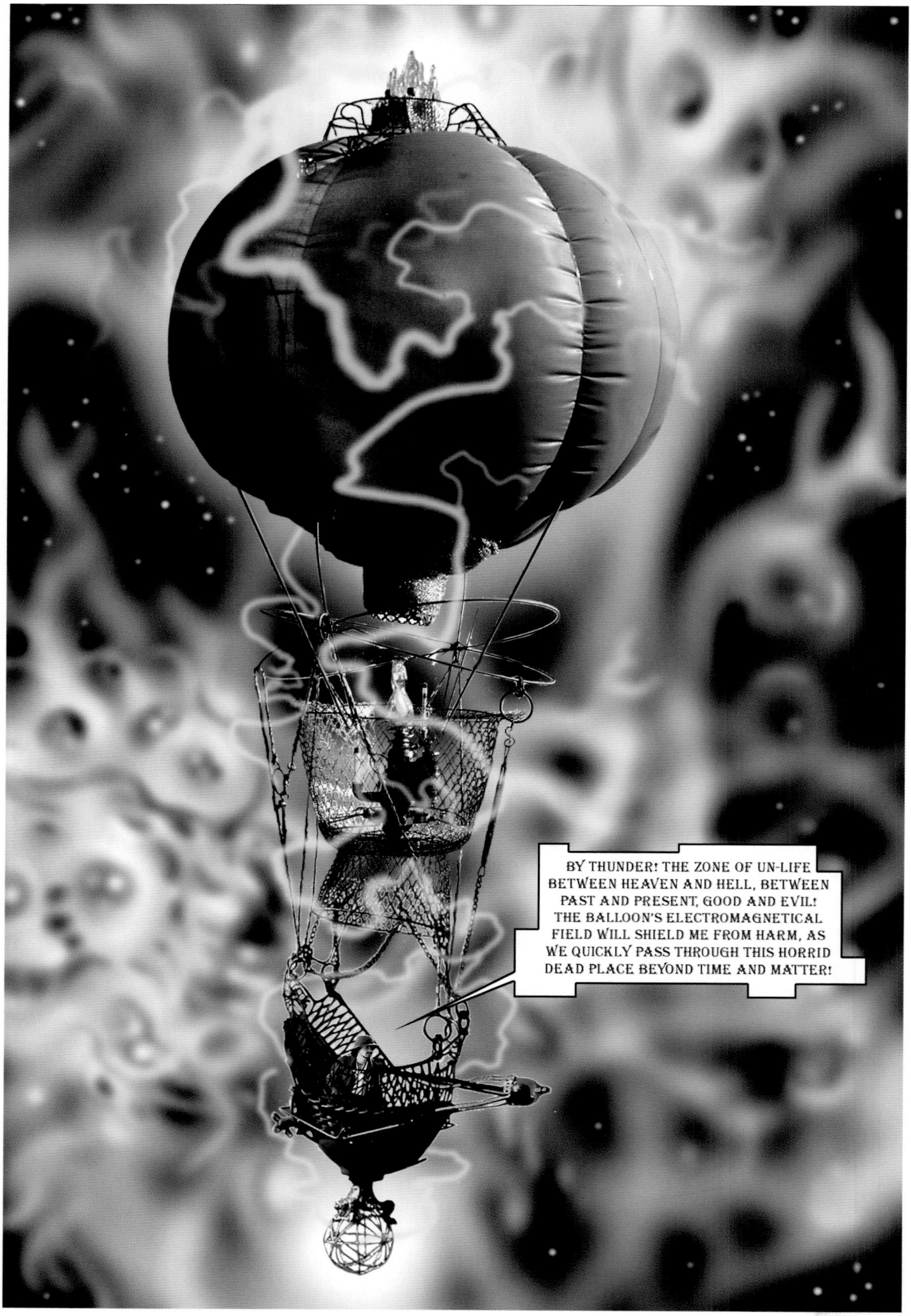
BY THUNDER! THE ZONE OF UN-LIFE BETWEEN HEAVEN AND HELL, BETWEEN PAST AND PRESENT, GOOD AND EVIL! THE BALLOON'S ELECTROMAGNETICAL FIELD WILL SHIELD ME FROM HARM, AS WE QUICKLY PASS THROUGH THIS HORRID DEAD PLACE BEYOND TIME AND MATTER!

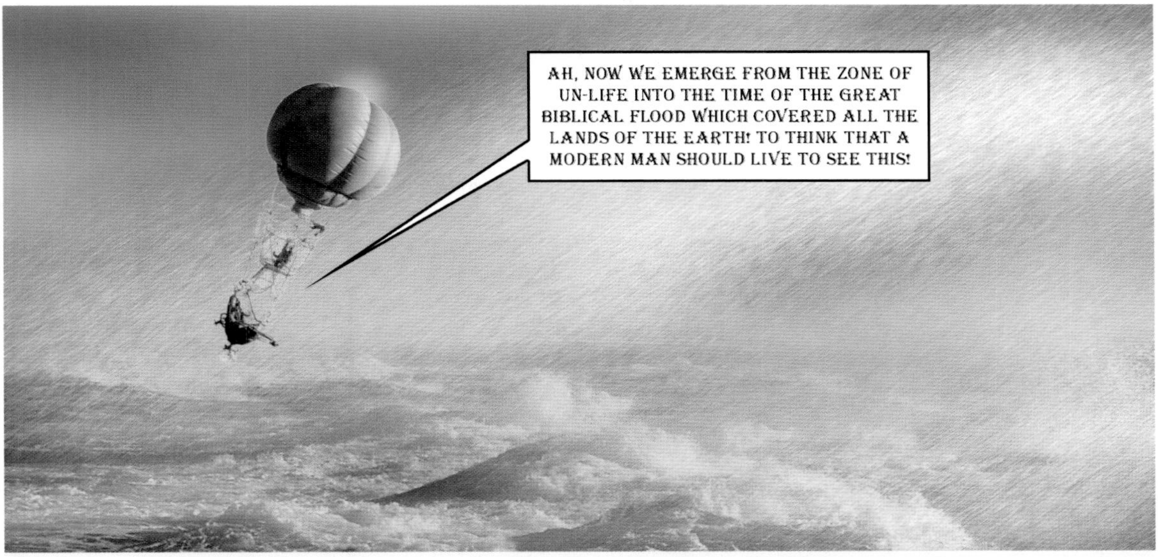
AH, NOW WE EMERGE FROM THE ZONE OF UN-LIFE INTO THE TIME OF THE GREAT BIBLICAL FLOOD WHICH COVERED ALL THE LANDS OF THE EARTH! TO THINK THAT A MODERN MAN SHOULD LIVE TO SEE THIS!

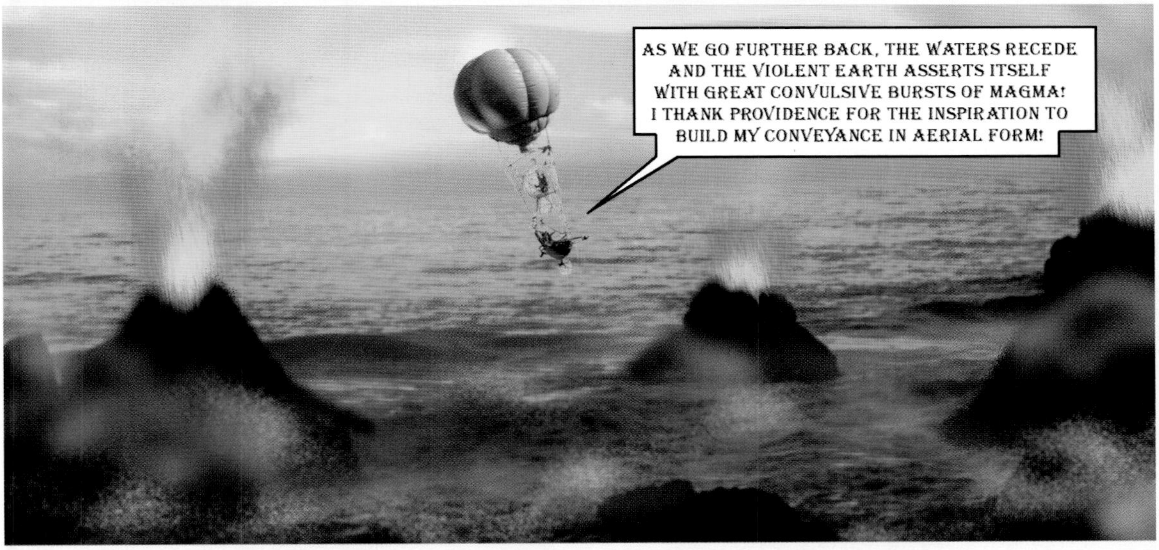
AS WE GO FURTHER BACK, THE WATERS RECEDE AND THE VIOLENT EARTH ASSERTS ITSELF WITH GREAT CONVULSIVE BURSTS OF MAGMA! I THANK PROVIDENCE FOR THE INSPIRATION TO BUILD MY CONVEYANCE IN AERIAL FORM!

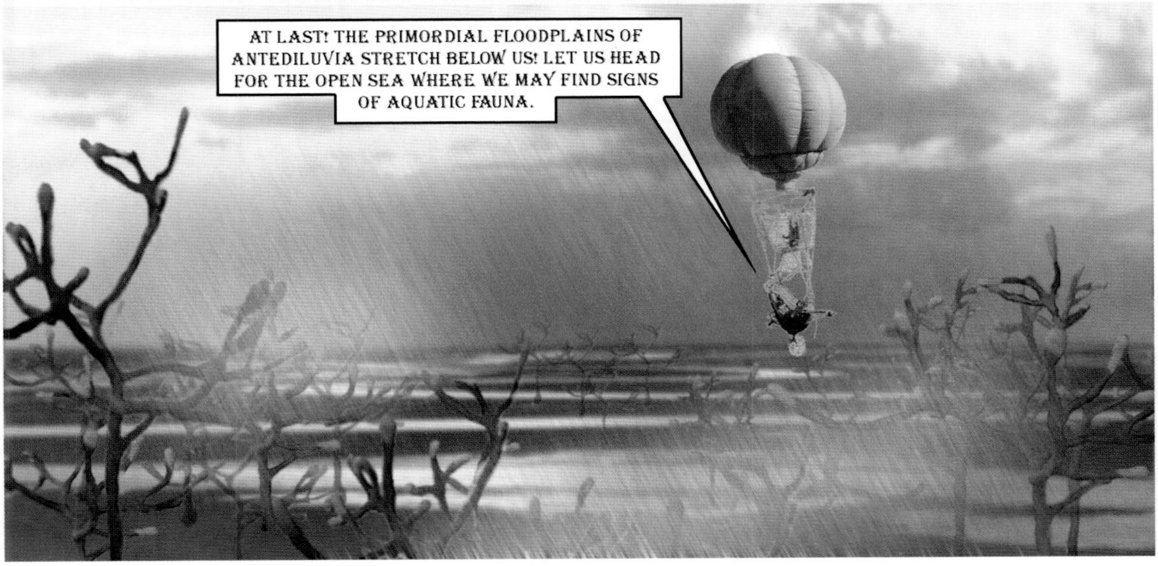
AT LAST! THE PRIMORDIAL FLOODPLAINS OF ANTEDILUVIA STRETCH BELOW US! LET US HEAD FOR THE OPEN SEA WHERE WE MAY FIND SIGNS OF AQUATIC FAUNA.

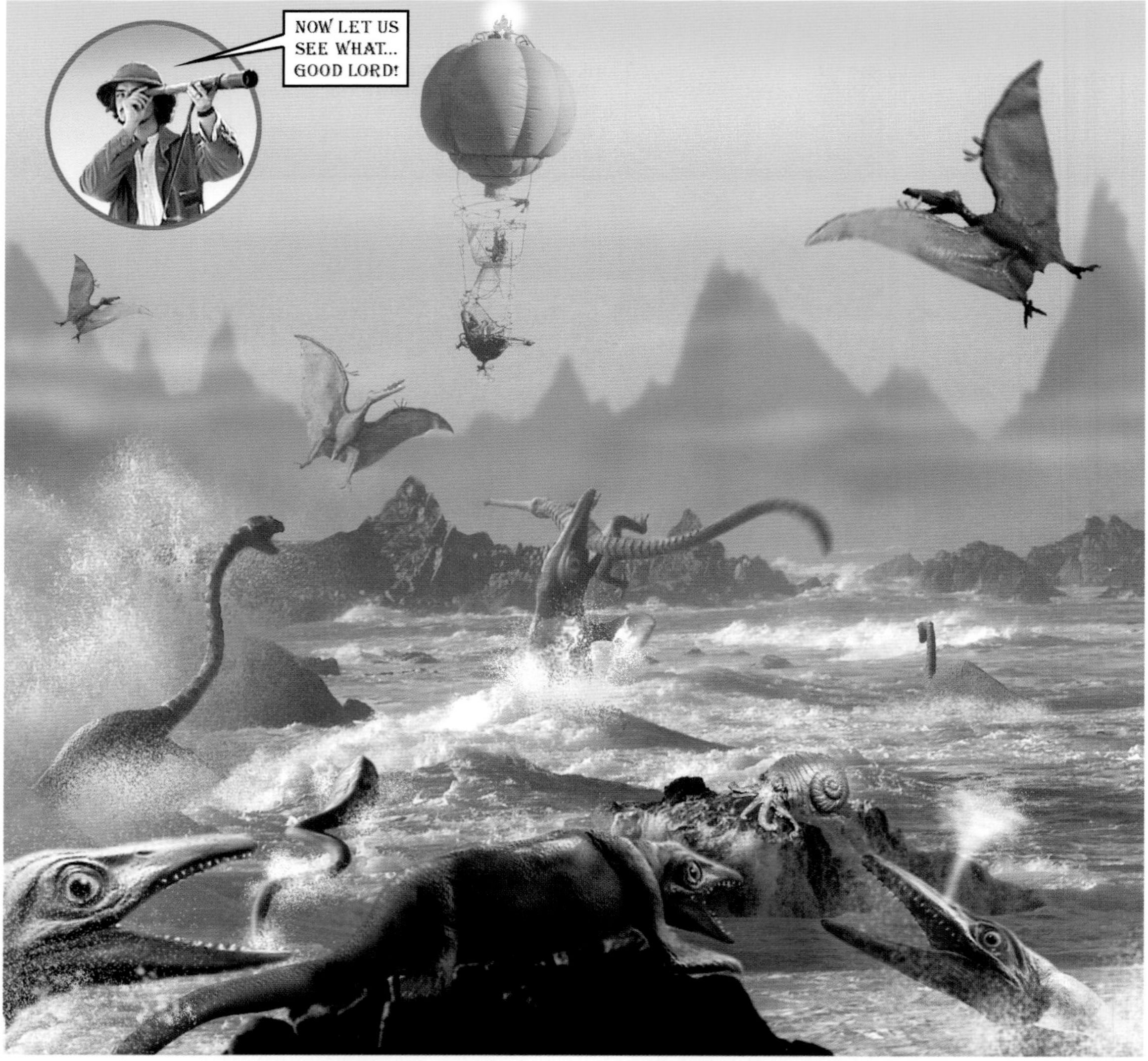
NOW LET US
SEE WHAT...
GOOD LORD!

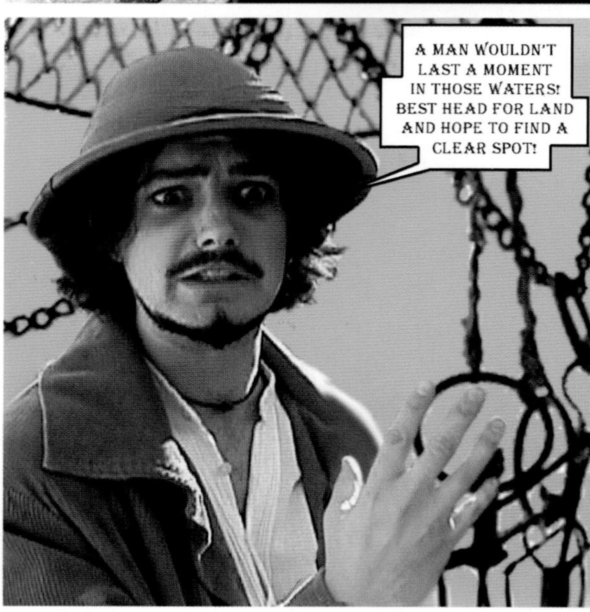
A MAN WOULDN'T LAST A MOMENT IN THOSE WATERS! BEST HEAD FOR LAND AND HOPE TO FIND A CLEAR SPOT!

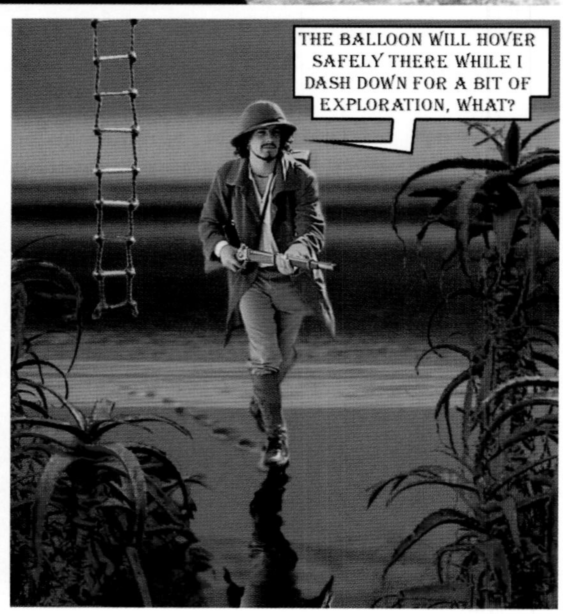
THE BALLOON WILL HOVER SAFELY THERE WHILE I DASH DOWN FOR A BIT OF EXPLORATION, WHAT?

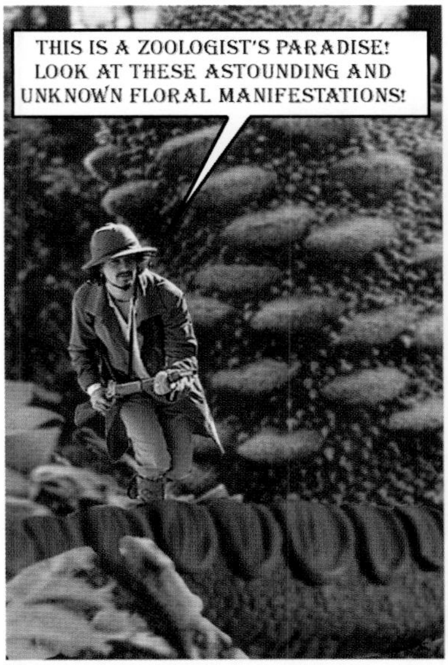
THIS IS A ZOOLOGIST'S PARADISE! LOOK AT THESE ASTOUNDING AND UNKNOWN FLORAL MANIFESTATIONS!

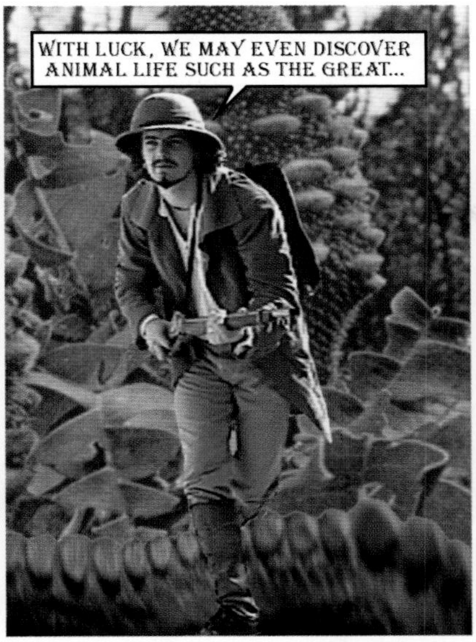
WITH LUCK, WE MAY EVEN DISCOVER ANIMAL LIFE SUCH AS THE GREAT...

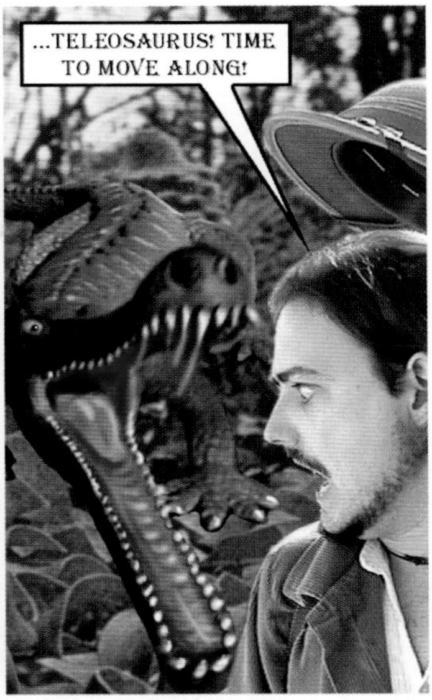
...TELEOSAURUS! TIME TO MOVE ALONG!

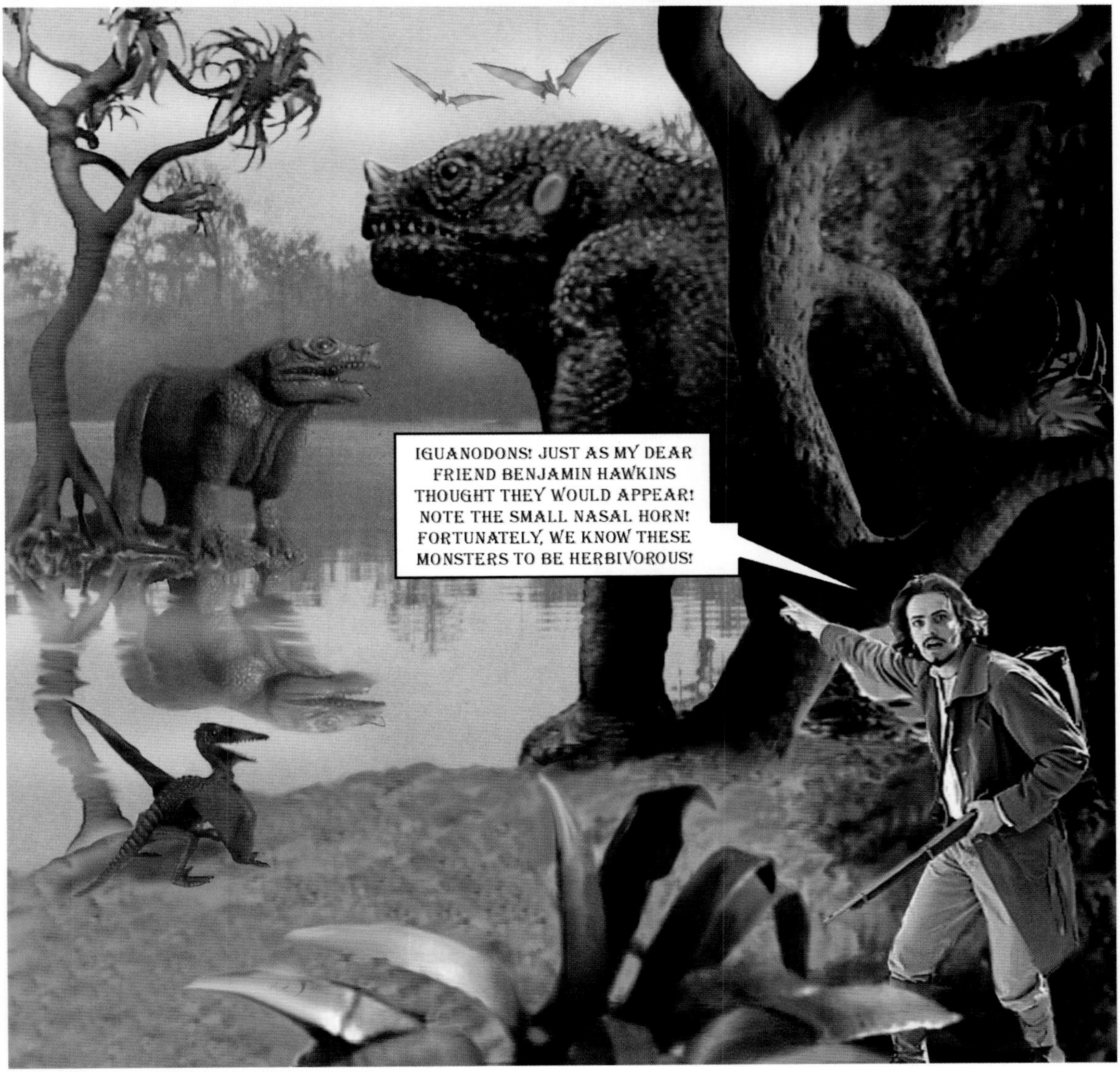
IGUANODONS! JUST AS MY DEAR FRIEND BENJAMIN HAWKINS THOUGHT THEY WOULD APPEAR! NOTE THE SMALL NASAL HORN! FORTUNATELY, WE KNOW THESE MONSTERS TO BE HERBIVOROUS!

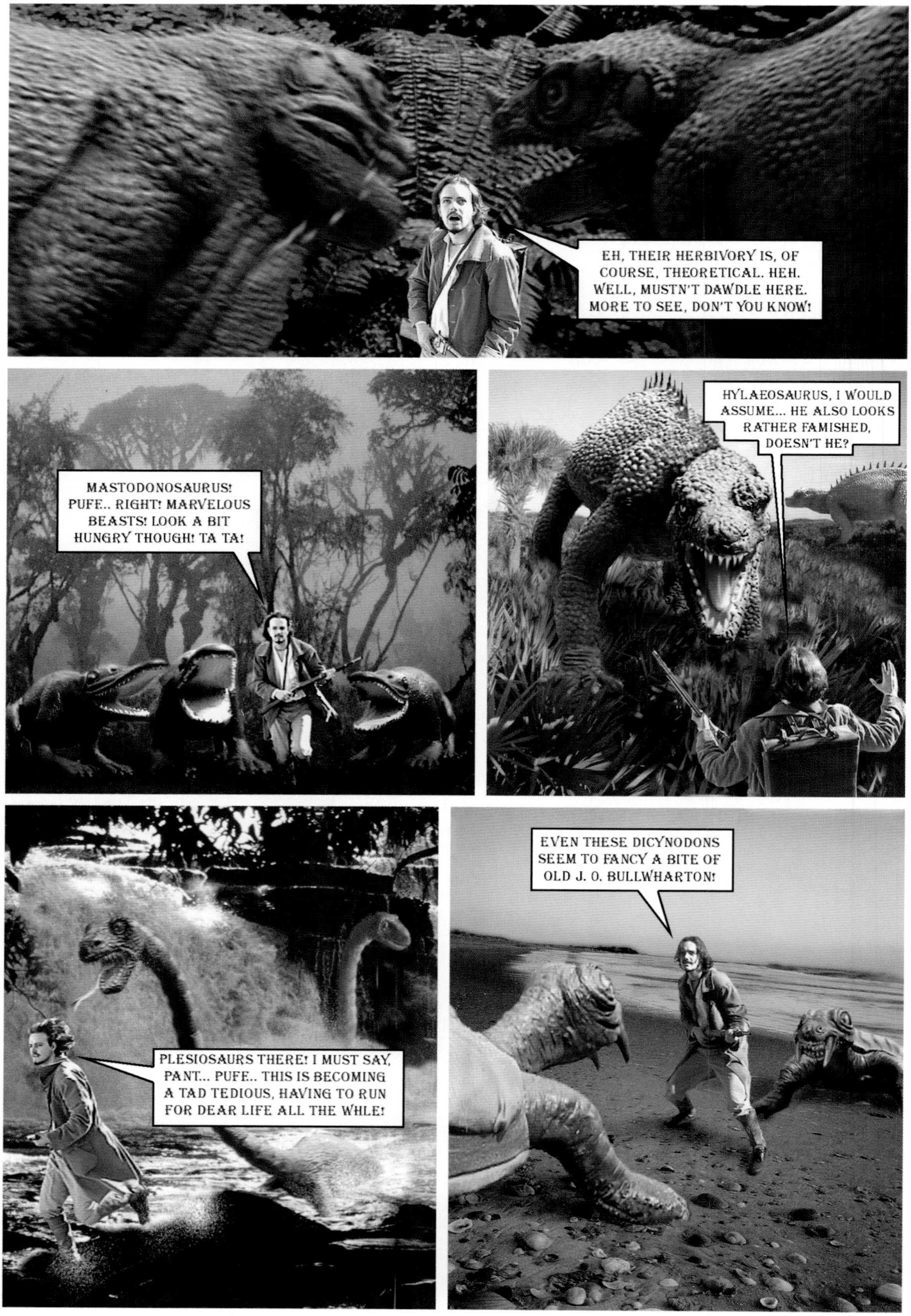
EH, THEIR HERBIVORY IS, OF COURSE, THEORETICAL. HEH. WELL, MUSTN'T DAWDLE HERE. MORE TO SEE, DON'T YOU KNOW!
MASTODONOSAURUS! PUFE.. RIGHT! MARVELOUS BEASTS! LOOK A BIT HUNGRY THOUGH! TA TA!
HYLAEOSAURUS, I WOULD ASSUME... HE ALSO LOOKS RATHER FAMISHED, DOESN'T HE?
PLESIOSAURS THERE! I MUST SAY, PANT... PUFE.. THIS IS BECOMING A TAD TEDIOUS, HAVING TO RUN FOR DEAR LIFE ALL THE WHLE!
EVEN THESE DICYNODONS SEEM TO FANCY A BITE OF OLD J. O. BULLWHARTON!

SNORT! SNUFFLE!

...SAUR.

BY HEAVEN, WHAT A SAVAGE WORLD THIS IS! I'D BEST MAKE MY WAY BACK TO THE BALLOON BEFORE I ENCOUNTER THE DREAD MEGALO...

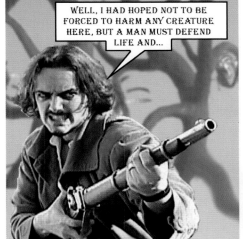

WELL, I HAD HOPED NOT TO BE FORCED TO HARM ANY CREATURE HERE, BUT A MAN MUST DEFEND LIFE AND...

KRUNTCH!

OH, BOTHER!

GROOAR!

PERHAPS IT'S TIME TO TAKE MY... PUFF PUFE... LEAVE OF THIS FABULOUS PLACE WHILE I STILL... PANT... MAY! MUST HAVE A CHAT WITH SIR RICHARD OWEN ABOUT THE ALLEGEDLY SLUGGISH REPTILIAN NATURE OF THE MEGALOSAUR UPON MY... PANT PANT... RETURN!

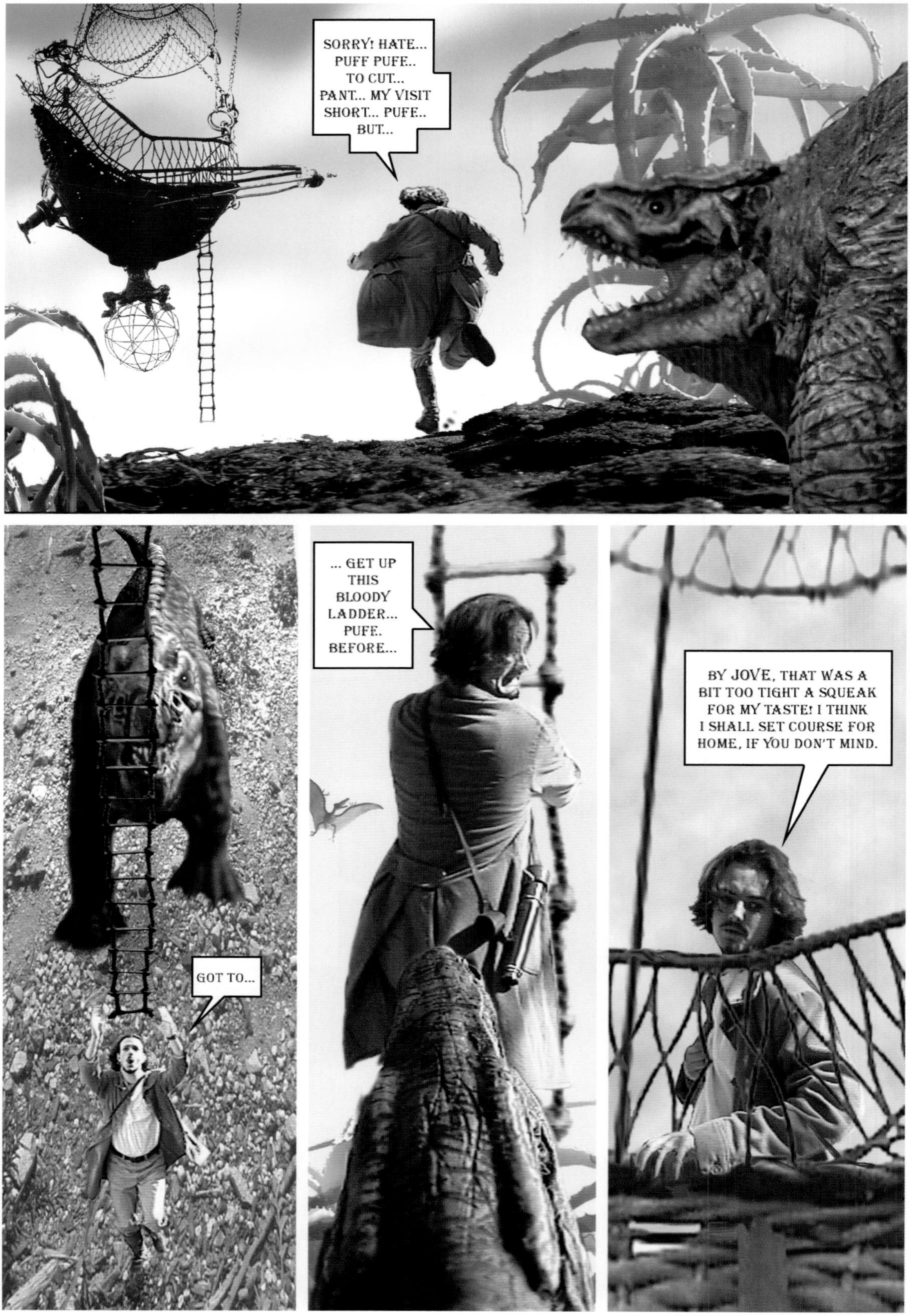
SORRY! HATE... PUFF PUFE.. TO CUT... PANT... MY VISIT SHORT... PUFE.. BUT...
GOT TO...
... GET UP THIS BLOODY LADDER... PUFE. BEFORE...
BY JOVE, THAT WAS A BIT TOO TIGHT A SQUEAK FOR MY TASTE! I THINK I SHALL SET COURSE FOR HOME, IF YOU DON'T MIND.

ONCE AGAIN, JEREMY'S ASTOUNDING MACHINE BRIDGES THE GAP OF TIME!

DEAR SWEET ENGLAND! I AM HOME.

THERE THERE, DEAREST! NOT ALL THE MONSTERS OF PRE-HISTORY COULD...

SKRAW! SKRAW!

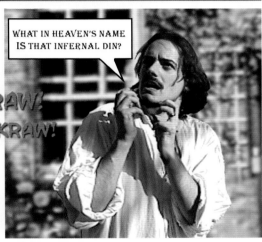

WHAT IN HEAVEN'S NAME IS THAT INFERNAL DIN?

SKRAW!

A PTERODACTYL! A BLEEDING PTERODACTYL HAS STOWED AWAY ATOP THE BALLOON!

SKREE!

IF I CAN ONLY... DAMN! THERE IT GOES! IT'S HEADING FOR THE SEA AND I HAVE NO HOPE OF STOPPING IT, BLAST IT ALL!

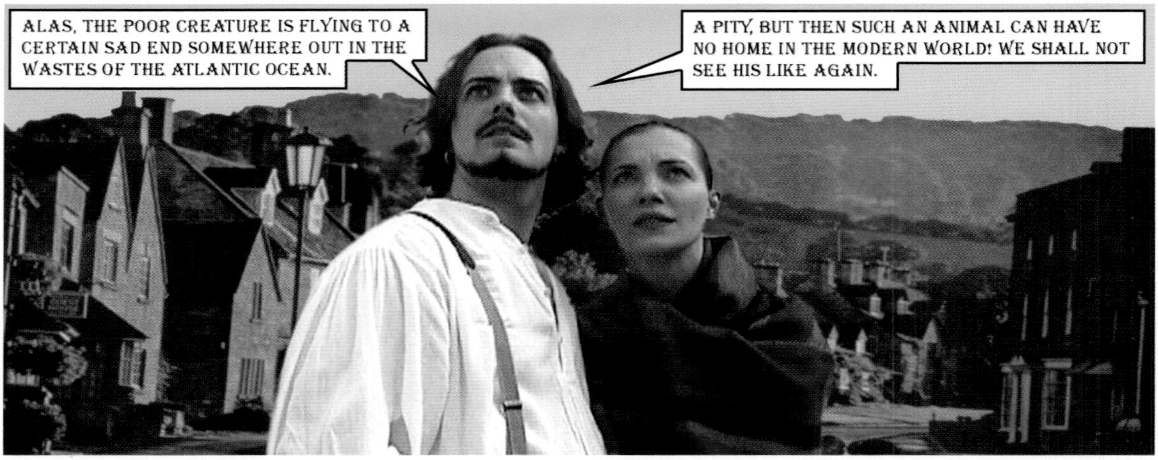
ALAS, THE POOR CREATURE IS FLYING TO A CERTAIN SAD END SOMEWHERE OUT IN THE WASTES OF THE ATLANTIC OCEAN.
A PITY, BUT THEN SUCH AN ANIMAL CAN HAVE NO HOME IN THE MODERN WORLD! WE SHALL NOT SEE HIS LIKE AGAIN.

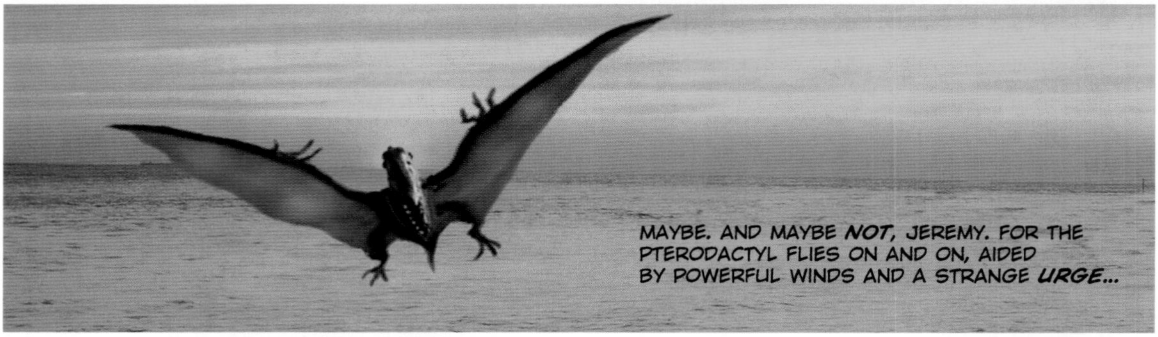
MAYBE. AND MAYBE *NOT*, JEREMY. FOR THE PTERODACTYL FLIES ON AND ON, AIDED BY POWERFUL WINDS AND A STRANGE *URGE*...

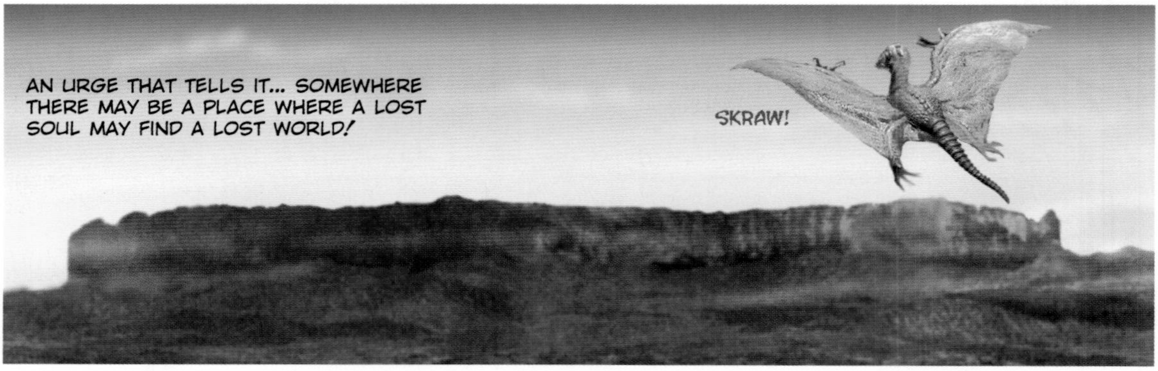
AN URGE THAT TELLS IT... SOMEWHERE THERE MAY BE A PLACE WHERE A LOST SOUL MAY FIND A LOST WORLD!
SKRAW!

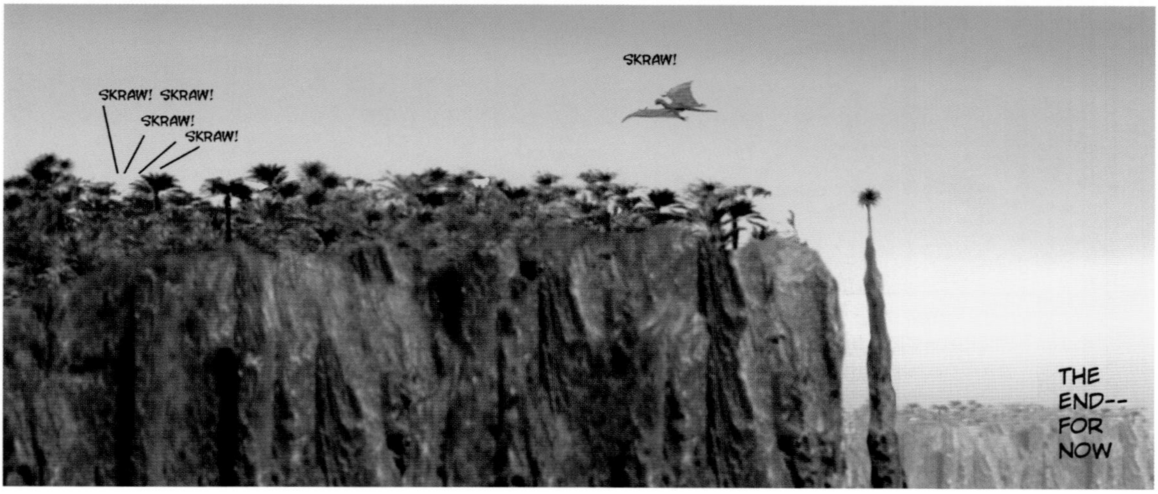
SKRAW! SKRAW!
SKRAW!
SKRAW!
SKRAW!
THE END--FOR NOW

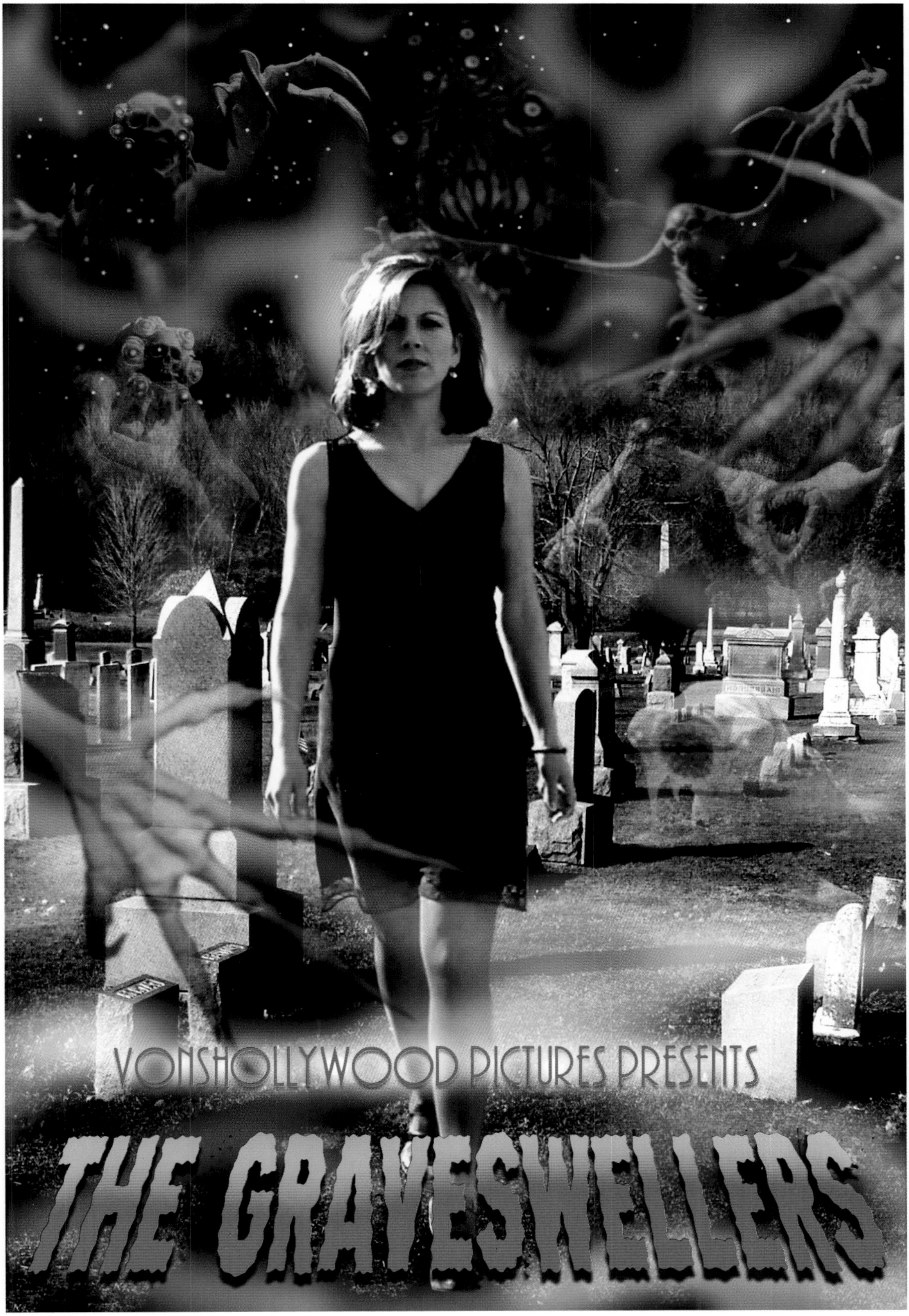
VONSHOLLYWOOD PICTURES PRESENTS
THE GRAVESWELLERS

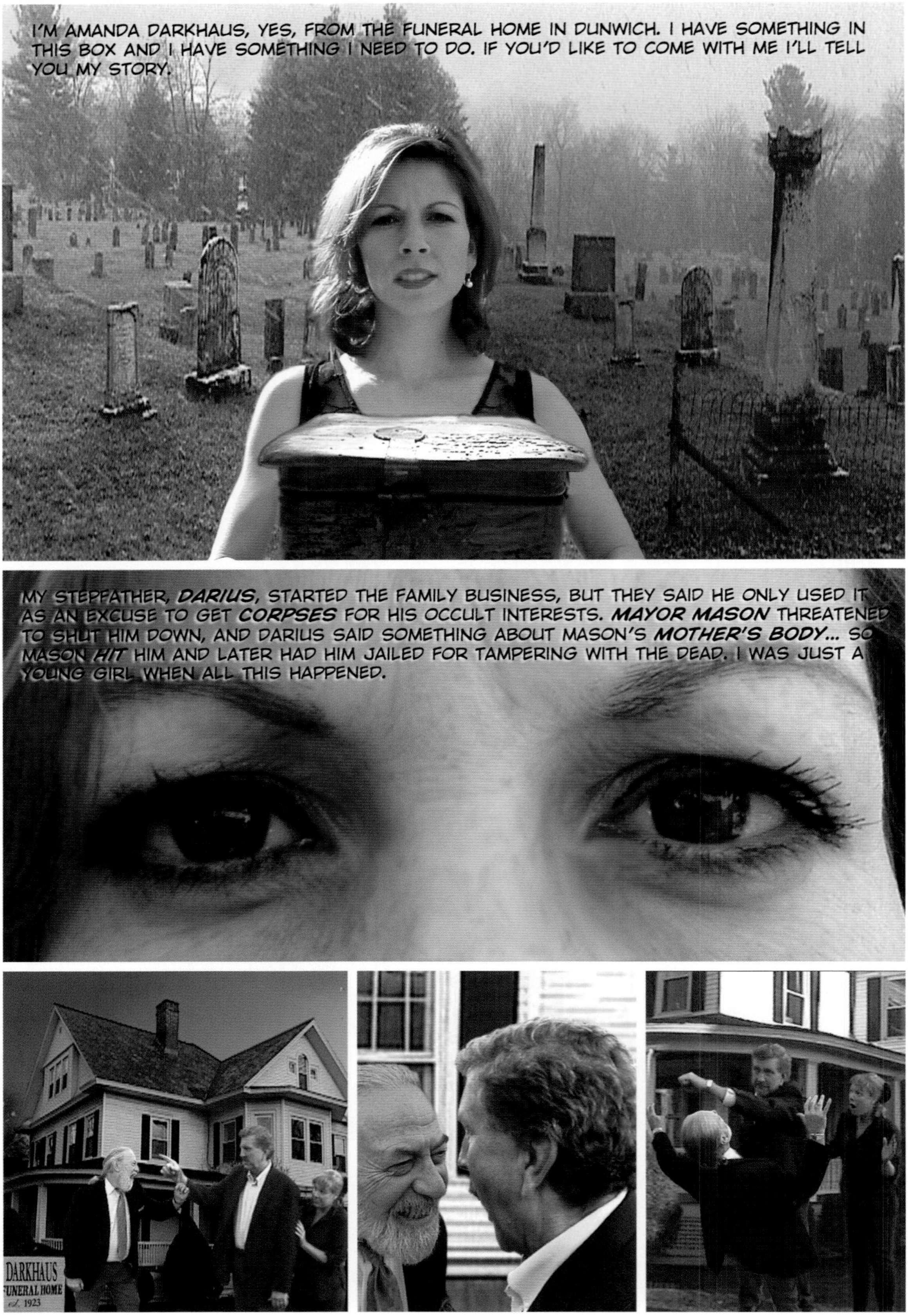
I'M AMANDA DARKHAUS, YES, FROM THE FUNERAL HOME IN DUNWICH. I HAVE SOMETHING IN THIS BOX AND I HAVE SOMETHING I NEED TO DO. IF YOU'D LIKE TO COME WITH ME I'LL TELL YOU MY STORY.
MY STEPFATHER, DARIUS, STARTED THE FAMILY BUSINESS, BUT THEY SAID HE ONLY USED IT AS AN EXCUSE TO GET CORPSES FOR HIS OCCULT INTERESTS. MAYOR MASON THREATENED TO SHUT HIM DOWN, AND DARIUS SAID SOMETHING ABOUT MASON'S MOTHER'S BODY... SO MASON HIT HIM AND LATER HAD HIM JAILED FOR TAMPERING WITH THE DEAD. I WAS JUST A YOUNG GIRL WHEN ALL THIS HAPPENED.
DARKHAUS
FUNERAL HOME
est. 1923

I'LL NEVER FORGET THE *LOOK* DARIUS GAVE MASON WHEN HE WAS SENTENCED TO PRISON...

WHEN I CAME OF AGE, IT WAS UP TO ME TO KEEP THE FAMILY BUSINESS GOING. IT WOULD NOT HAVE BEEN MY CHOICE, BUT CAREERS IN DUNWICH ARE HARD TO COME BY.

THEN THEY LET HIM OUT.

Dunwich Mirror

**DARKHAUS FREE**

HE WANTED ME TO KEEP THE MORTUARY GOING. HE WOULD TAKE WHAT MONEY HE NEEDED FROM THE BUSINESS WHILE HE FOUND A NEW PLACE FOR HIMSELF.

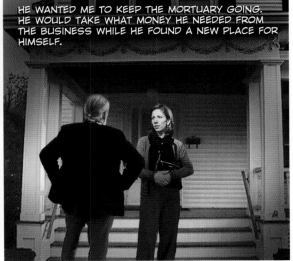

A PLACE WHERE HE COULD RESUME HIS "STUDIES."

WHERE HE COULD PORE OVER STRANGE BOOKS AND SCROLLS SENT BY FOREIGN CORRESPONDENTS.

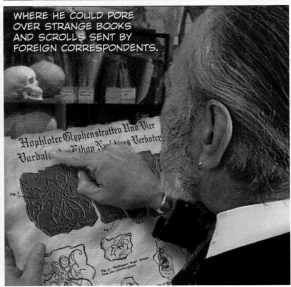

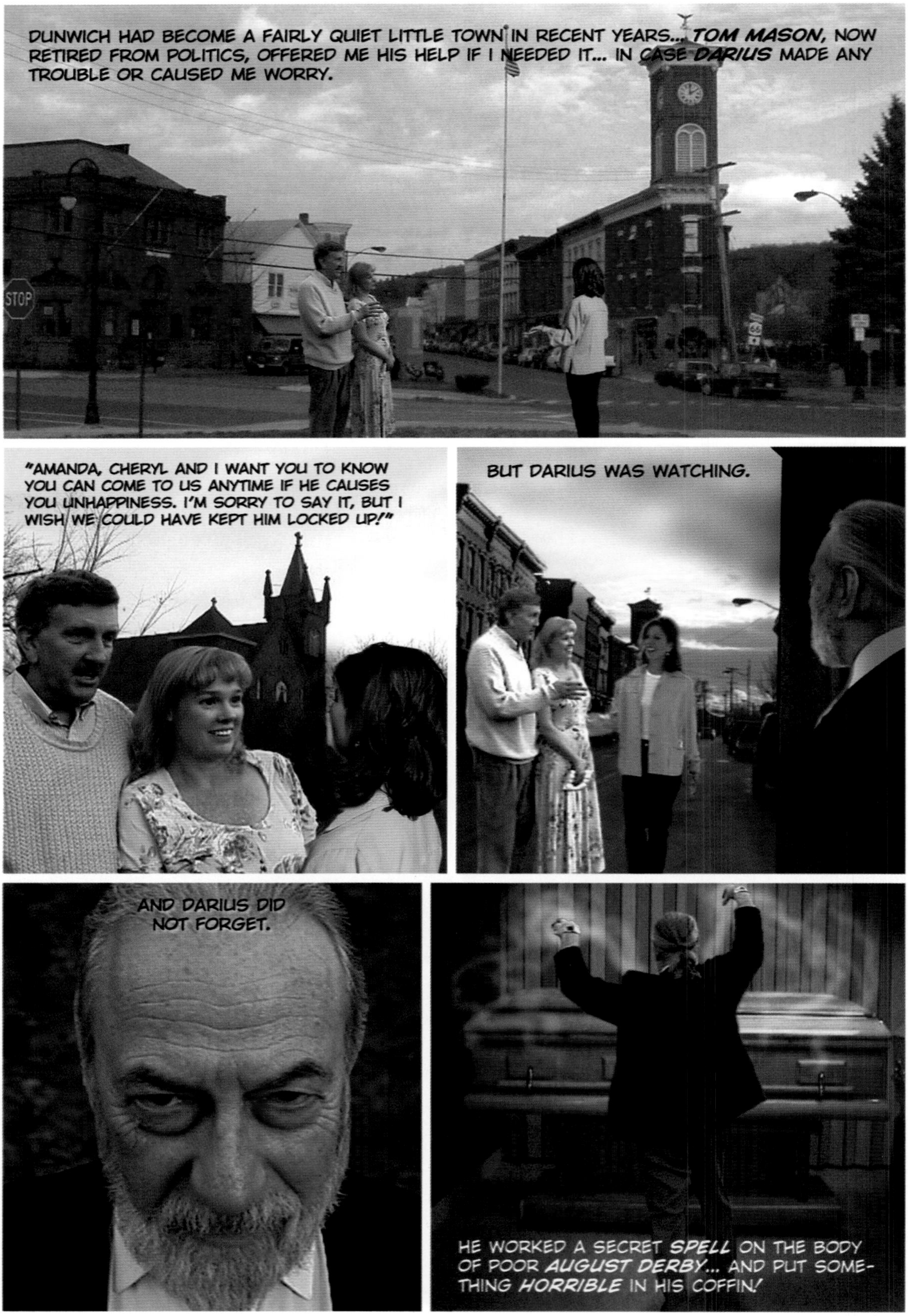
DUNWICH HAD BECOME A FAIRLY QUIET LITTLE TOWN IN RECENT YEARS... *TOM MASON,* NOW RETIRED FROM POLITICS, OFFERED ME HIS HELP IF I NEEDED IT... IN CASE *DARIUS* MADE ANY TROUBLE OR CAUSED ME WORRY.
STOP
"AMANDA, CHERYL AND I WANT YOU TO KNOW YOU CAN COME TO US ANYTIME IF HE CAUSES YOU UNHAPPINESS. I'M SORRY TO SAY IT, BUT I WISH WE COULD HAVE KEPT HIM LOCKED UP!"
BUT DARIUS WAS WATCHING.
AND DARIUS DID NOT FORGET.
HE WORKED A SECRET *SPELL* ON THE BODY OF POOR *AUGUST DERBY*... AND PUT SOME-THING *HORRIBLE* IN HIS COFFIN!

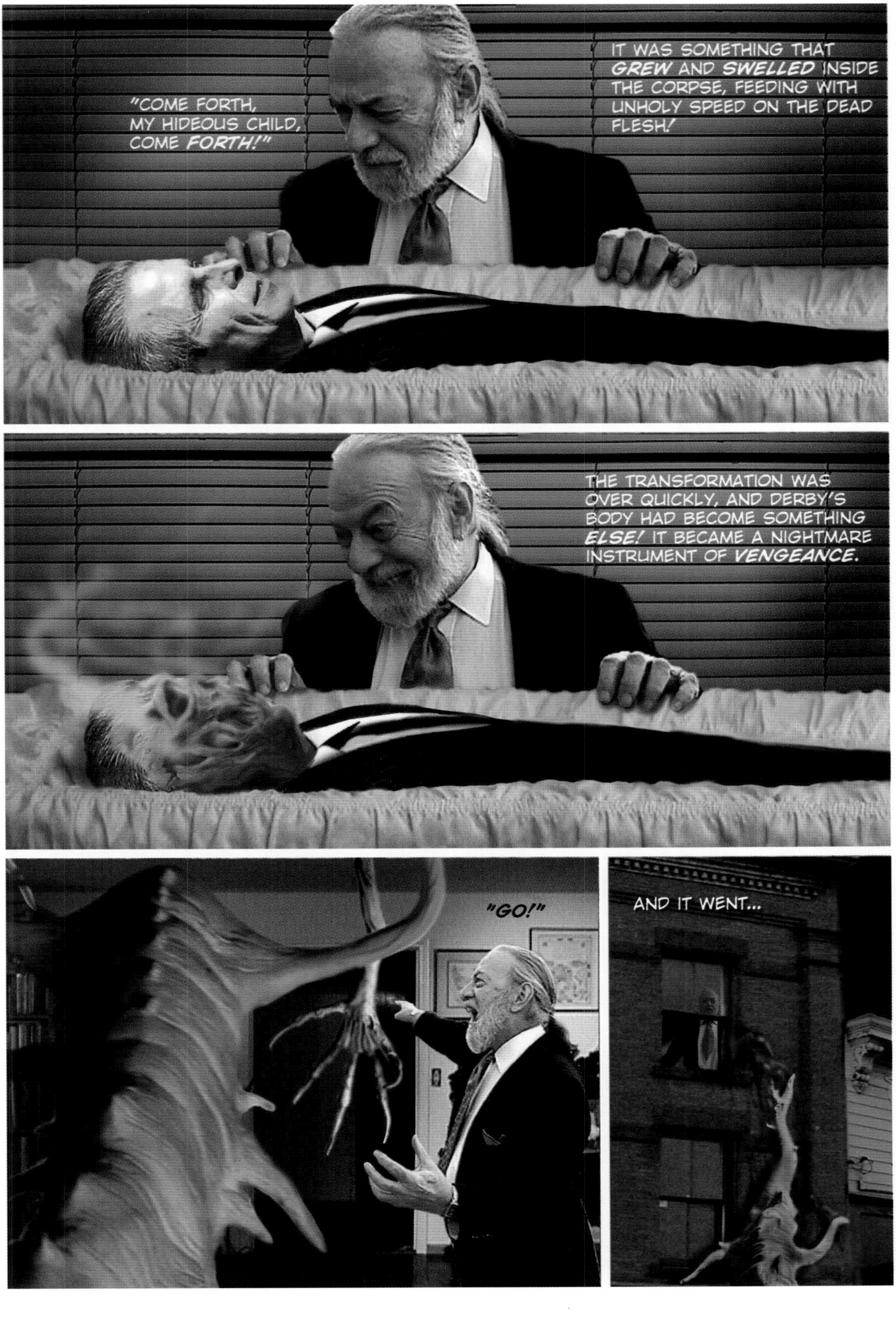
"COME FORTH, MY HIDEOUS CHILD, COME FORTH!"
IT WAS SOMETHING THAT GREW AND SWELLED INSIDE THE CORPSE, FEEDING WITH UNHOLY SPEED ON THE DEAD FLESH!
THE TRANSFORMATION WAS OVER QUICKLY, AND DERBY'S BODY HAD BECOME SOMETHING ELSE! IT BECAME A NIGHTMARE INSTRUMENT OF VENGEANCE.
"GO!"
AND IT WENT...

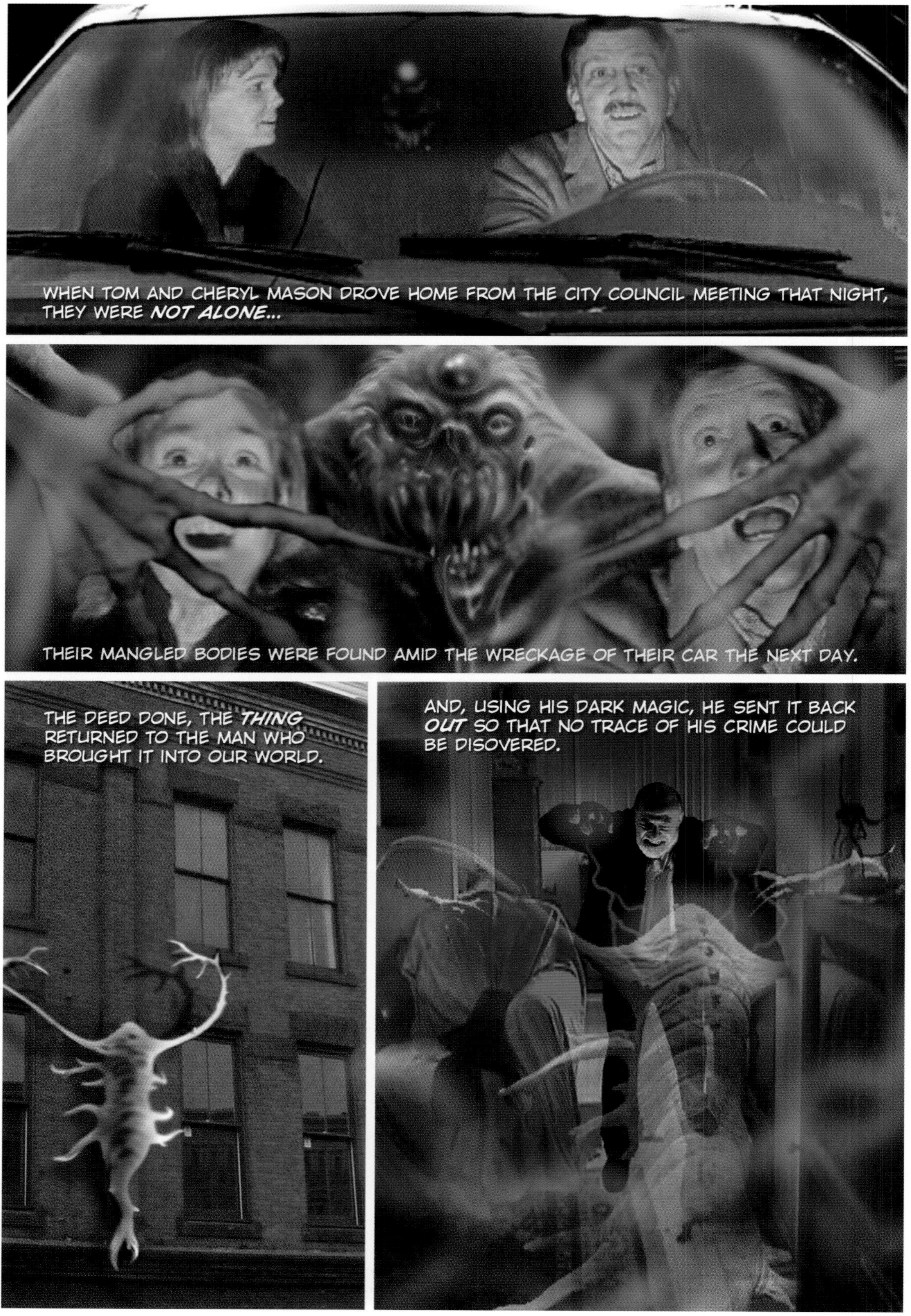
WHEN TOM AND CHERYL MASON DROVE HOME FROM THE CITY COUNCIL MEETING THAT NIGHT, THEY WERE ***NOT ALONE...***
THEIR MANGLED BODIES WERE FOUND AMID THE WRECKAGE OF THEIR CAR THE NEXT DAY.
THE DEED DONE, THE ***THING*** RETURNED TO THE MAN WHO BROUGHT IT INTO OUR WORLD.
AND, USING HIS DARK MAGIC, HE SENT IT BACK ***OUT*** SO THAT NO TRACE OF HIS CRIME COULD BE DISOVERED.

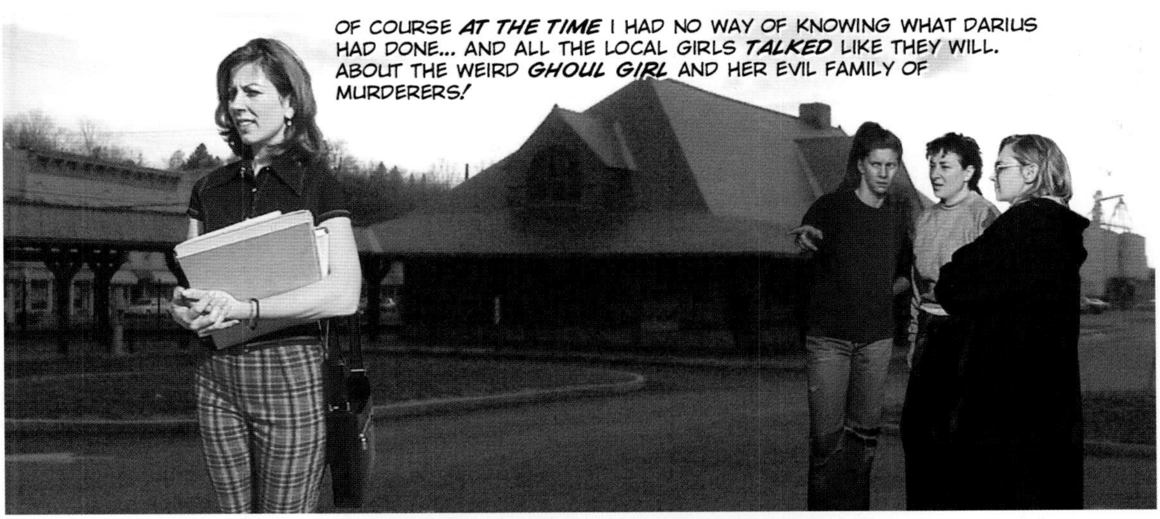
OF COURSE AT THE TIME I HAD NO WAY OF KNOWING WHAT DARIUS HAD DONE... AND ALL THE LOCAL GIRLS TALKED LIKE THEY WILL. ABOUT THE WEIRD GHOUL GIRL AND HER EVIL FAMILY OF MURDERERS!

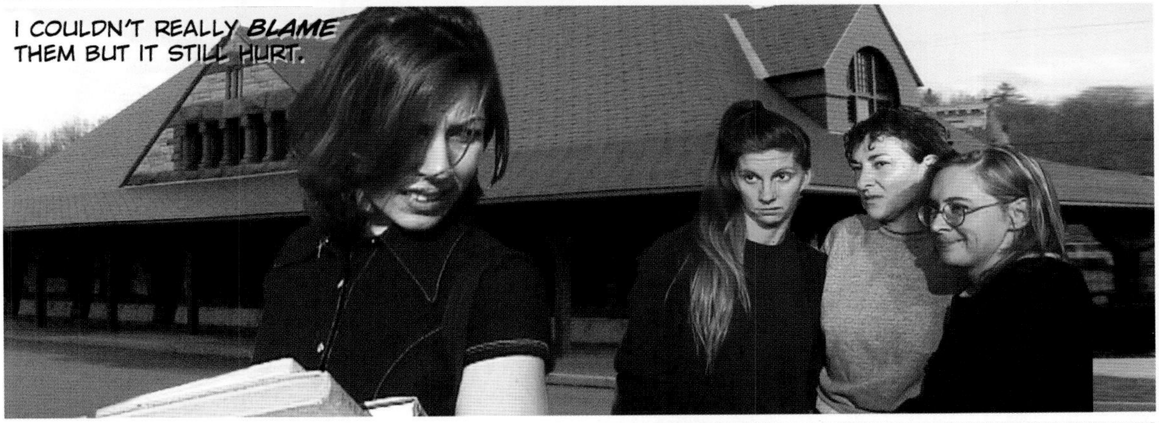
I COULDN'T REALLY BLAME THEM BUT IT STILL HURT.

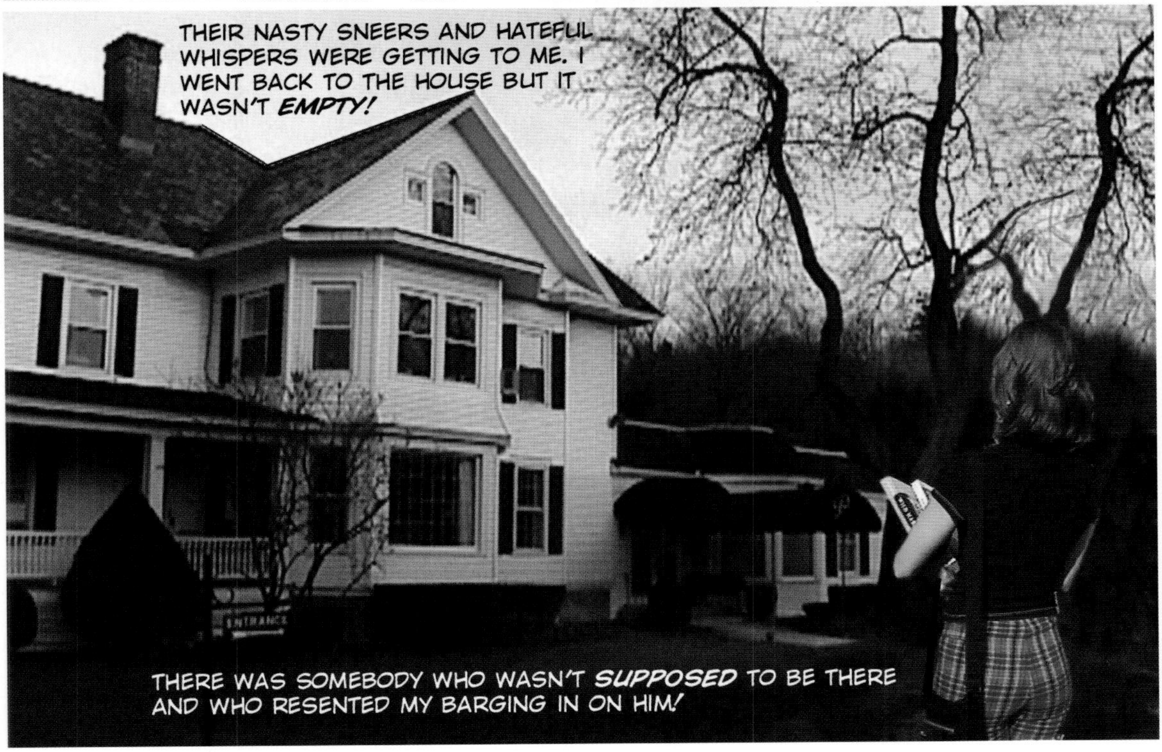
THEIR NASTY SNEERS AND HATEFUL WHISPERS WERE GETTING TO ME. I WENT BACK TO THE HOUSE BUT IT WASN'T EMPTY!
ENTRANCE
THERE WAS SOMEBODY WHO WASN'T SUPPOSED TO BE THERE AND WHO RESENTED MY BARGING IN ON HIM!

"HOW *DARE* YOU SNEAK UP ON ME LIKE THIS?"

"WHAT... WHAT ARE YOU..."

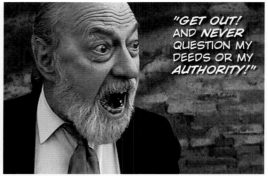

"*GET OUT!* AND *NEVER* QUESTION MY DEEDS OR MY *AUTHORITY!*"

I RAN FROM THE FUNERAL PARLOR IN TEARS, FILLED WITH LOATHING AND TERROR! I DIDN'T EVEN NOTICE *HER* WATCHING.

THE NEXT DAY I WENT TO THE LIBRARY TO READ UP ON DARIUS' TRIAL. I DIDN'T KNOW THE EXTENT OF HIS ALLEGED CRIMES.

IT WAS TOO HORRIBLE TO CONTEMPLATE HOW HE'D CUT UP BODIES AND PERFORMED OBSCENE RITES UPON THEM.

AND SUDDENLY *KARLA* WAS THERE.

SHE WAS HIS *REAL* DAUGHTER, BACK FROM WHERE HER MOTHER HAD HIDDEN HER.

SHE SHOWED ME THE BOOKS ON *MAGIC* AND WE FOUND OUT WHAT DARIUS WAS DOING.

AND ABOUT THE *GRAVESWELLERS!*

"OH MY GOD..."

THERE WAS A PICTURE OF THE VERY *BOX* I SAW HIM WITH. THE BOX THAT HELD THE HEAD OF THE SORCEROR, *IBNZAK!*

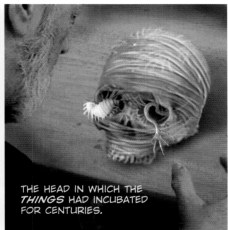

THE HEAD IN WHICH THE *THINGS* HAD INCUBATED FOR CENTURIES.

ALL ONE HAD TO DO, PROVIDING ONE POSSESSED THE REQUIRED *FORMULAE*, WAS ALLOW THEM TO *EMERGE*, NOURISH THEM ON *CARRION*, AND *PLANT THEM* IN A PLACE WHERE THEY COULD THRIVE!

THEY WOULD *GROW* IN THE *CORPSE-FILLED EARTH*, AWAITING THE NIGHT OF *ARISING* WHEN THEY COULD EMERGE AND DESTROY THE *ENEMIES* OF THEIR GUARDIAN!

IT WAS TO BE THE NIGHT OF THE *DEAD MOON... THAT VERY NIGHT!* BY MORNING ALL OF DUNWICH WOULD BE *WIPED OUT*. THE THINGS WOULD BE FIERCELY *LOYAL* TO DARIUS AS LONG AS HE SERVED AND PROTECTED THEM. IF WE COULD GET HIM TO TURN AGAINST THEM, THERE WOULD BE HOPE, BUT HOW COULD WE DO *THAT?*

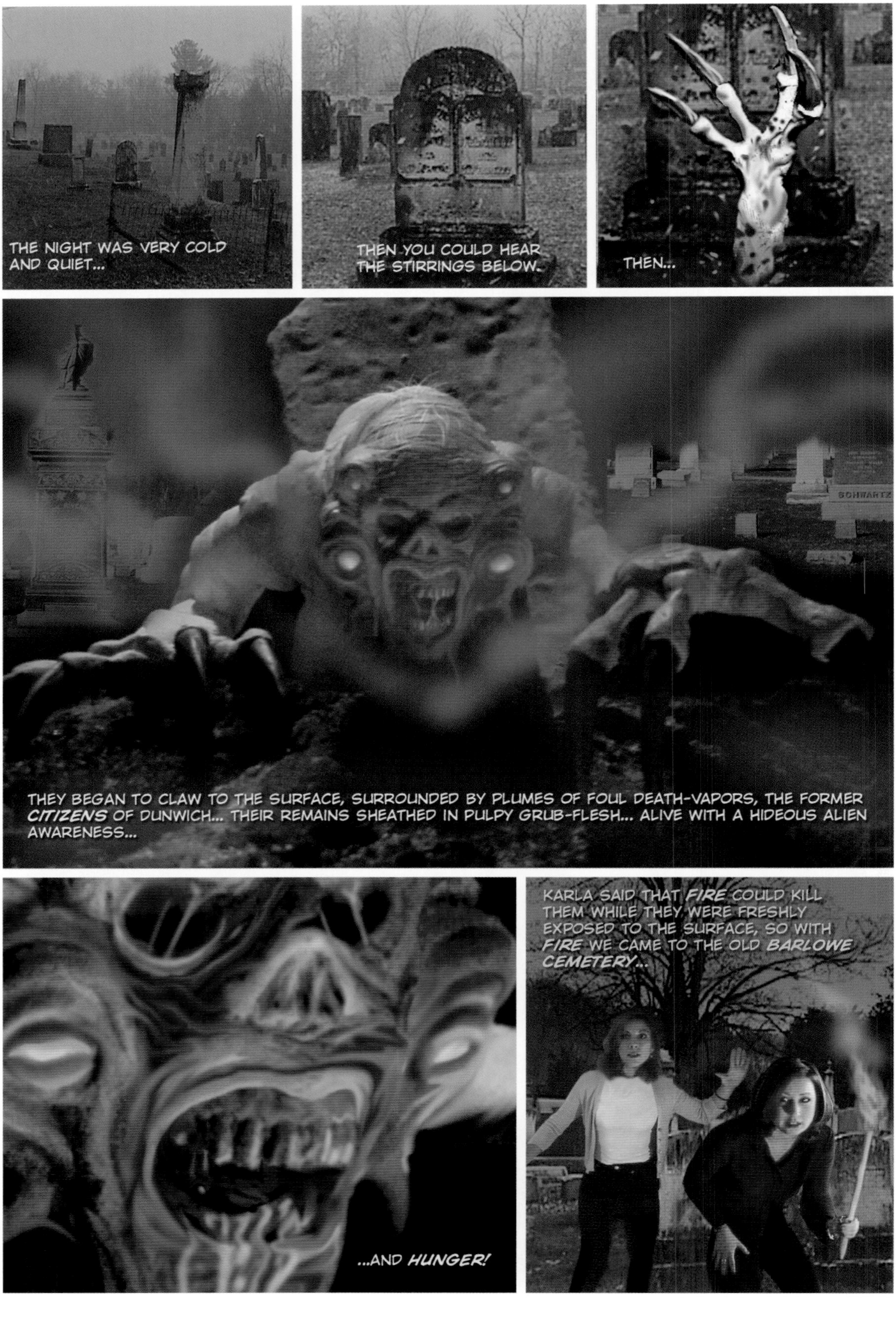
THE NIGHT WAS VERY COLD AND QUIET...
THEN YOU COULD HEAR THE STIRRINGS BELOW.
THEN...
SCHWARTZ
THEY BEGAN TO CLAW TO THE SURFACE, SURROUNDED BY PLUMES OF FOUL DEATH-VAPORS, THE FORMER *CITIZENS* OF DUNWICH... THEIR REMAINS SHEATHED IN PULPY GRUB-FLESH... ALIVE WITH A HIDEOUS ALIEN AWARENESS...
...AND *HUNGER!*
KARLA SAID THAT *FIRE* COULD KILL THEM WHILE THEY WERE FRESHLY EXPOSED TO THE SURFACE, SO WITH *FIRE* WE CAME TO THE OLD *BARLOWE CEMETERY*...

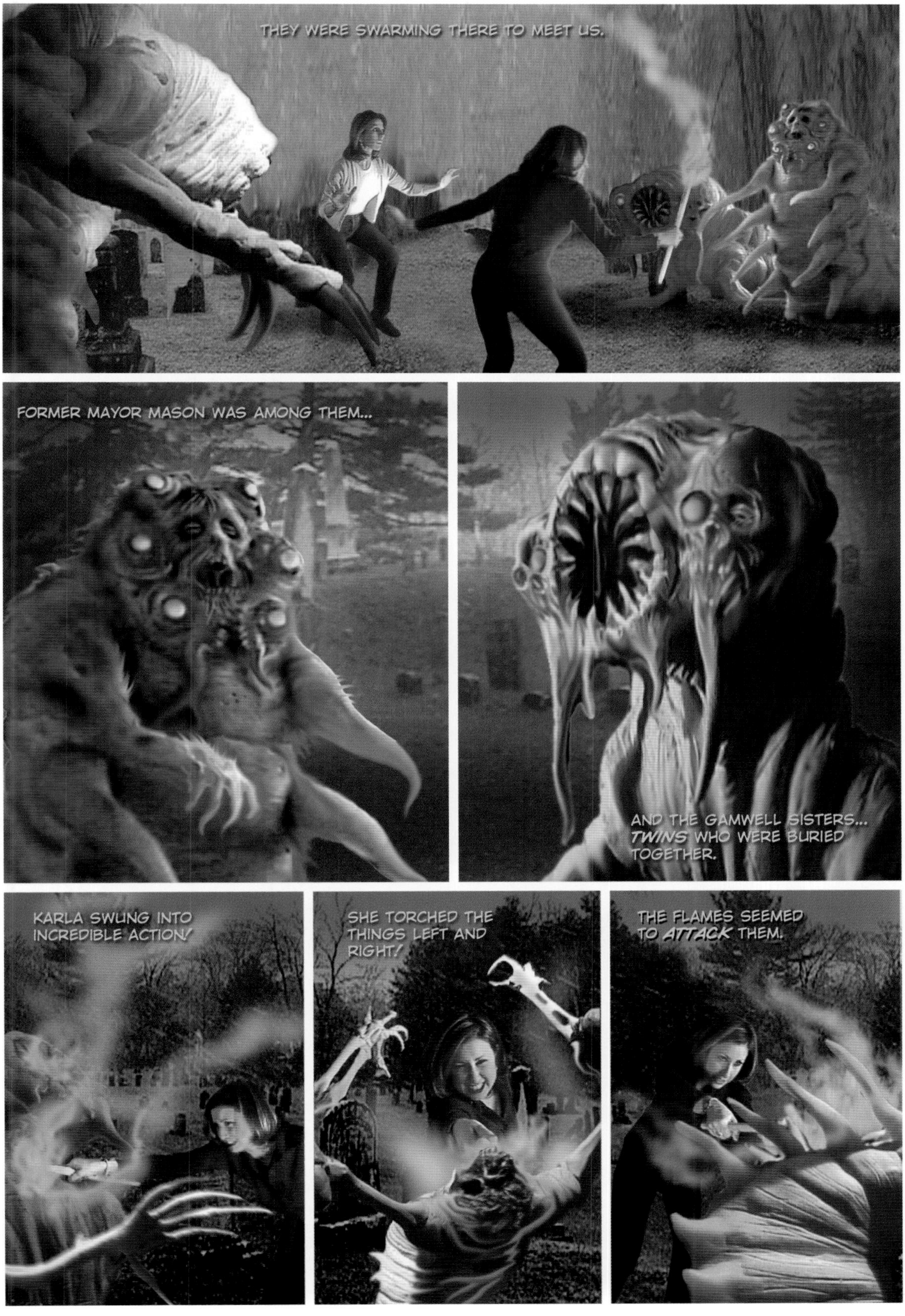
THEY WERE SWARMING THERE TO MEET US.
FORMER MAYOR MASON WAS AMONG THEM...
AND THE GAMWELL SISTERS... *TWINS* WHO WERE BURIED TOGETHER.
KARLA SWUNG INTO INCREDIBLE ACTION!
SHE TORCHED THE THINGS LEFT AND RIGHT!
THE FLAMES SEEMED TO *ATTACK* THEM.

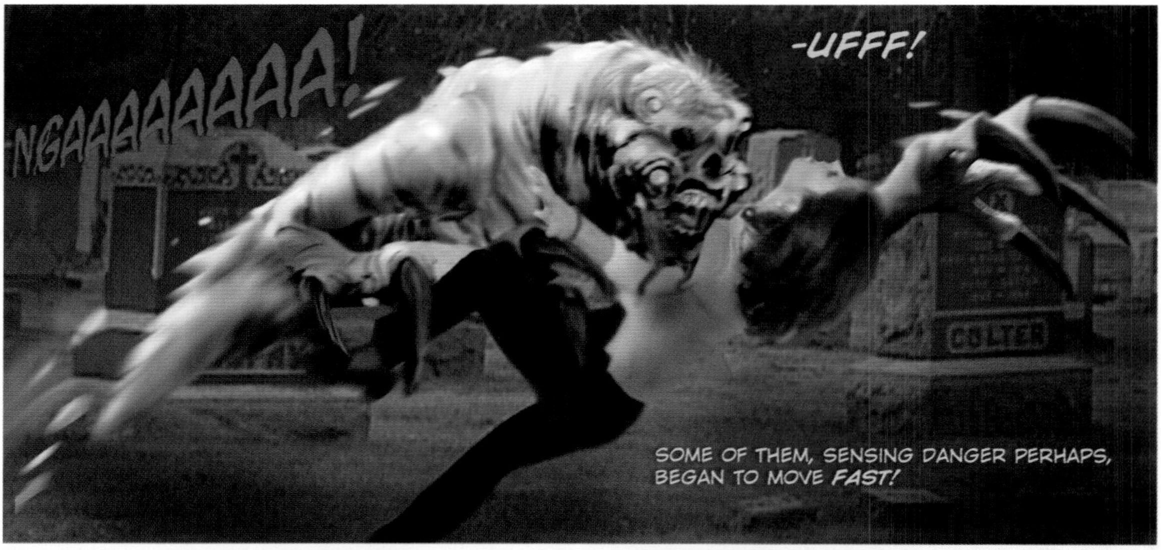
NGAAAAAAAA!
-UFFF!
CULTER
SOME OF THEM, SENSING DANGER PERHAPS, BEGAN TO MOVE *FAST!*

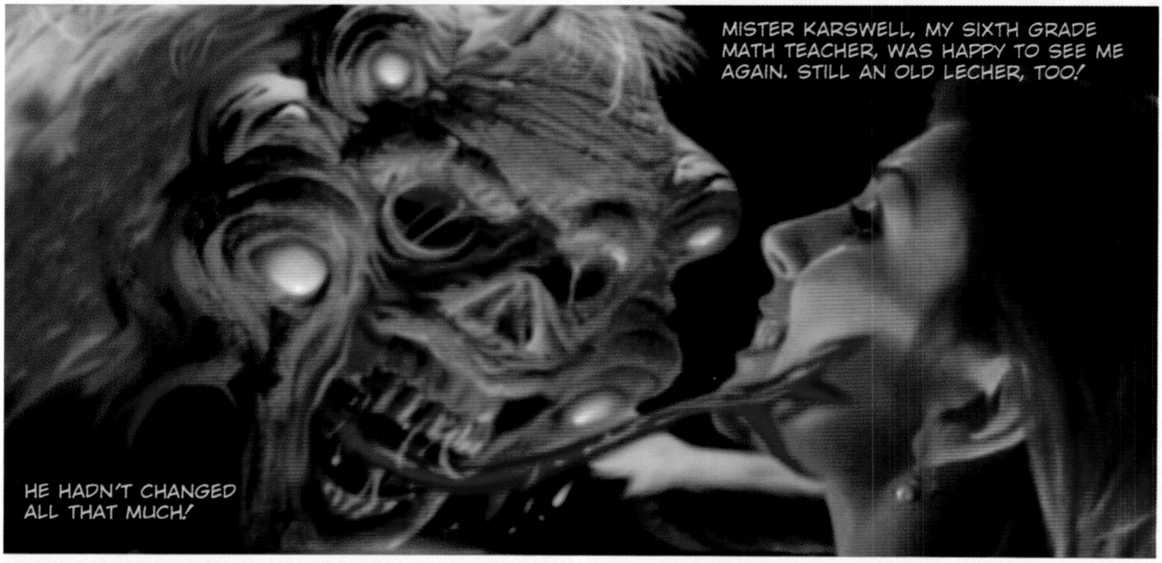
MISTER KARSWELL, MY SIXTH GRADE MATH TEACHER, WAS HAPPY TO SEE ME AGAIN. STILL AN OLD LECHER, TOO!
HE HADN'T CHANGED ALL THAT MUCH!

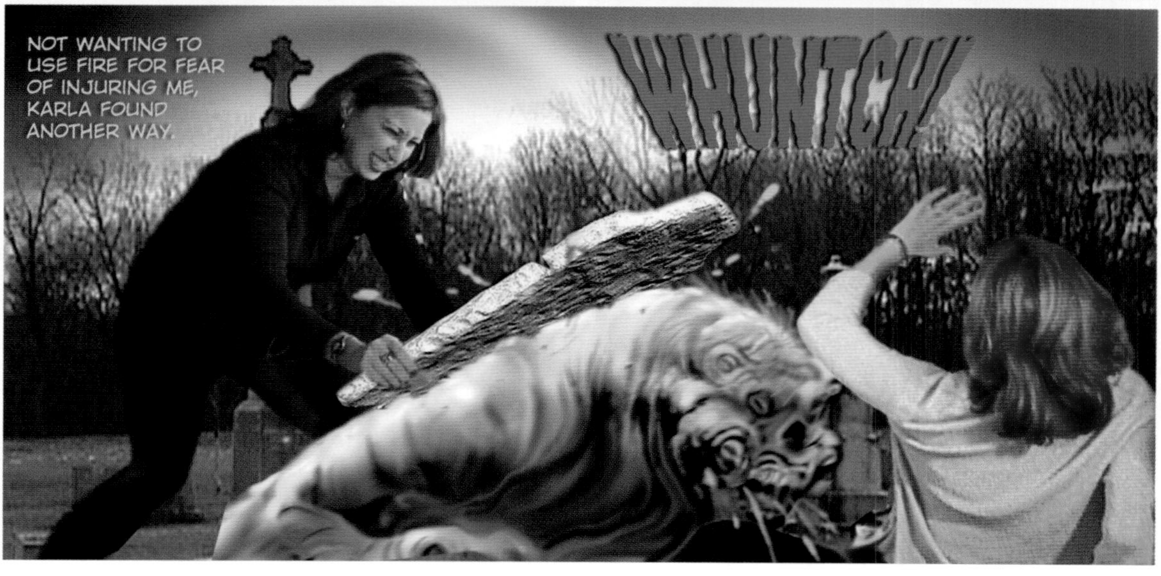
NOT WANTING TO USE FIRE FOR FEAR OF INJURING ME, KARLA FOUND ANOTHER WAY.
WHUNTCH!

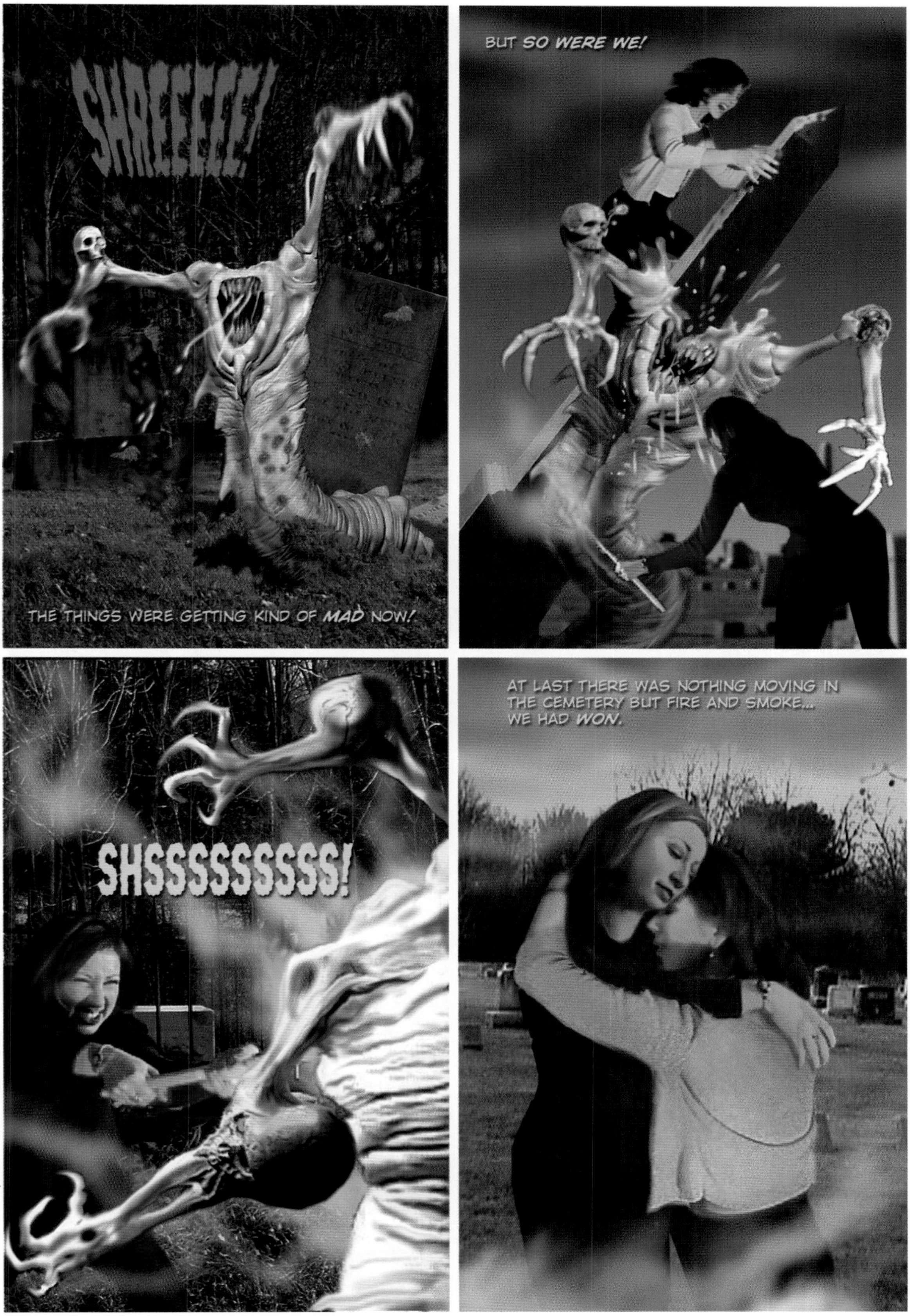
SHREEEEE!
THE THINGS WERE GETTING KIND OF MAD NOW!
BUT SO WERE WE!
SHSSSSSSSSS!
AT LAST THERE WAS NOTHING MOVING IN THE CEMETERY BUT FIRE AND SMOKE... WE HAD WON.

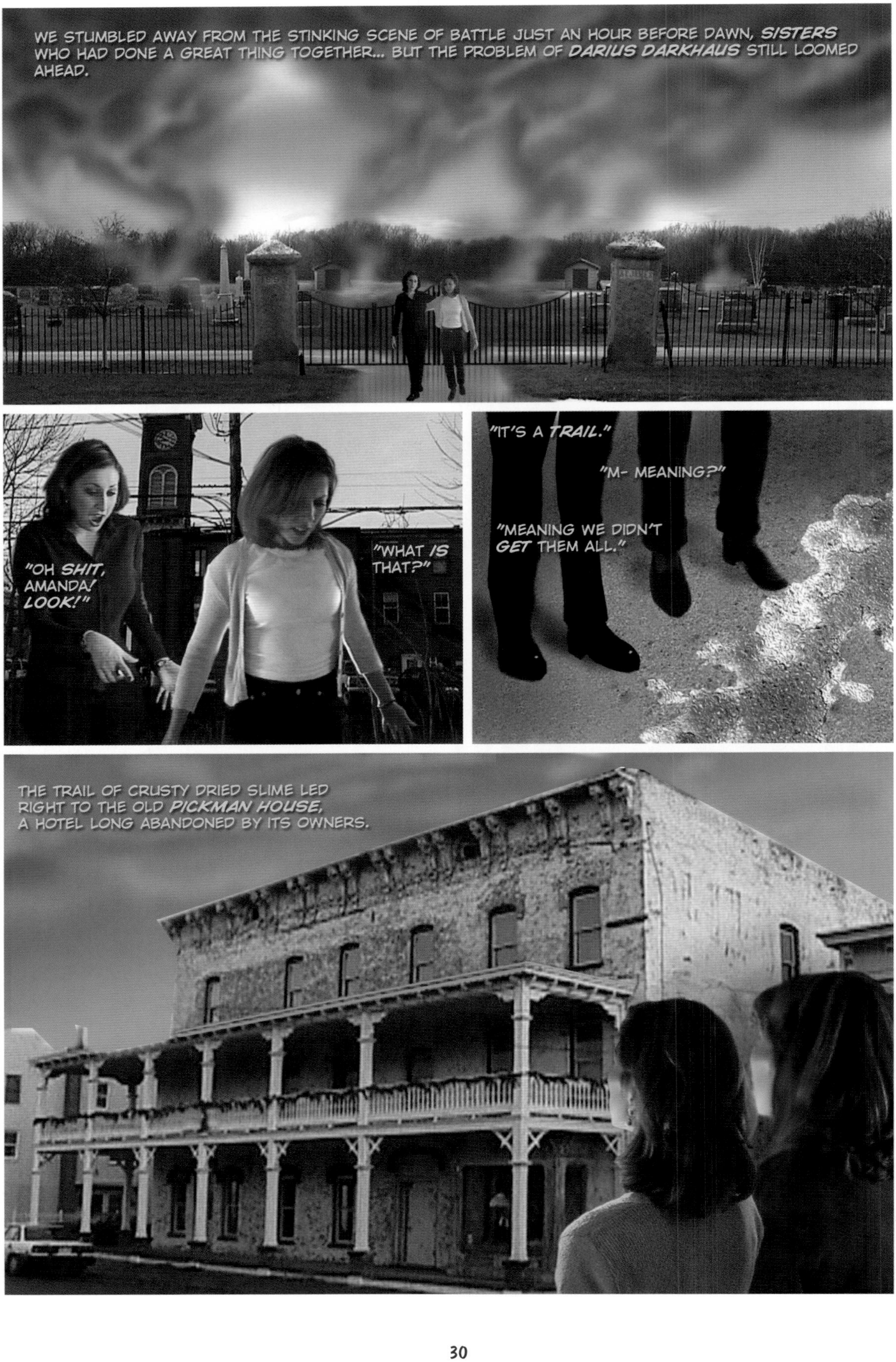
WE STUMBLED AWAY FROM THE STINKING SCENE OF BATTLE JUST AN HOUR BEFORE DAWN, *SISTERS* WHO HAD DONE A GREAT THING TOGETHER... BUT THE PROBLEM OF *DARIUS DARKHAUS* STILL LOOMED AHEAD.
"OH *SHIT*, AMANDA! *LOOK!*"
"WHAT *IS* THAT?"
"IT'S A *TRAIL*."
"M- MEANING?"
"MEANING WE DIDN'T *GET* THEM ALL."
THE TRAIL OF CRUSTY DRIED SLIME LED RIGHT TO THE OLD *PICKMAN HOUSE*, A HOTEL LONG ABANDONED BY ITS OWNERS.

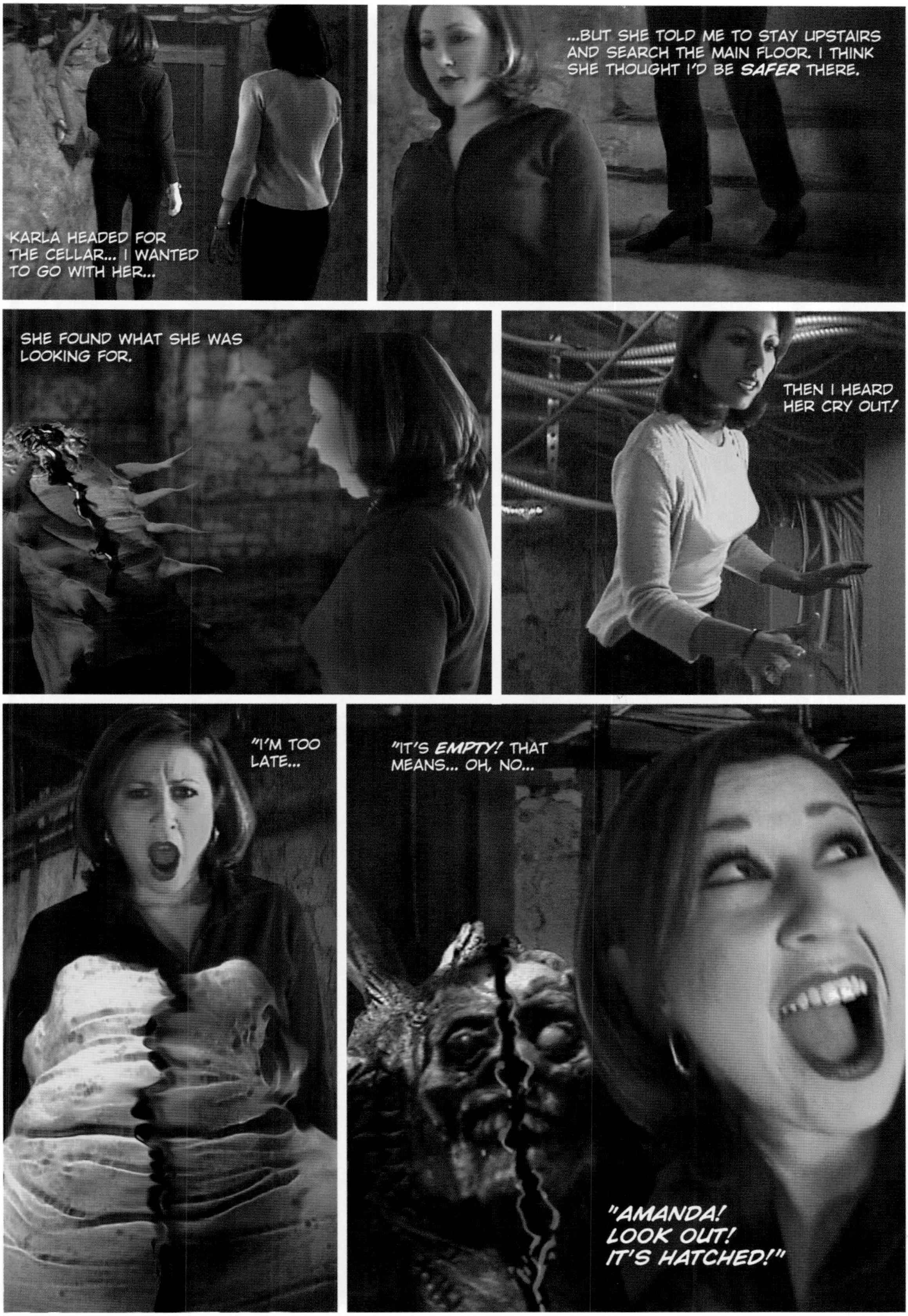
KARLA HEADED FOR THE CELLAR... I WANTED TO GO WITH HER...
...BUT SHE TOLD ME TO STAY UPSTAIRS AND SEARCH THE MAIN FLOOR. I THINK SHE THOUGHT I'D BE SAFER THERE.
SHE FOUND WHAT SHE WAS LOOKING FOR.
THEN I HEARD HER CRY OUT!
"I'M TOO LATE...
"IT'S EMPTY! THAT MEANS... OH, NO...
"AMANDA! LOOK OUT! IT'S HATCHED!"

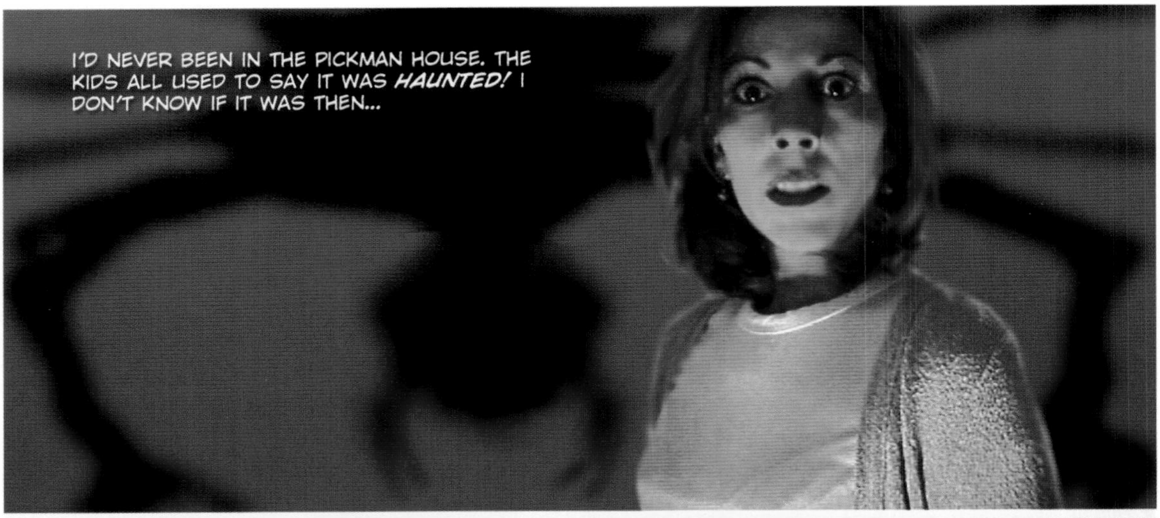
I'D NEVER BEEN IN THE PICKMAN HOUSE. THE KIDS ALL USED TO SAY IT WAS *HAUNTED!* I DON'T KNOW IF IT WAS THEN...

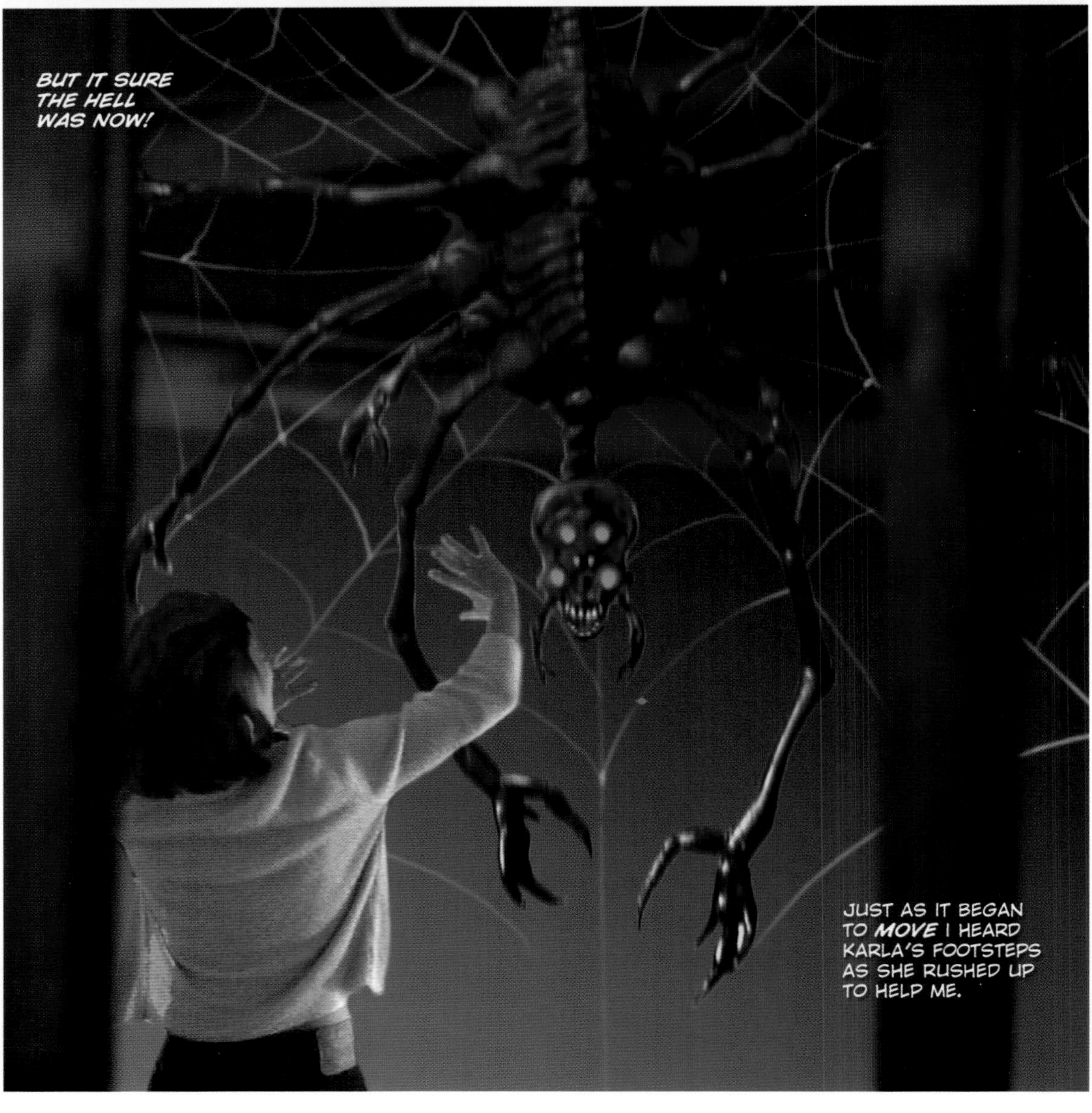
*BUT IT SURE THE HELL WAS NOW!*
JUST AS IT BEGAN TO ***MOVE*** I HEARD KARLA'S FOOTSTEPS AS SHE RUSHED UP TO HELP ME.

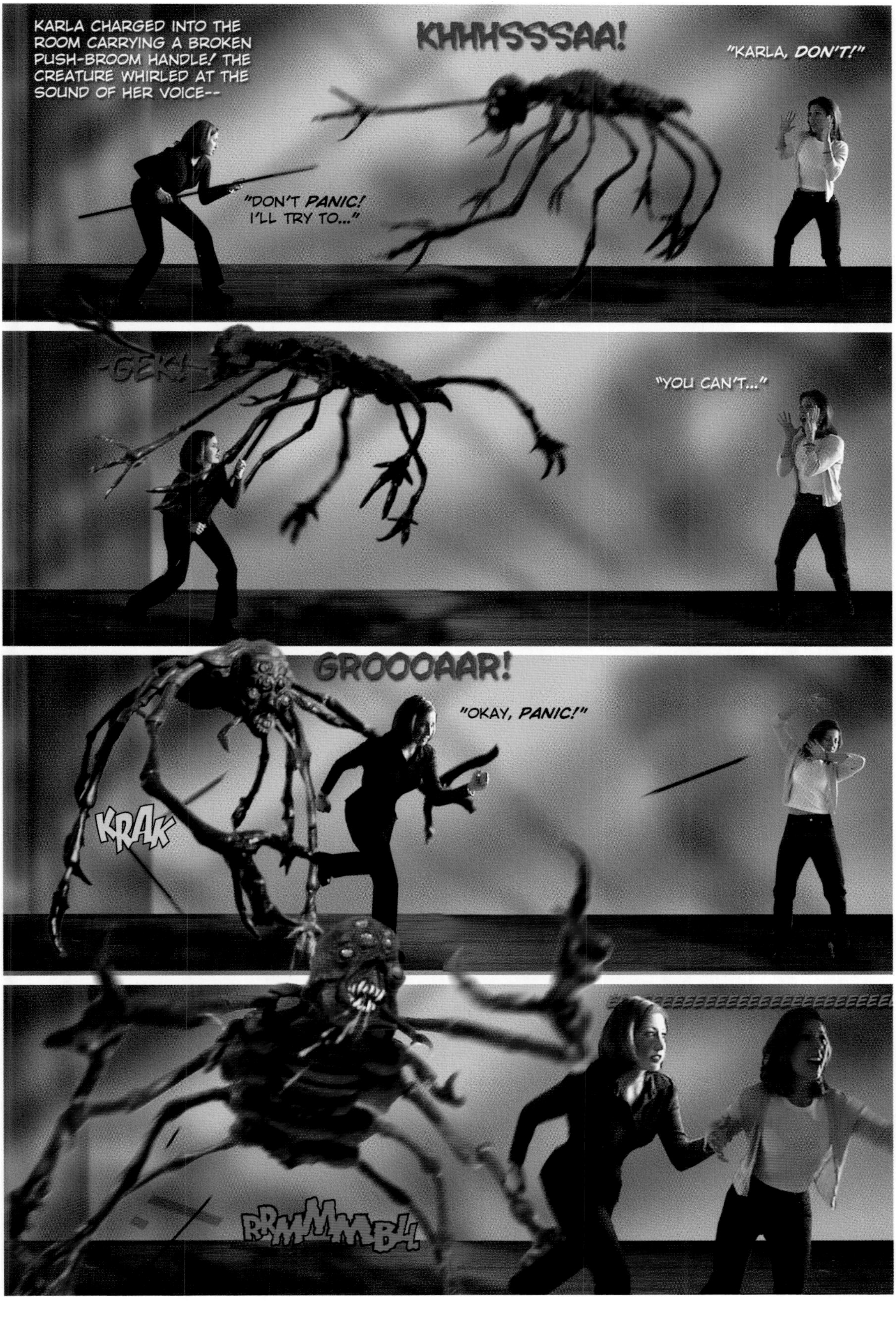
KARLA CHARGED INTO THE ROOM CARRYING A BROKEN PUSH-BROOM HANDLE! THE CREATURE WHIRLED AT THE SOUND OF HER VOICE--
KHHHSSSAA!
"KARLA, DON'T!"
"DON'T PANIC! I'LL TRY TO..."
-GEK!
"YOU CAN'T..."
GROOOAAR!
"OKAY, PANIC!"
KRAK
EEEEEEEEEEEEEEEEEEEEEEEEEEE
RRMMMMBL!

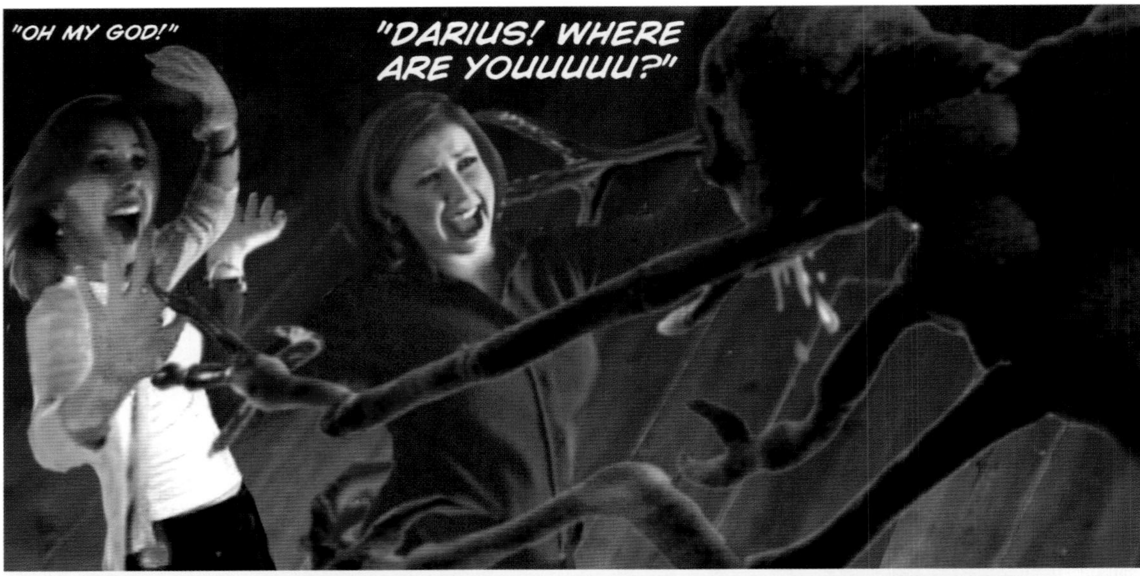
"OH MY GOD!"
"DARIUS! WHERE ARE YOUUUUU?"

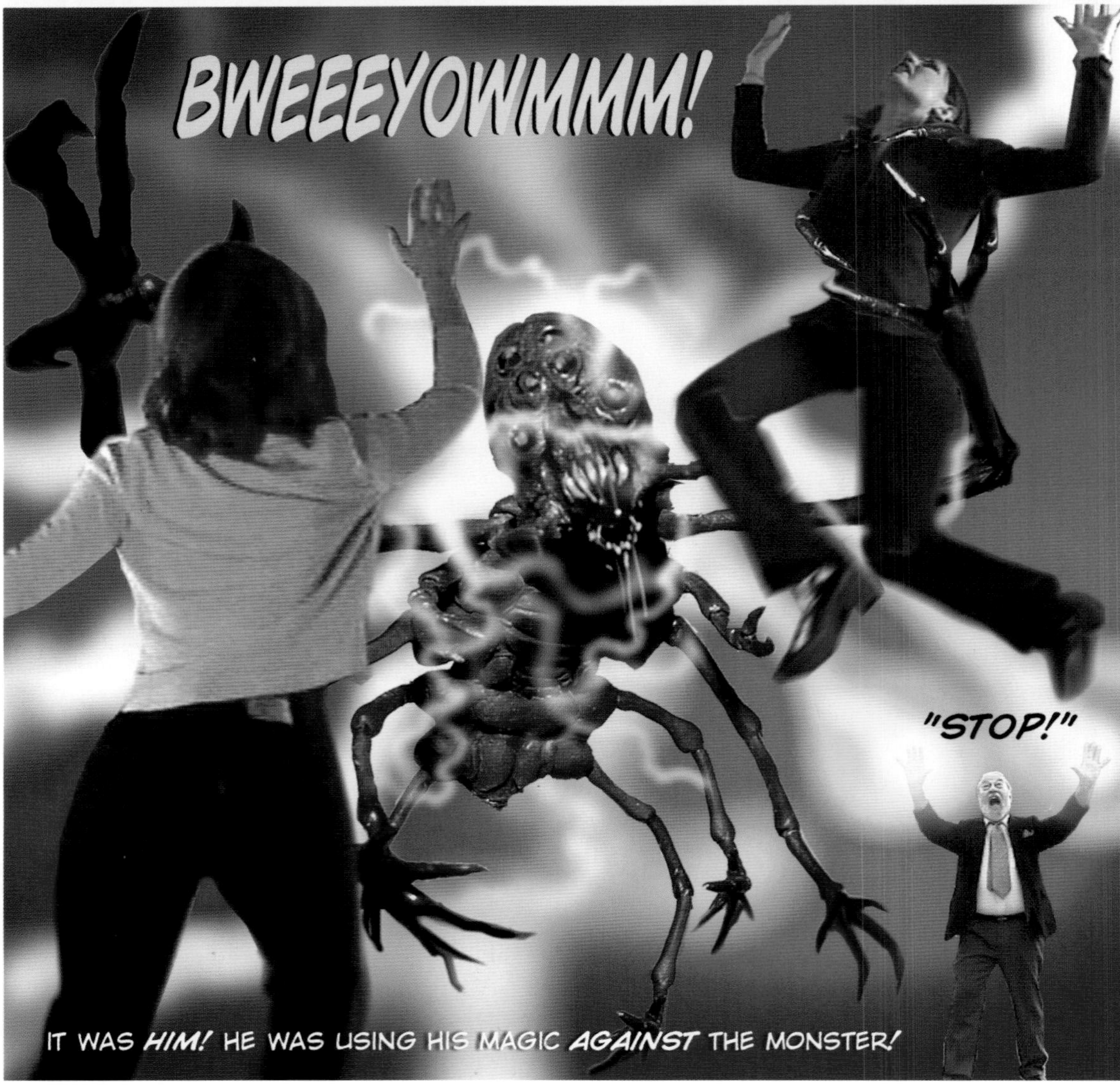
BWEEEYOWMMM!
"STOP!"
IT WAS HIM! HE WAS USING HIS MAGIC AGAINST THE MONSTER!

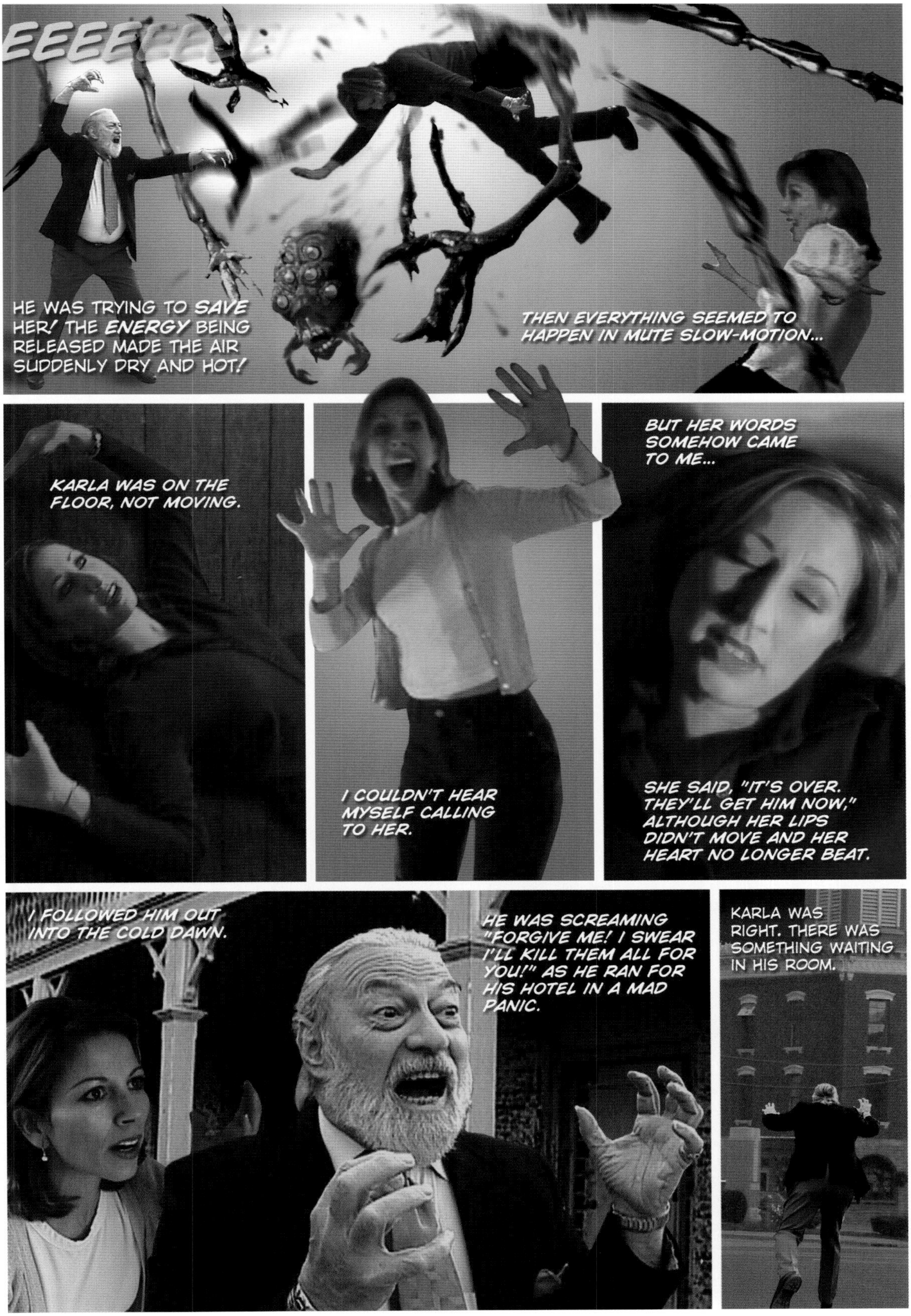
EEEEEEE
HE WAS TRYING TO SAVE HER! THE ENERGY BEING RELEASED MADE THE AIR SUDDENLY DRY AND HOT!
THEN EVERYTHING SEEMED TO HAPPEN IN MUTE SLOW-MOTION...
KARLA WAS ON THE FLOOR, NOT MOVING.
I COULDN'T HEAR MYSELF CALLING TO HER.
BUT HER WORDS SOMEHOW CAME TO ME...
SHE SAID, "IT'S OVER. THEY'LL GET HIM NOW," ALTHOUGH HER LIPS DIDN'T MOVE AND HER HEART NO LONGER BEAT.
I FOLLOWED HIM OUT INTO THE COLD DAWN.
HE WAS SCREAMING "FORGIVE ME! I SWEAR I'LL KILL THEM ALL FOR YOU!" AS HE RAN FOR HIS HOTEL IN A MAD PANIC.
KARLA WAS RIGHT. THERE WAS SOMETHING WAITING IN HIS ROOM.

HE WAS WEAK, *DISLOYAL!*

HE DIDN'T WANT KARLA TO DIE, AND HE WOULD HAVE TO PAY FOR THAT.

HIS HEAD WAS *SEEDED, REMOVED, WRAPPED IN SILK* AND PUT INTO THE *BOX!* ITS WORK FINISHED, ITS LINK TO EARTH DESTROYED, THE LAST GRAVESWELLER VANISHED. THE OLD *BOOKS* TOLD ME THIS.

AND NOW TO DO WHAT *I* MUST DO. THANKS FOR COMING ALONG.

IT'S A LONG WALK TO *POINT WILBUR.*

DARIUS' BRAIN IS THEIR HOME NOW. THERE THEY WILL THRIVE AND BIDE THEIR TIME. SOMEONE WILL FIND THEM AGAIN.

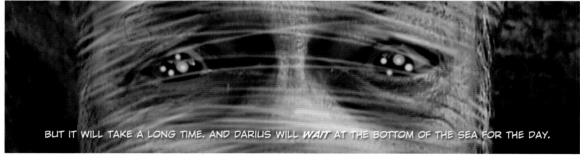

BUT IT WILL TAKE A LONG TIME. AND DARIUS WILL *WAIT* AT THE BOTTOM OF THE SEA FOR THE DAY.

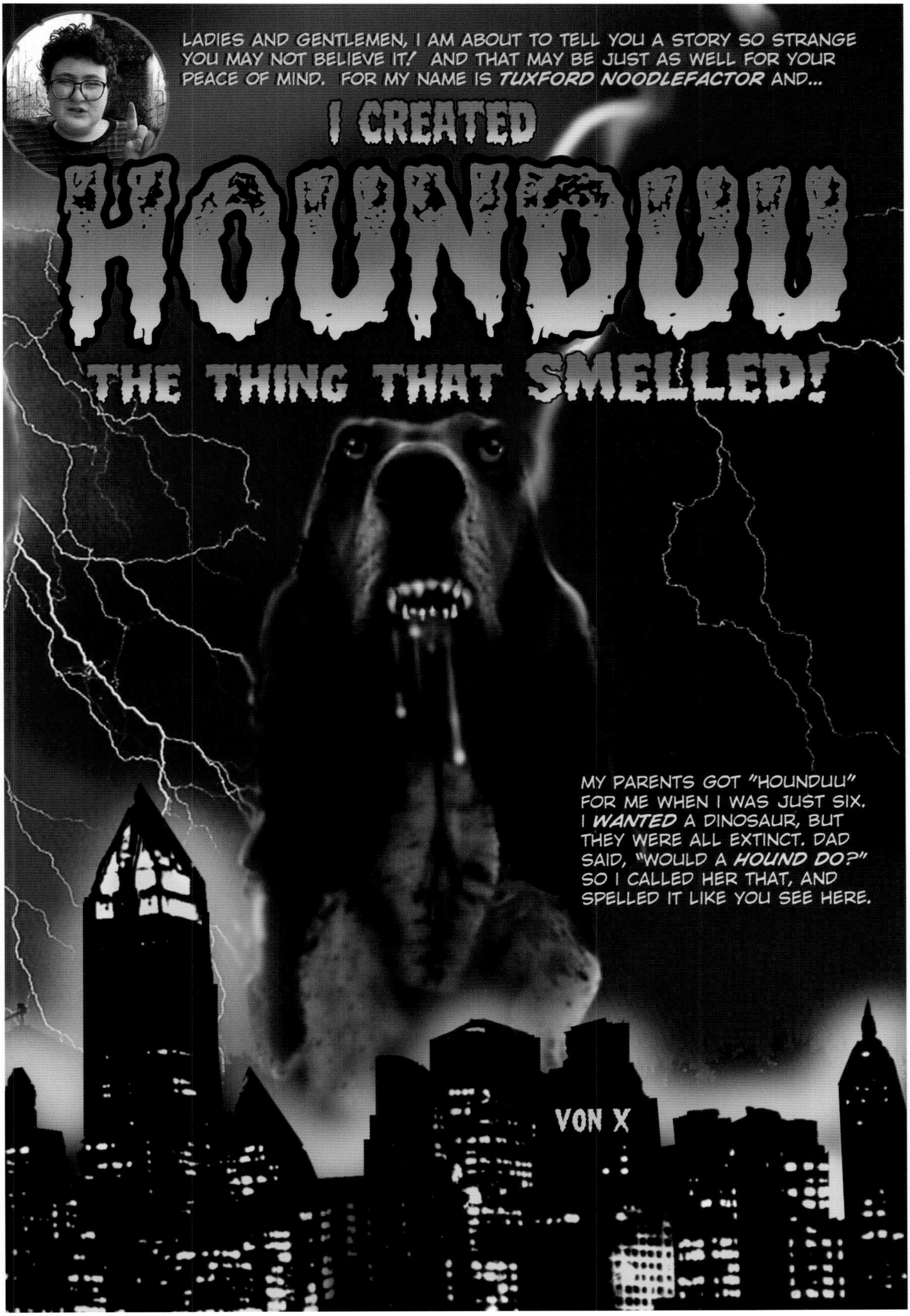

LADIES AND GENTLEMEN, I AM ABOUT TO TELL YOU A STORY SO STRANGE YOU MAY NOT BELIEVE IT! AND THAT MAY BE JUST AS WELL FOR YOUR PEACE OF MIND. FOR MY NAME IS *TUXFORD NOODLEFACTOR* AND...
I CREATED
HOUNDUU
THE THING THAT SMELLED!
MY PARENTS GOT "HOUNDUU" FOR ME WHEN I WAS JUST SIX. I *WANTED* A DINOSAUR, BUT THEY WERE ALL EXTINCT. DAD SAID, "WOULD A *HOUND DO?*" SO I CALLED HER THAT, AND SPELLED IT LIKE YOU SEE HERE.
VON X

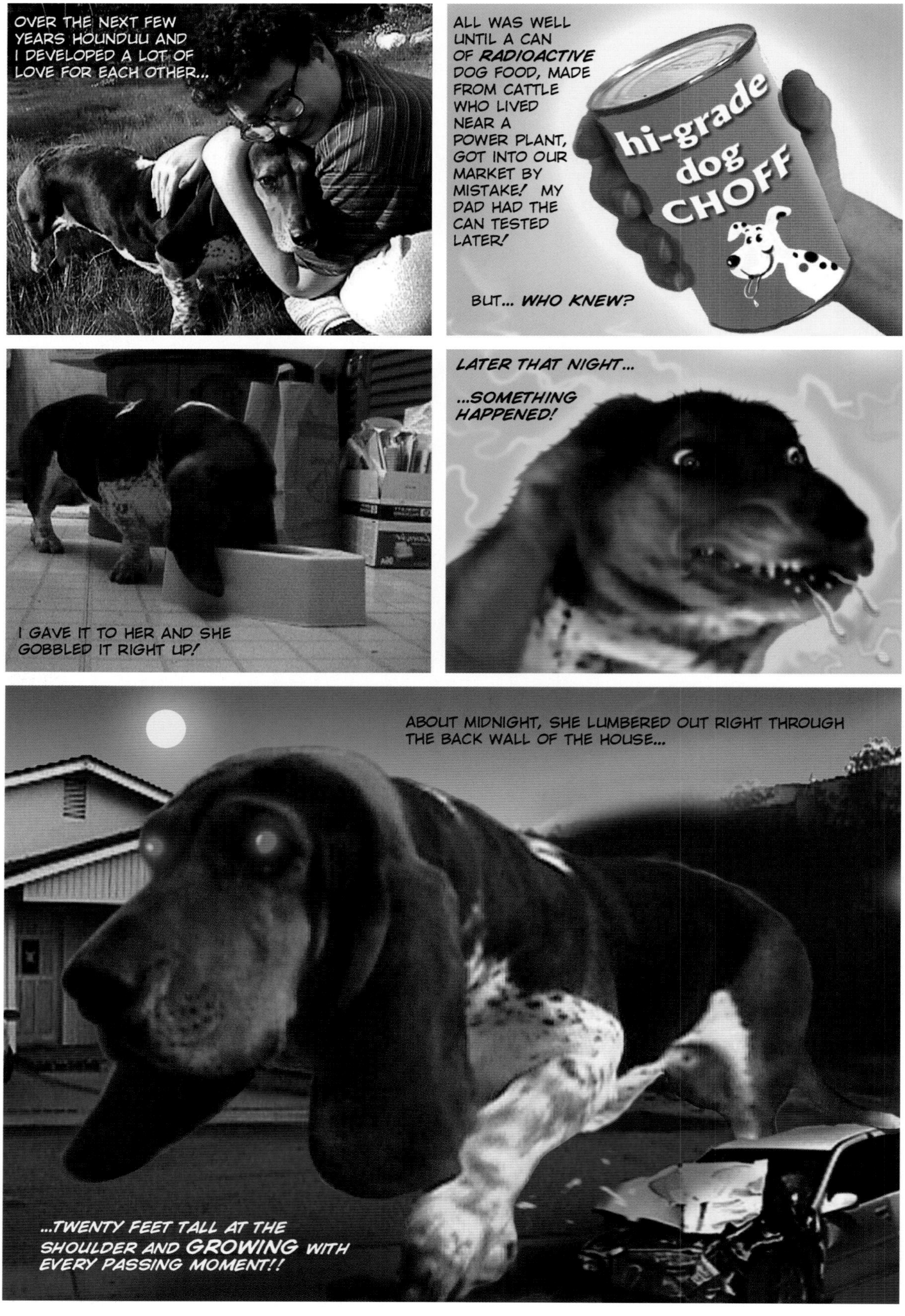
OVER THE NEXT FEW YEARS HOUNDUU AND I DEVELOPED A LOT OF LOVE FOR EACH OTHER...
ALL WAS WELL UNTIL A CAN OF RADIOACTIVE DOG FOOD, MADE FROM CATTLE WHO LIVED NEAR A POWER PLANT, GOT INTO OUR MARKET BY MISTAKE! MY DAD HAD THE CAN TESTED LATER!
hi-grade dog CHOFF
BUT... WHO KNEW?
I GAVE IT TO HER AND SHE GOBBLED IT RIGHT UP!
LATER THAT NIGHT...
...SOMETHING HAPPENED!
ABOUT MIDNIGHT, SHE LUMBERED OUT RIGHT THROUGH THE BACK WALL OF THE HOUSE...
...TWENTY FEET TALL AT THE SHOULDER AND GROWING WITH EVERY PASSING MOMENT!!

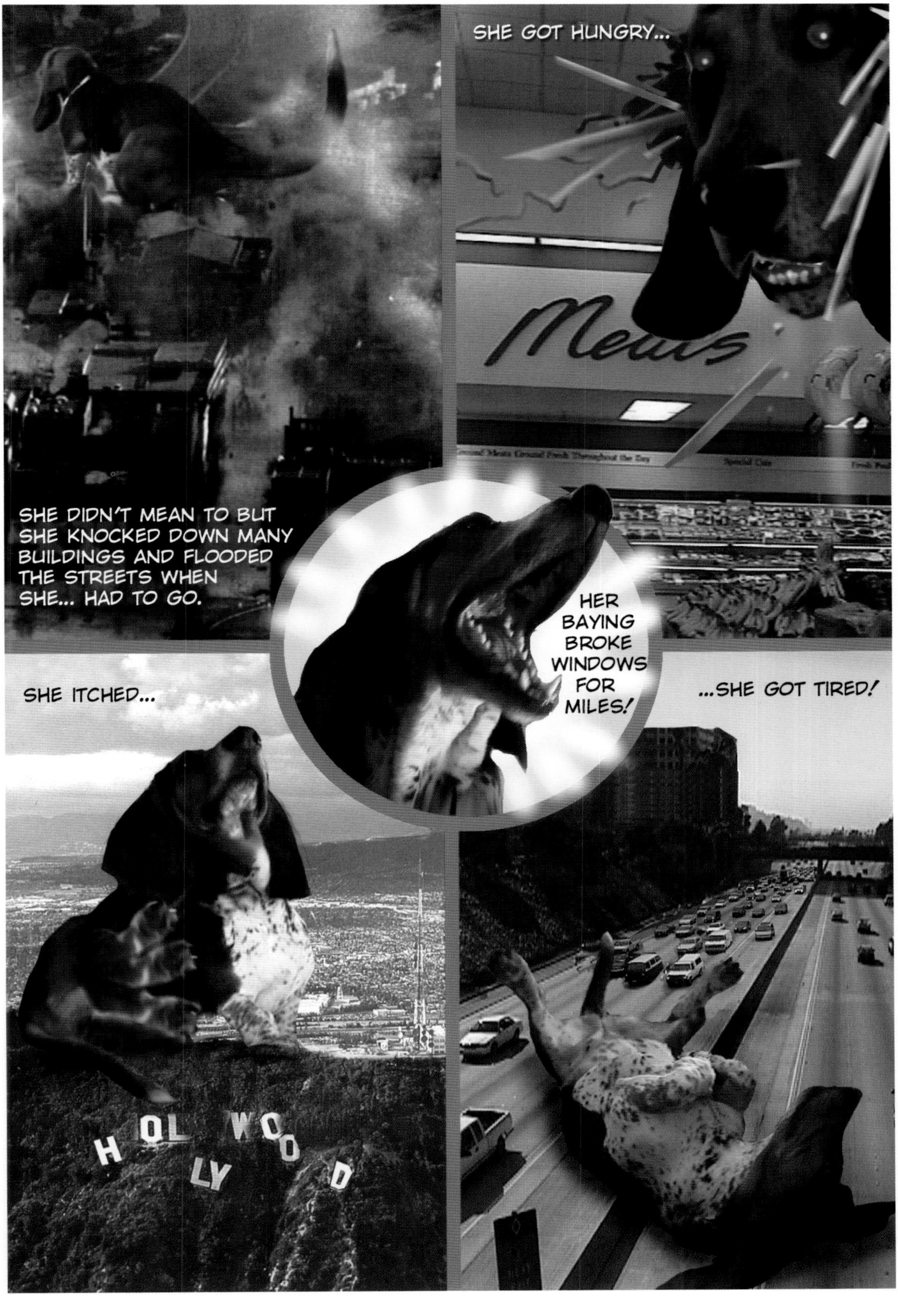
SHE DIDN'T MEAN TO BUT SHE KNOCKED DOWN MANY BUILDINGS AND FLOODED THE STREETS WHEN SHE... HAD TO GO.
SHE GOT HUNGRY...
Meats
HER BAYING BROKE WINDOWS FOR MILES!
SHE ITCHED...
...SHE GOT TIRED!

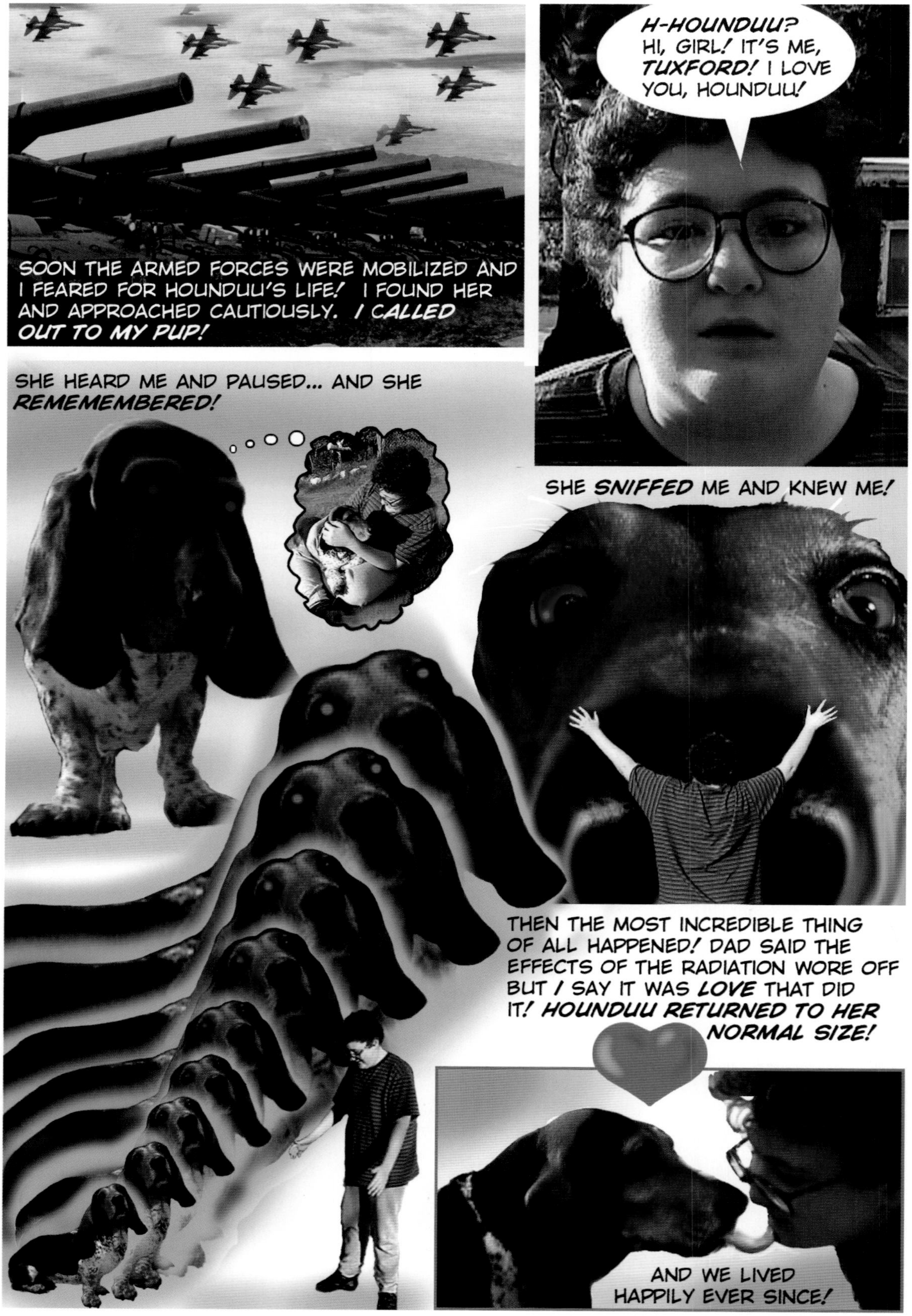
SOON THE ARMED FORCES WERE MOBILIZED AND I FEARED FOR HOUNDUU'S LIFE! I FOUND HER AND APPROACHED CAUTIOUSLY. I CALLED OUT TO MY PUP!
H-HOUNDUU? HI, GIRL! IT'S ME, TUXFORD! I LOVE YOU, HOUNDUU!
SHE HEARD ME AND PAUSED... AND SHE REMEMEMBERED!
SHE SNIFFED ME AND KNEW ME!
THEN THE MOST INCREDIBLE THING OF ALL HAPPENED! DAD SAID THE EFFECTS OF THE RADIATION WORE OFF BUT I SAY IT WAS LOVE THAT DID IT! HOUNDUU RETURNED TO HER NORMAL SIZE!
AND WE LIVED HAPPILY EVER SINCE!

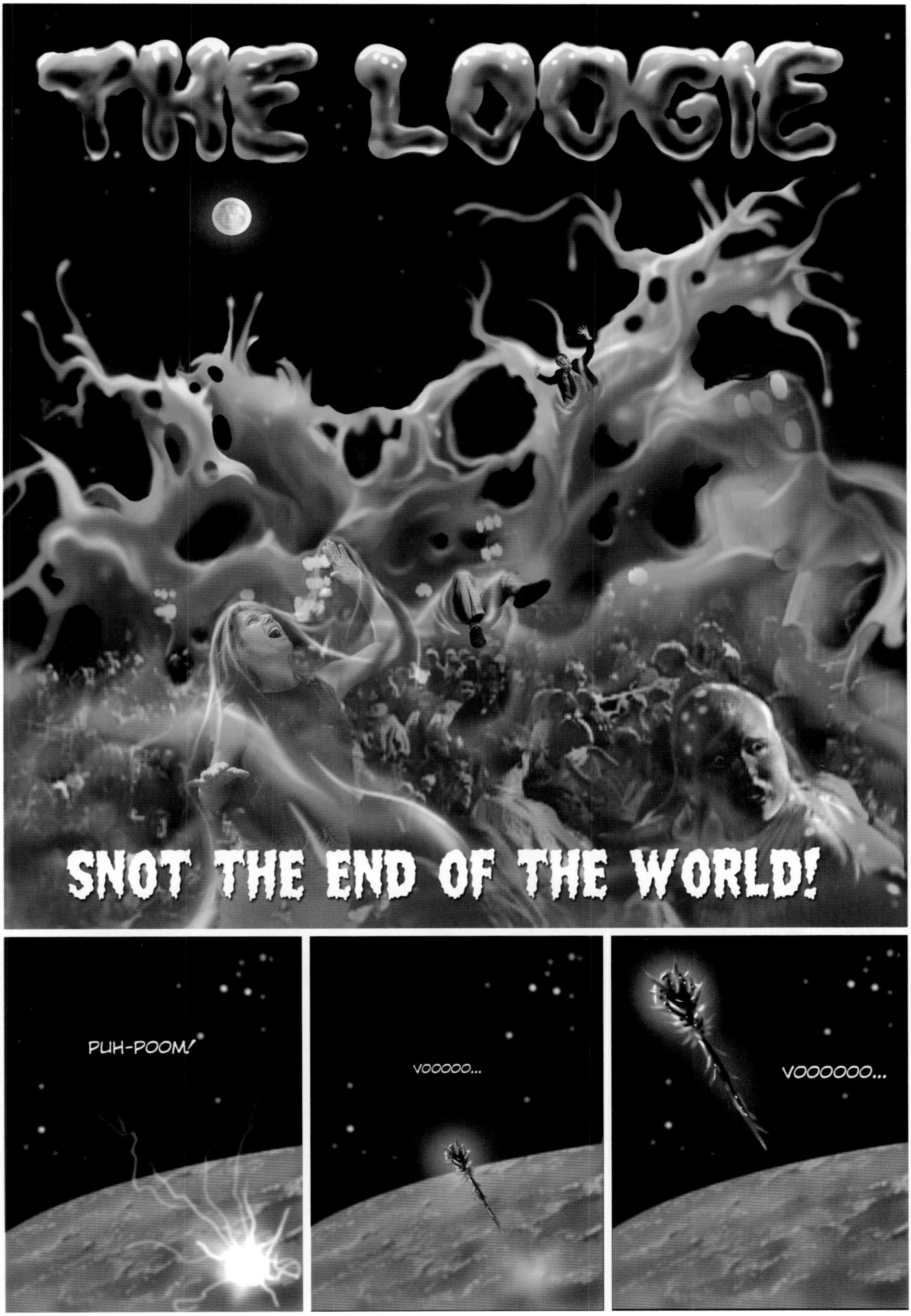
THE LOOGIE
SNOT THE END OF THE WORLD!
PUH-POOM!
VOOOOO...
VOOOOOO...

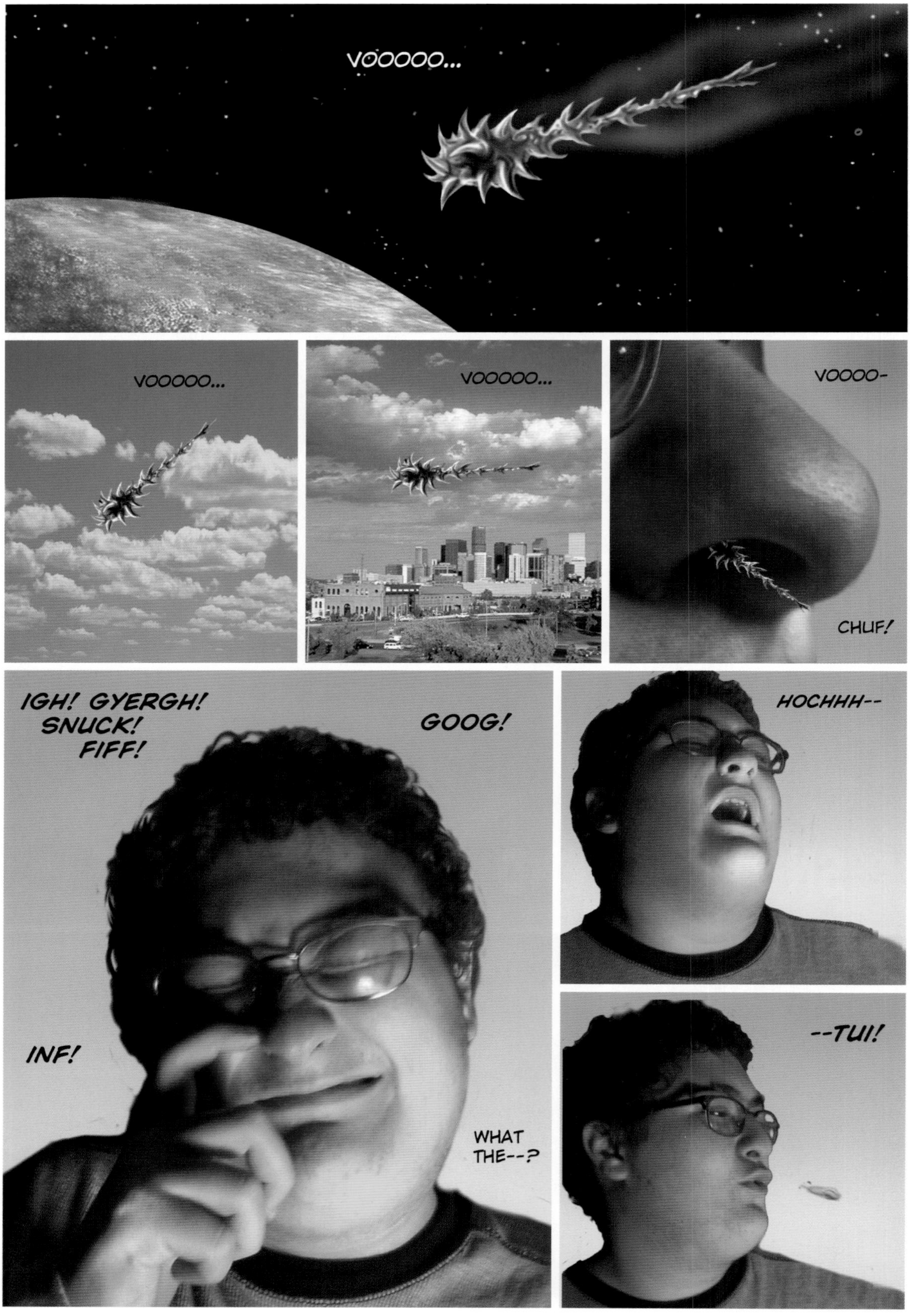
VOOOOO...
VOOOOO...
VOOOOO...
VOOOO-
CHUF!
IGH! GYERGH!
SNUCK!
FIFF!
GOOG!
INF!
WHAT
THE--?
HOCHHH--
--TUI!

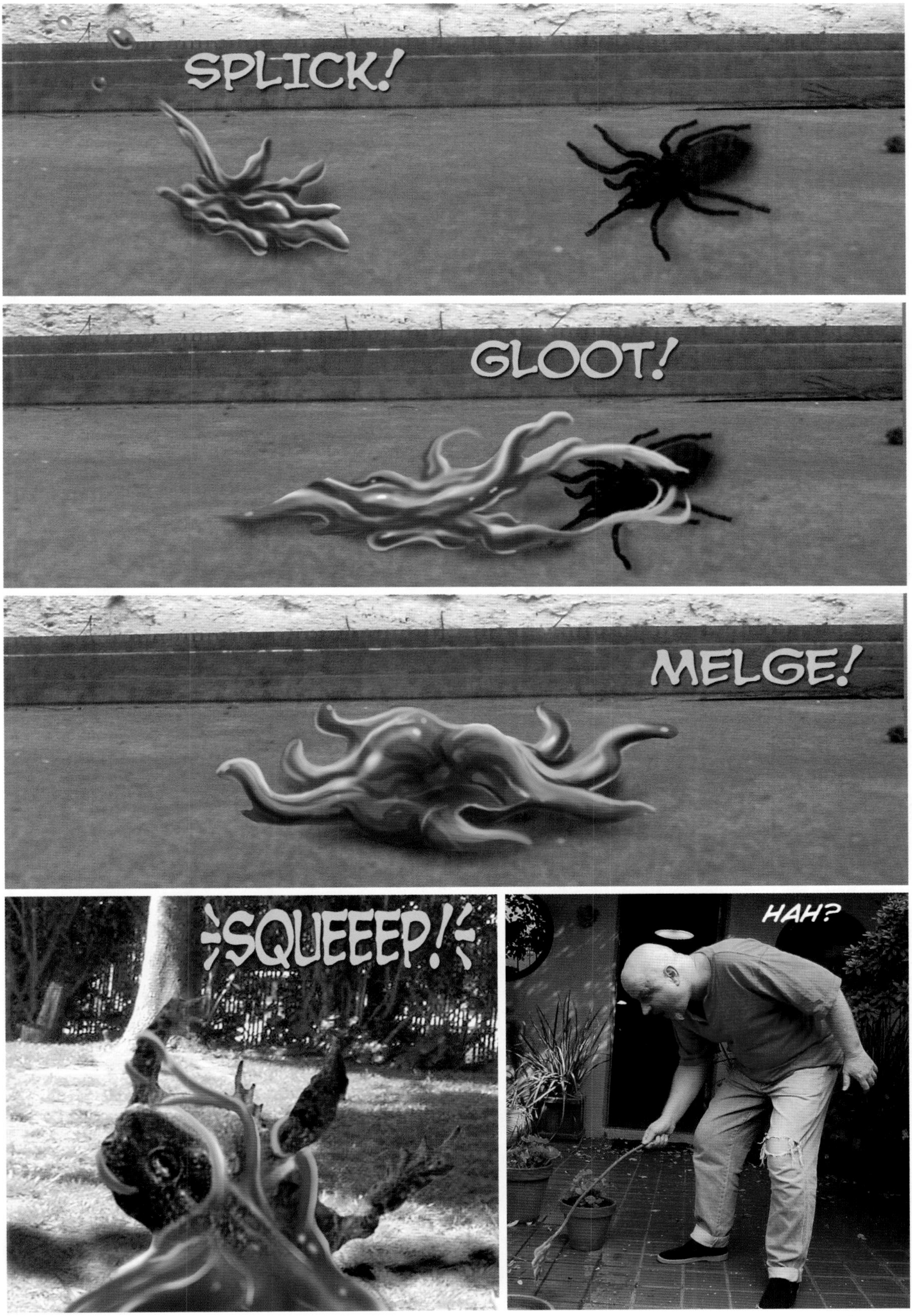
SPLICK!
GLOOT!
MELGE!
SQUEEEP!
HAH?

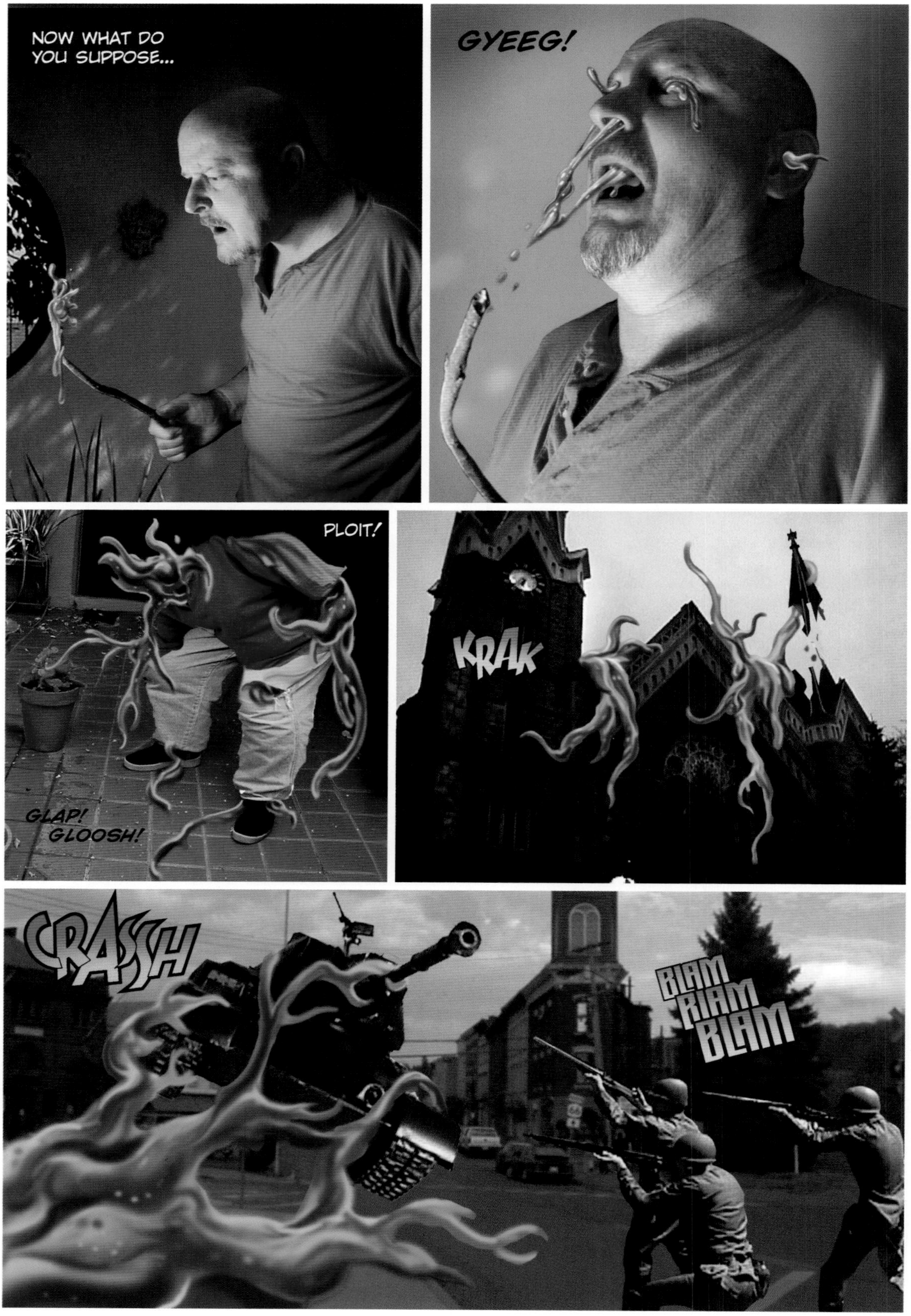
NOW WHAT DO YOU SUPPOSE...
GYEEG!
PLOIT!
GLAP! GLOOSH!
KRAK
CRASSH
BLAM BLAM BLAM

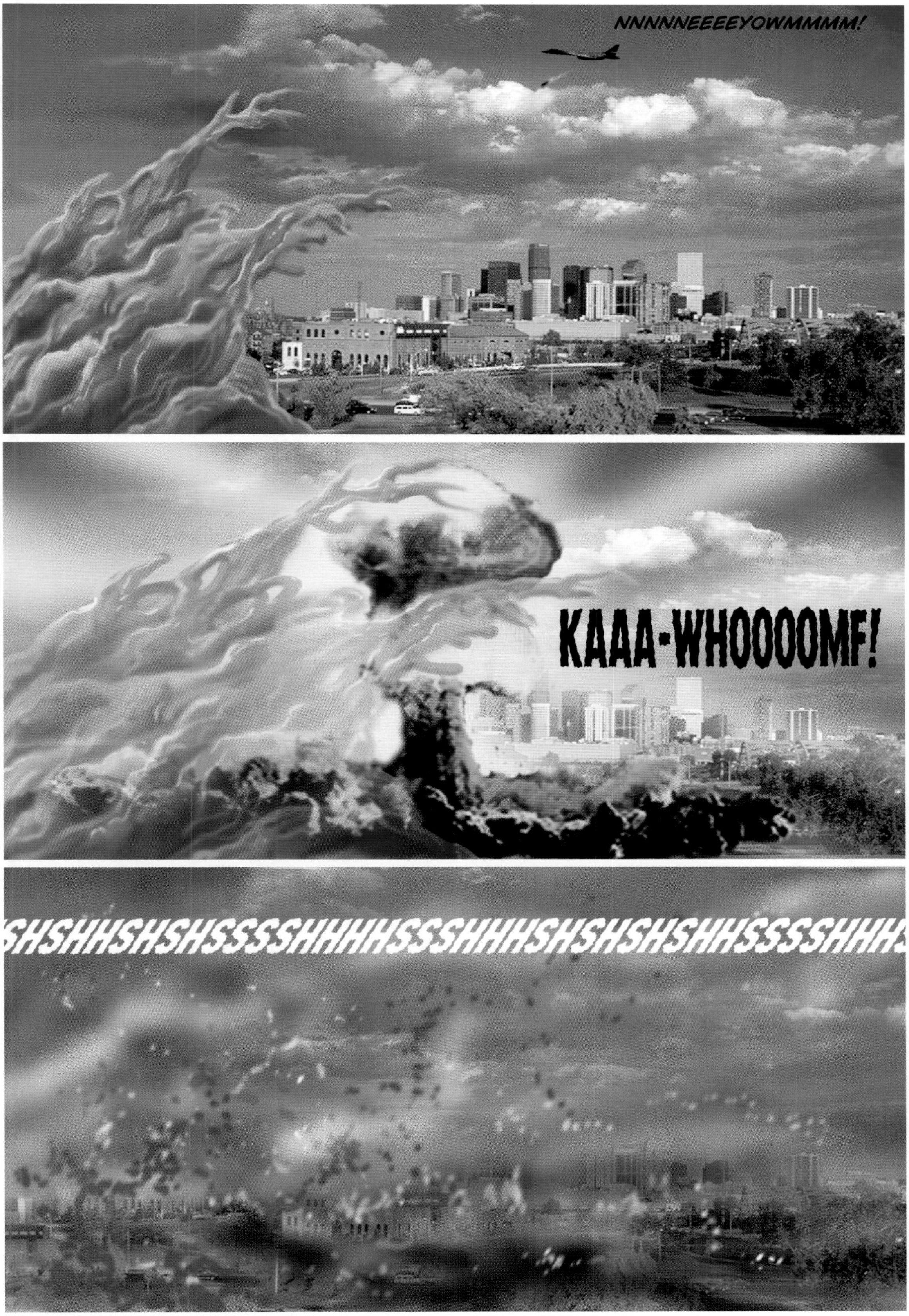
NNNNNEEEEYOWMMMM!
KAAA-WHOOOOMF!
SHSHHSHSHSSSSHHHHSSSSHHHHSHSHSHSHHSSSSHHHS

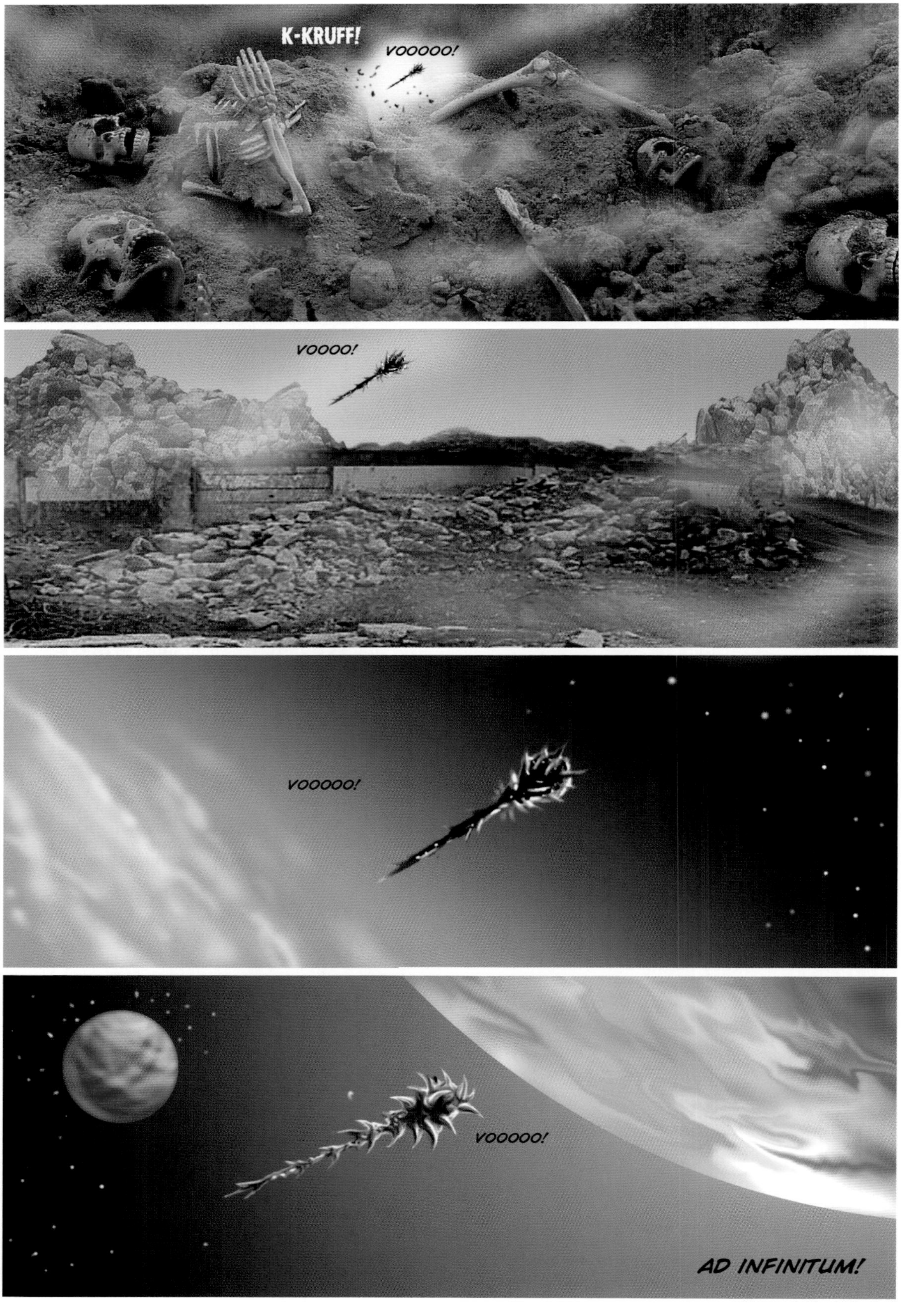
K-KRUFF!
VOOOOO!
VOOOO!
VOOOOO!
VOOOOO!
AD INFINITUM!

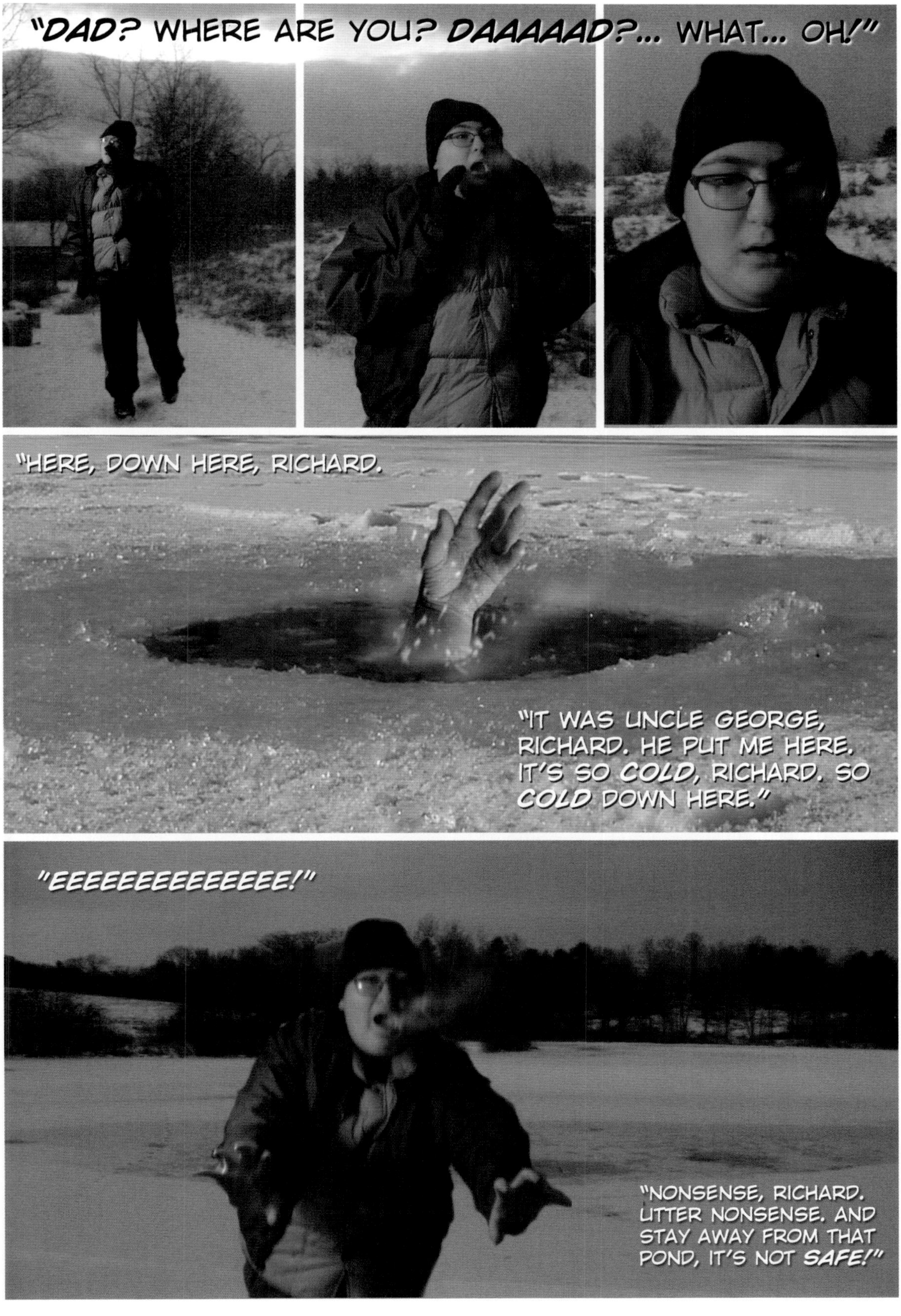
"DAD? WHERE ARE YOU? DAAAAAD?... WHAT... OH!"
"HERE, DOWN HERE, RICHARD.
"IT WAS UNCLE GEORGE, RICHARD. HE PUT ME HERE. IT'S SO COLD, RICHARD. SO COLD DOWN HERE."
"EEEEEEEEEEEEEE!"
"NONSENSE, RICHARD. UTTER NONSENSE. AND STAY AWAY FROM THAT POND, IT'S NOT SAFE!"

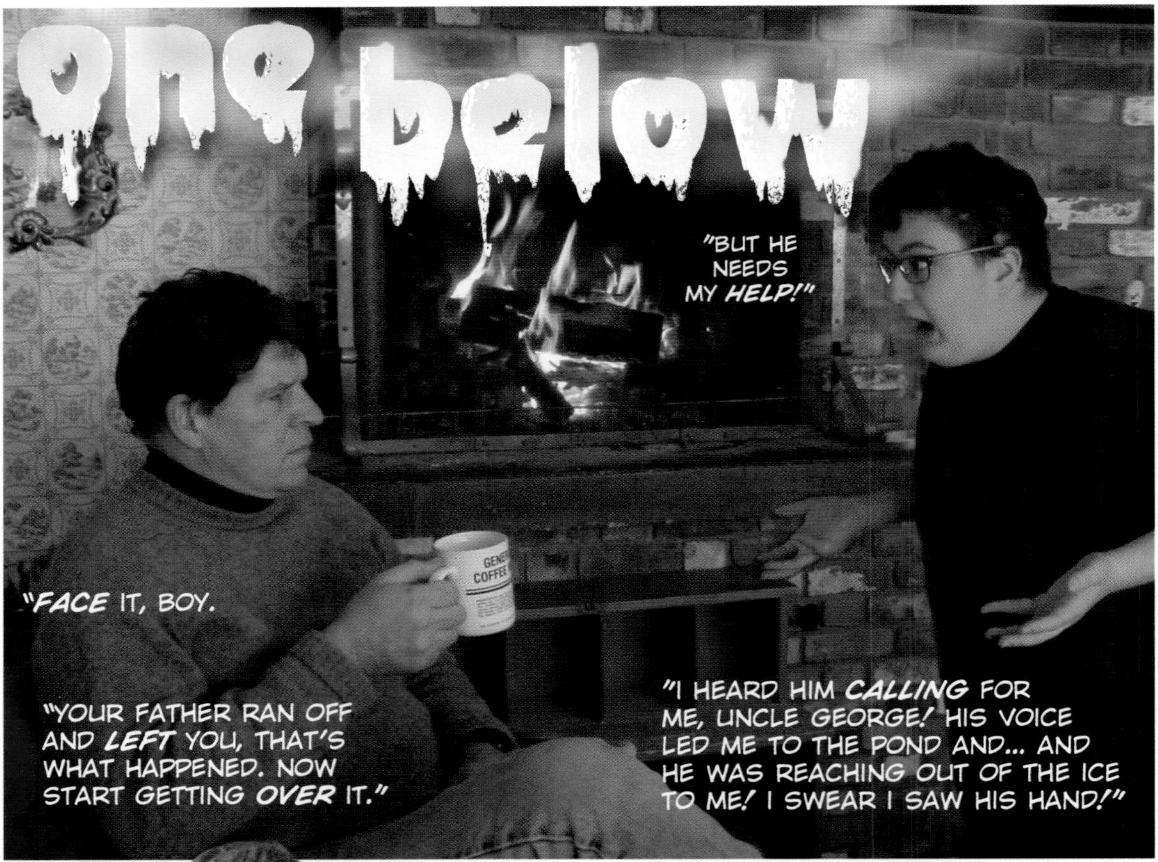
one below
"BUT HE NEEDS MY HELP!"
"FACE IT, BOY.
"YOUR FATHER RAN OFF AND LEFT YOU, THAT'S WHAT HAPPENED. NOW START GETTING OVER IT."
"I HEARD HIM CALLING FOR ME, UNCLE GEORGE! HIS VOICE LED ME TO THE POND AND... AND HE WAS REACHING OUT OF THE ICE TO ME! I SWEAR I SAW HIS HAND!"

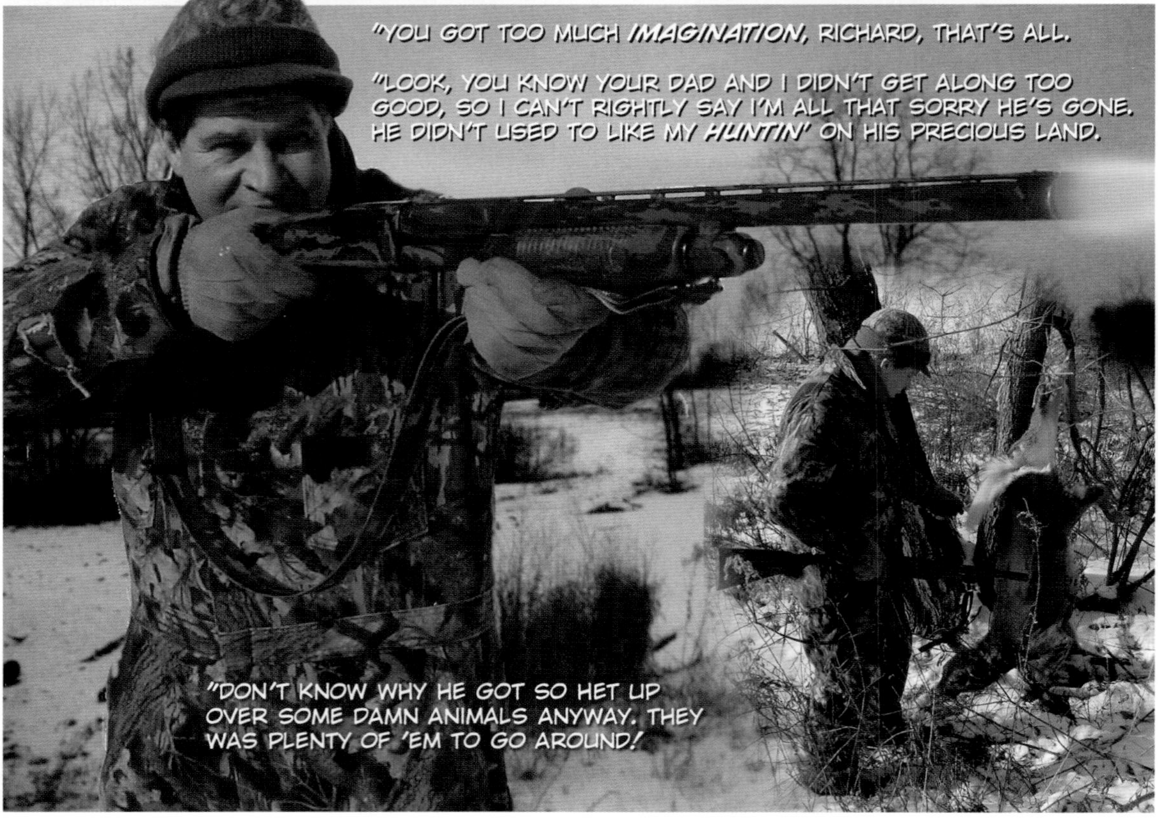
"YOU GOT TOO MUCH IMAGINATION, RICHARD, THAT'S ALL.
"LOOK, YOU KNOW YOUR DAD AND I DIDN'T GET ALONG TOO GOOD, SO I CAN'T RIGHTLY SAY I'M ALL THAT SORRY HE'S GONE. HE DIDN'T USED TO LIKE MY HUNTIN' ON HIS PRECIOUS LAND.
"DON'T KNOW WHY HE GOT SO HET UP OVER SOME DAMN ANIMALS ANYWAY. THEY WAS PLENTY OF 'EM TO GO AROUND!

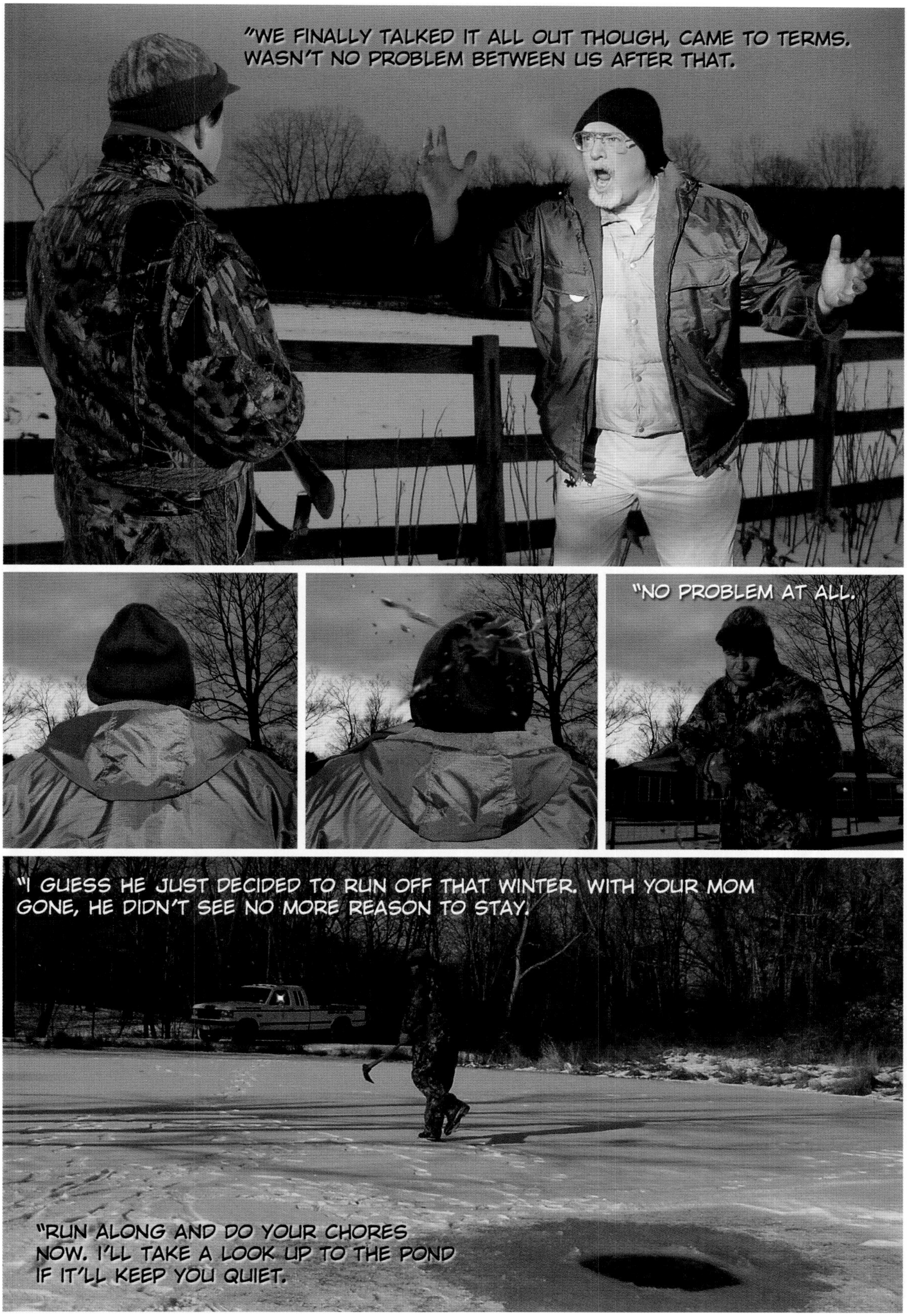
"WE FINALLY TALKED IT ALL OUT THOUGH, CAME TO TERMS. WASN'T NO PROBLEM BETWEEN US AFTER THAT.
"NO PROBLEM AT ALL.
"I GUESS HE JUST DECIDED TO RUN OFF THAT WINTER. WITH YOUR MOM GONE, HE DIDN'T SEE NO MORE REASON TO STAY.
"RUN ALONG AND DO YOUR CHORES NOW. I'LL TAKE A LOOK UP TO THE POND IF IT'LL KEEP YOU QUIET.

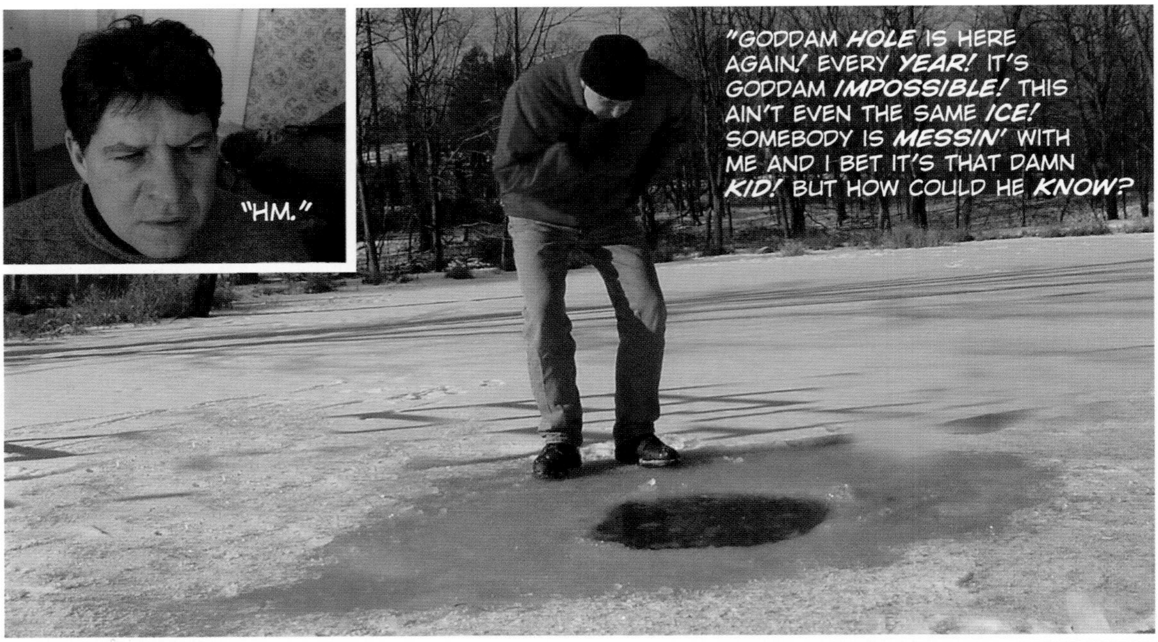
"HM."
"GODDAM HOLE IS HERE AGAIN! EVERY YEAR! IT'S GODDAM IMPOSSIBLE! THIS AIN'T EVEN THE SAME ICE! SOMEBODY IS MESSIN' WITH ME AND I BET IT'S THAT DAMN KID! BUT HOW COULD HE KNOW?

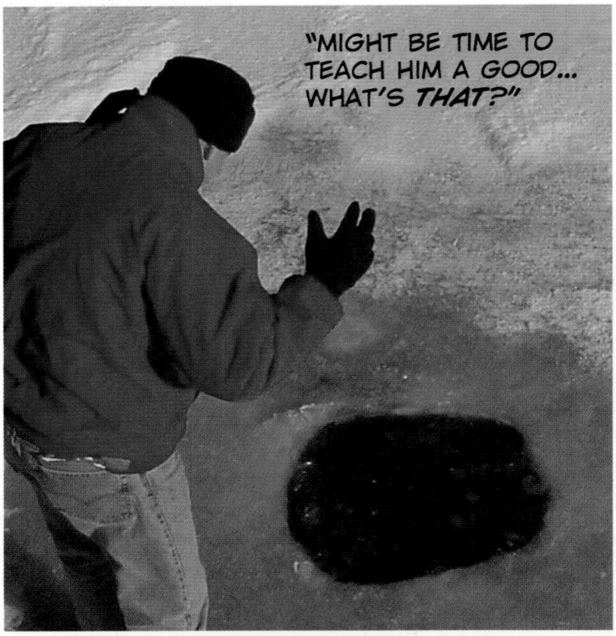
"MIGHT BE TIME TO TEACH HIM A GOOD... WHAT'S THAT?"

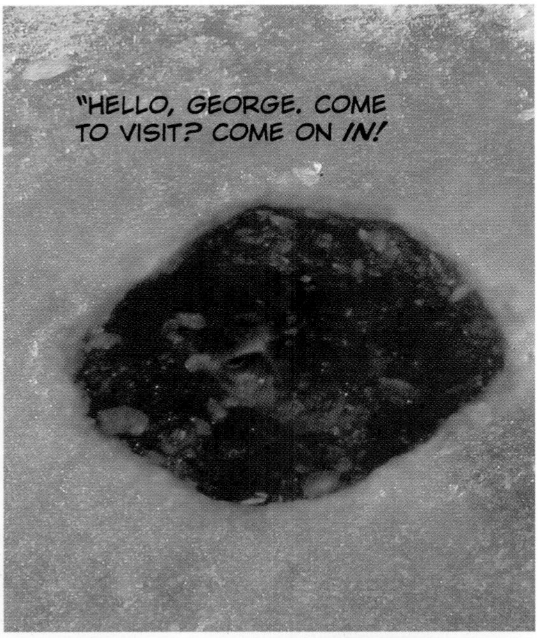
"HELLO, GEORGE. COME TO VISIT? COME ON IN!

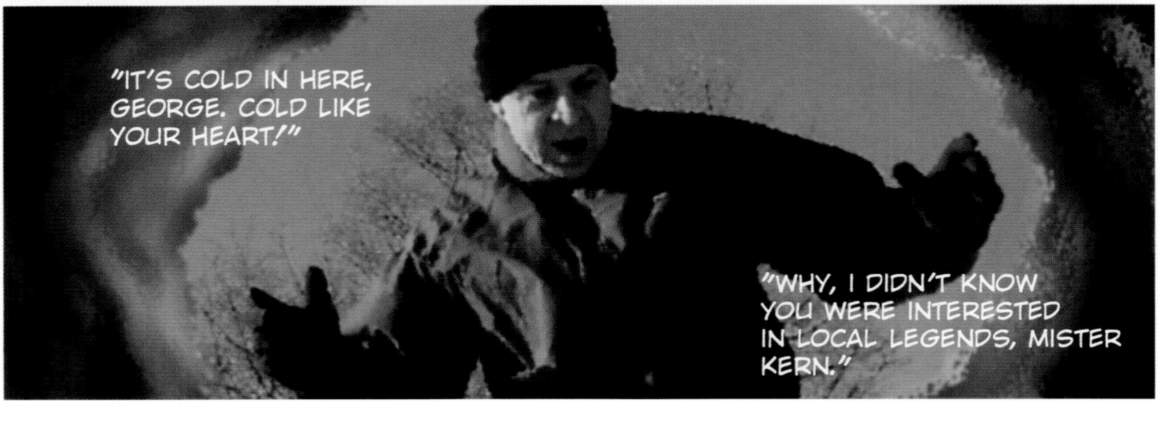
"IT'S COLD IN HERE, GEORGE. COLD LIKE YOUR HEART!"
"WHY, I DIDN'T KNOW YOU WERE INTERESTED IN LOCAL LEGENDS, MISTER KERN."

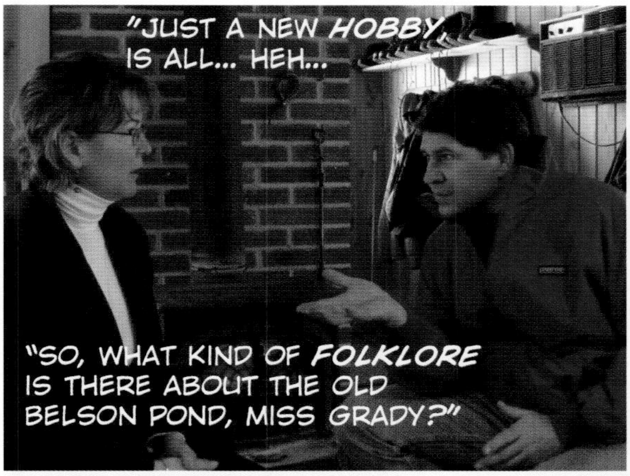
"JUST A NEW HOBBY, IS ALL... HEH...
"SO, WHAT KIND OF FOLKLORE IS THERE ABOUT THE OLD BELSON POND, MISS GRADY?"

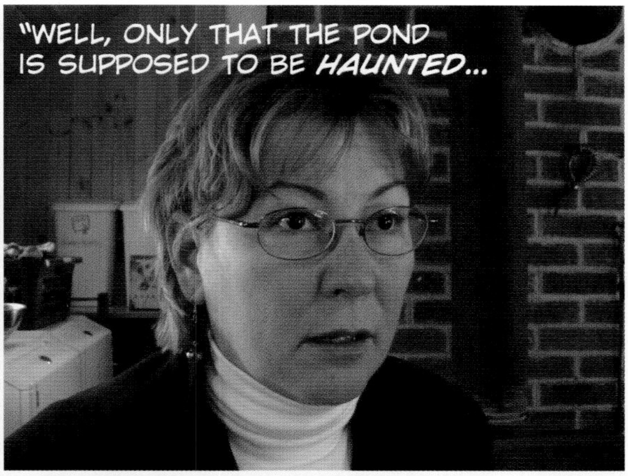
"WELL, ONLY THAT THE POND IS SUPPOSED TO BE HAUNTED...

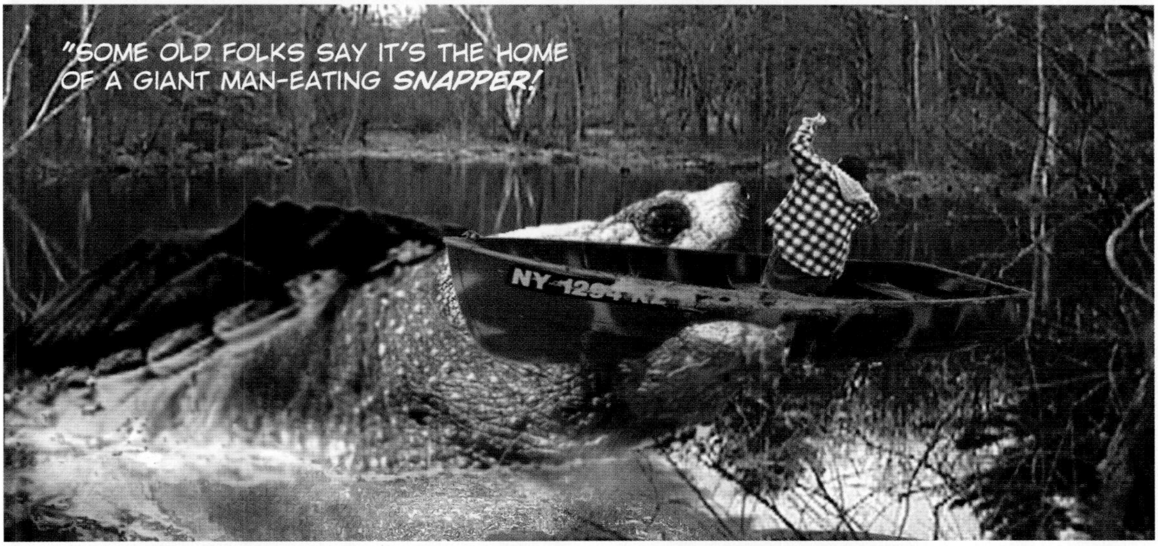
"SOME OLD FOLKS SAY IT'S THE HOME OF A GIANT MAN-EATING SNAPPER!
NY-1294-KL

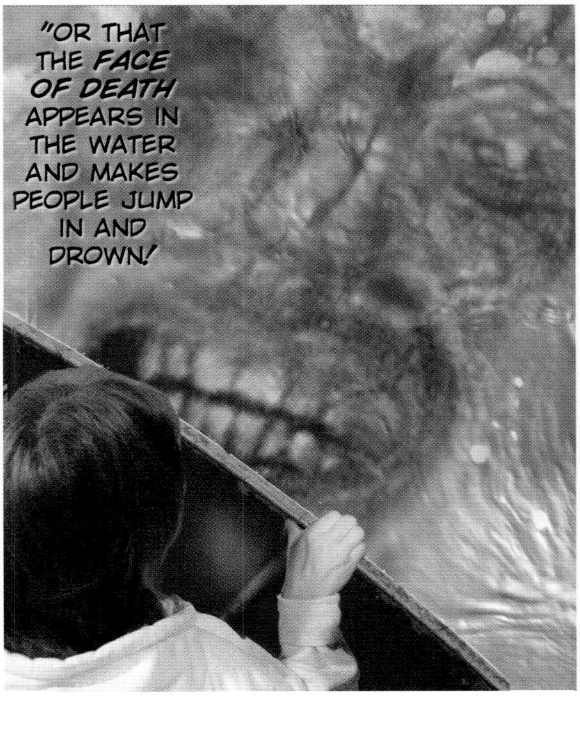
"OR THAT THE FACE OF DEATH APPEARS IN THE WATER AND MAKES PEOPLE JUMP IN AND DROWN!

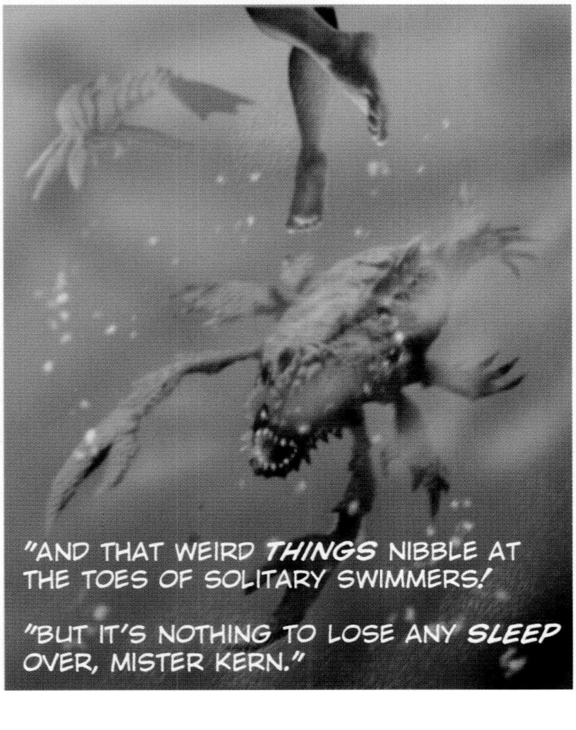
"AND THAT WEIRD THINGS NIBBLE AT THE TOES OF SOLITARY SWIMMERS!
"BUT IT'S NOTHING TO LOSE ANY SLEEP OVER, MISTER KERN."

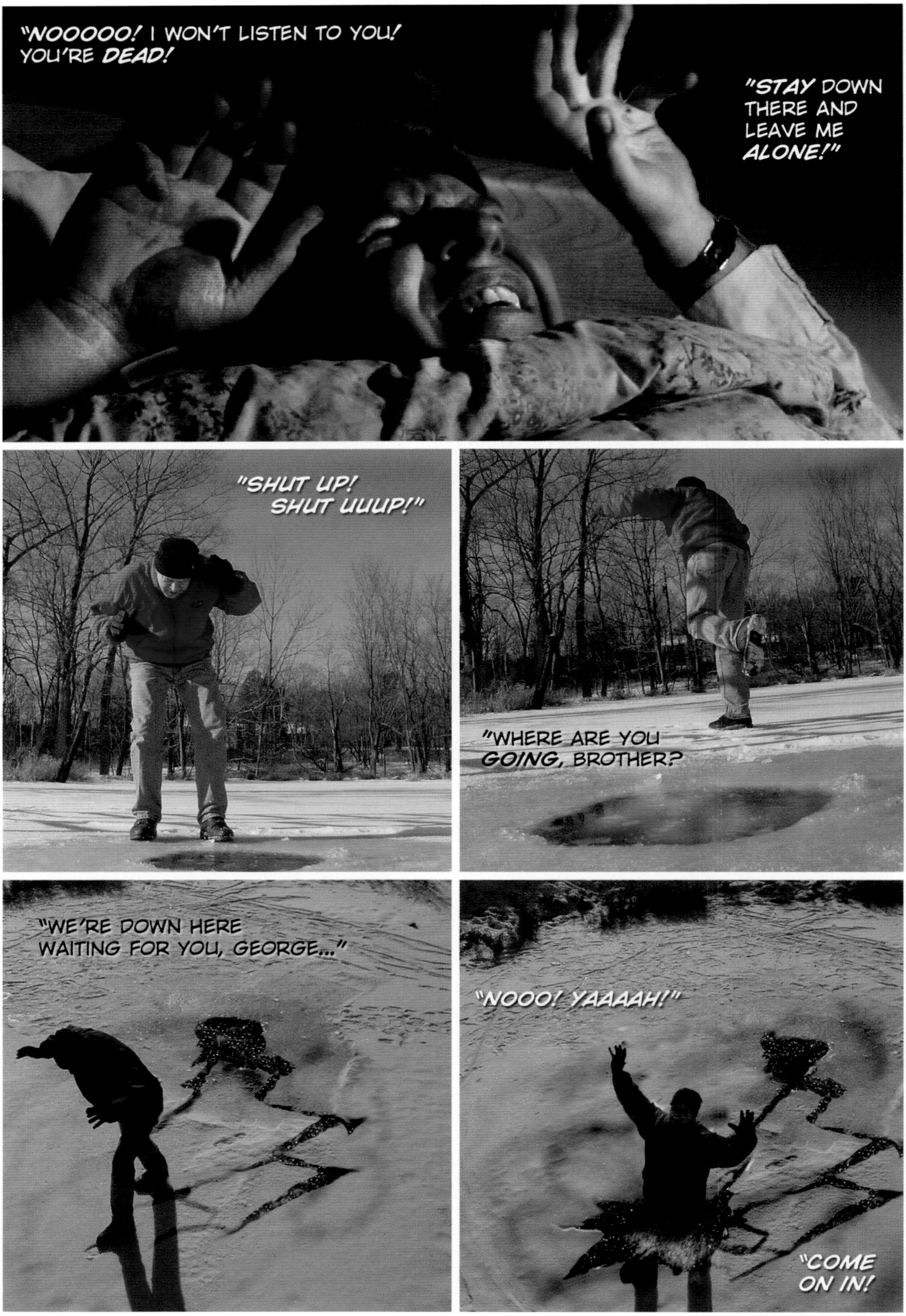
"NOOOOO! I WON'T LISTEN TO YOU! YOU'RE DEAD!
"STAY DOWN THERE AND LEAVE ME ALONE!"
"SHUT UP! SHUT UUUP!"
"WHERE ARE YOU GOING, BROTHER?
"WE'RE DOWN HERE WAITING FOR YOU, GEORGE..."
"NOOO! YAAAAH!"
"COME ON IN!

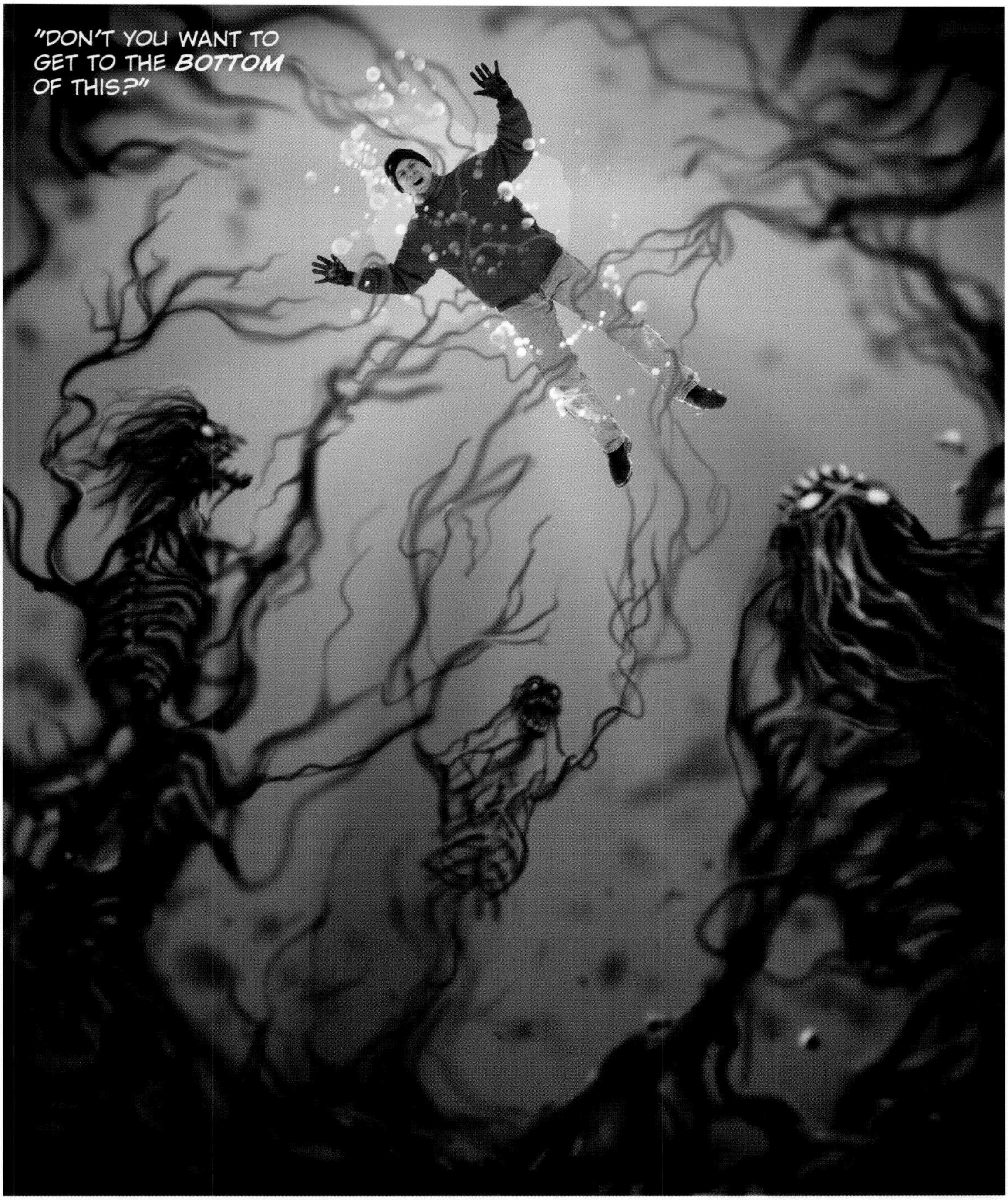
"DON'T YOU WANT TO GET TO THE *BOTTOM* OF THIS?"

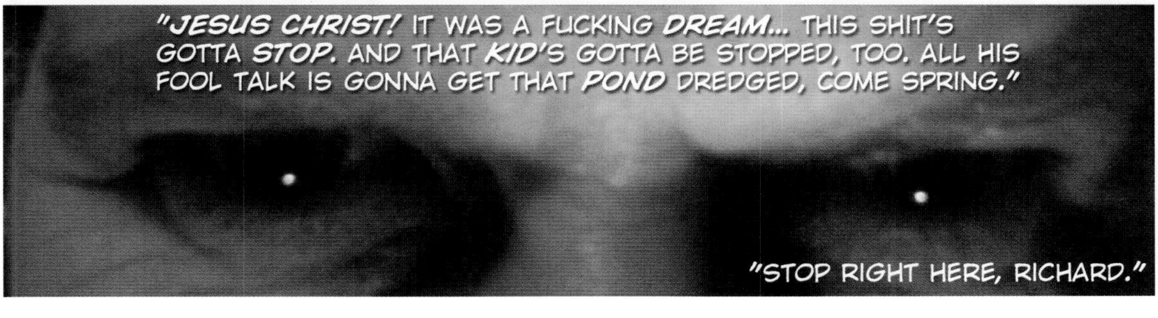
"*JESUS CHRIST!* IT WAS A FUCKING *DREAM*... THIS SHIT'S GOTTA *STOP*. AND THAT *KID'S* GOTTA BE STOPPED, TOO. ALL HIS FOOL TALK IS GONNA GET THAT *POND* DREDGED, COME SPRING."
"STOP RIGHT HERE, RICHARD."

"WHY DID YOU **BRING** ME HERE, UNCLE GEORGE?"

"IT'S **SPRINGTIME**, RICHARD. AIN'T NO MORE ICE AND SNOW. TIME THE **SHERIFF** MIGHT COME LOOKING AROUND... IF YOU WAS TO KEEP THAT **MOUTH** GOING..."

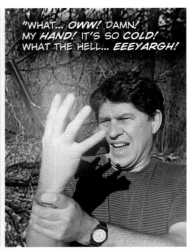

"WHAT... **OWW!** DAMN! MY **HAND!** IT'S SO **COLD!** WHAT THE HELL... **EEEYARGH!**

"C-C-CAN'T... MUH... M-M-MOOOVE... CHHH... KKHHHH..."

"UNCLE GEORGE? OH, MY **GOD!**"

*FREEZE FRAME!*

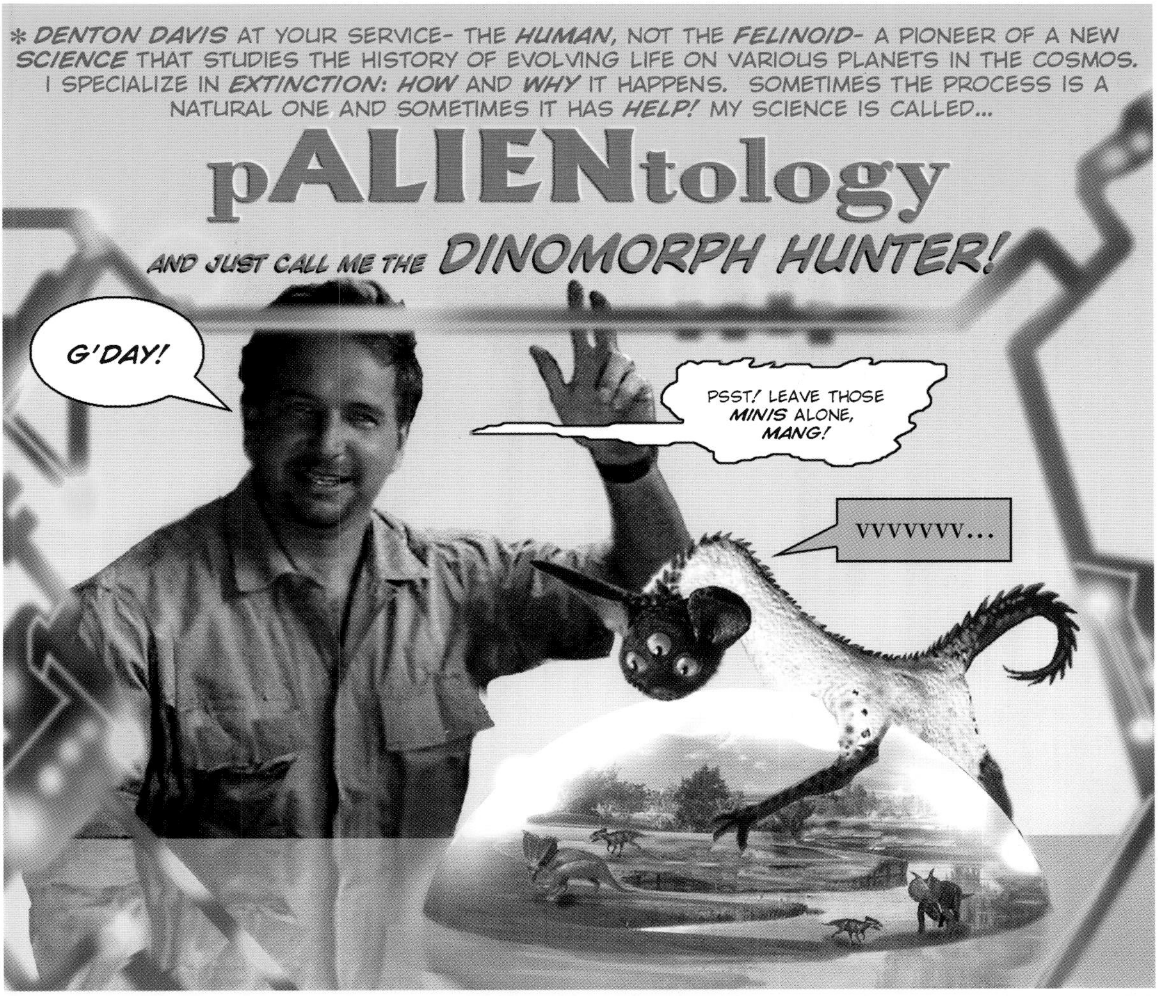
* DENTON DAVIS AT YOUR SERVICE- THE HUMAN, NOT THE FELINOID- A PIONEER OF A NEW SCIENCE THAT STUDIES THE HISTORY OF EVOLVING LIFE ON VARIOUS PLANETS IN THE COSMOS. I SPECIALIZE IN EXTINCTION: HOW AND WHY IT HAPPENS. SOMETIMES THE PROCESS IS A NATURAL ONE AND SOMETIMES IT HAS HELP! MY SCIENCE IS CALLED...
pALIENtology
AND JUST CALL ME THE DINOMORPH HUNTER!
G'DAY!
PSST! LEAVE THOSE MINIS ALONE, MANG!
VVVVVVV...

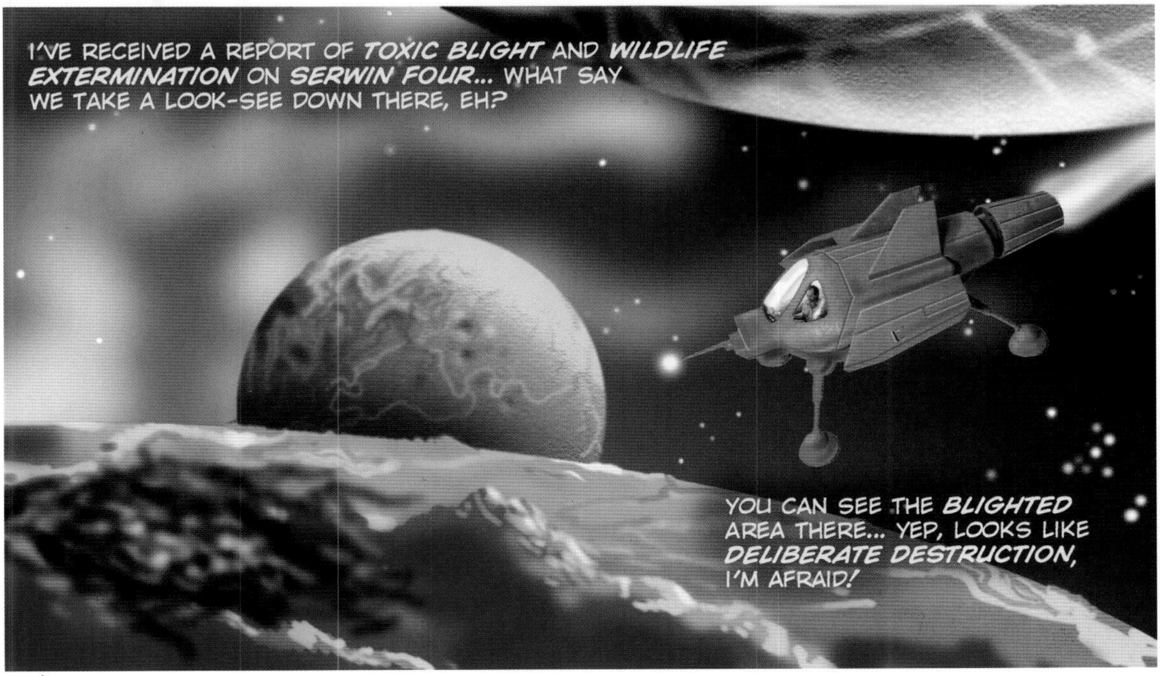
I'VE RECEIVED A REPORT OF TOXIC BLIGHT AND WILDLIFE EXTERMINATION ON SERWIN FOUR... WHAT SAY WE TAKE A LOOK-SEE DOWN THERE, EH?
YOU CAN SEE THE BLIGHTED AREA THERE... YEP, LOOKS LIKE DELIBERATE DESTRUCTION, I'M AFRAID!

* YOU HAVE TO IMAGINE ALL THIS AS BEING SPOKEN WITH A HEAVY AUSSIE ACCENT.

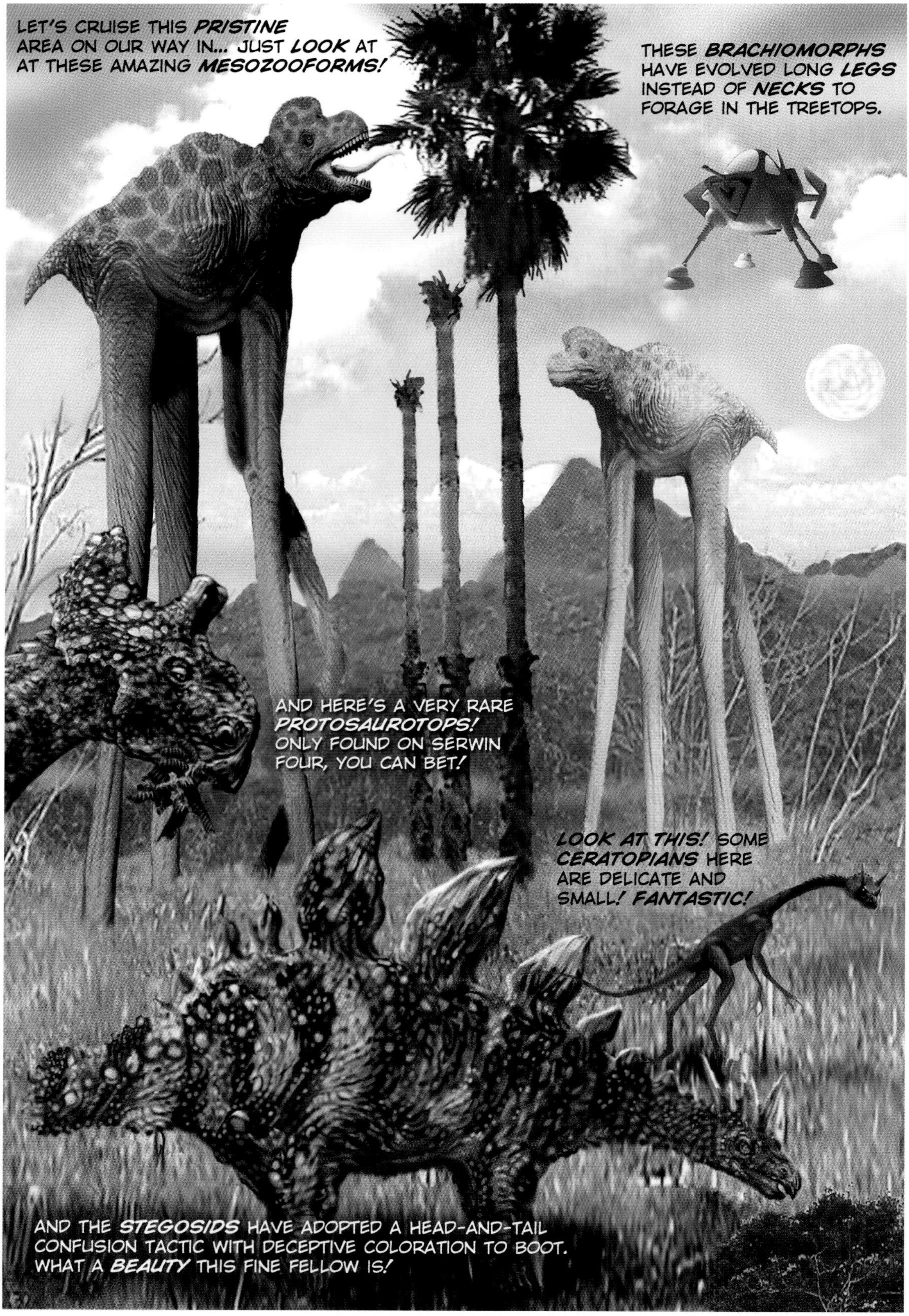
LET'S CRUISE THIS PRISTINE AREA ON OUR WAY IN... JUST LOOK AT AT THESE AMAZING MESOZOOFORMS!
THESE BRACHIOMORPHS HAVE EVOLVED LONG LEGS INSTEAD OF NECKS TO FORAGE IN THE TREETOPS.
AND HERE'S A VERY RARE PROTOSAUROTOPS! ONLY FOUND ON SERWIN FOUR, YOU CAN BET!
LOOK AT THIS! SOME CERATOPIANS HERE ARE DELICATE AND SMALL! FANTASTIC!
AND THE STEGOSIDS HAVE ADOPTED A HEAD-AND-TAIL CONFUSION TACTIC WITH DECEPTIVE COLORATION TO BOOT. WHAT A BEAUTY THIS FINE FELLOW IS!

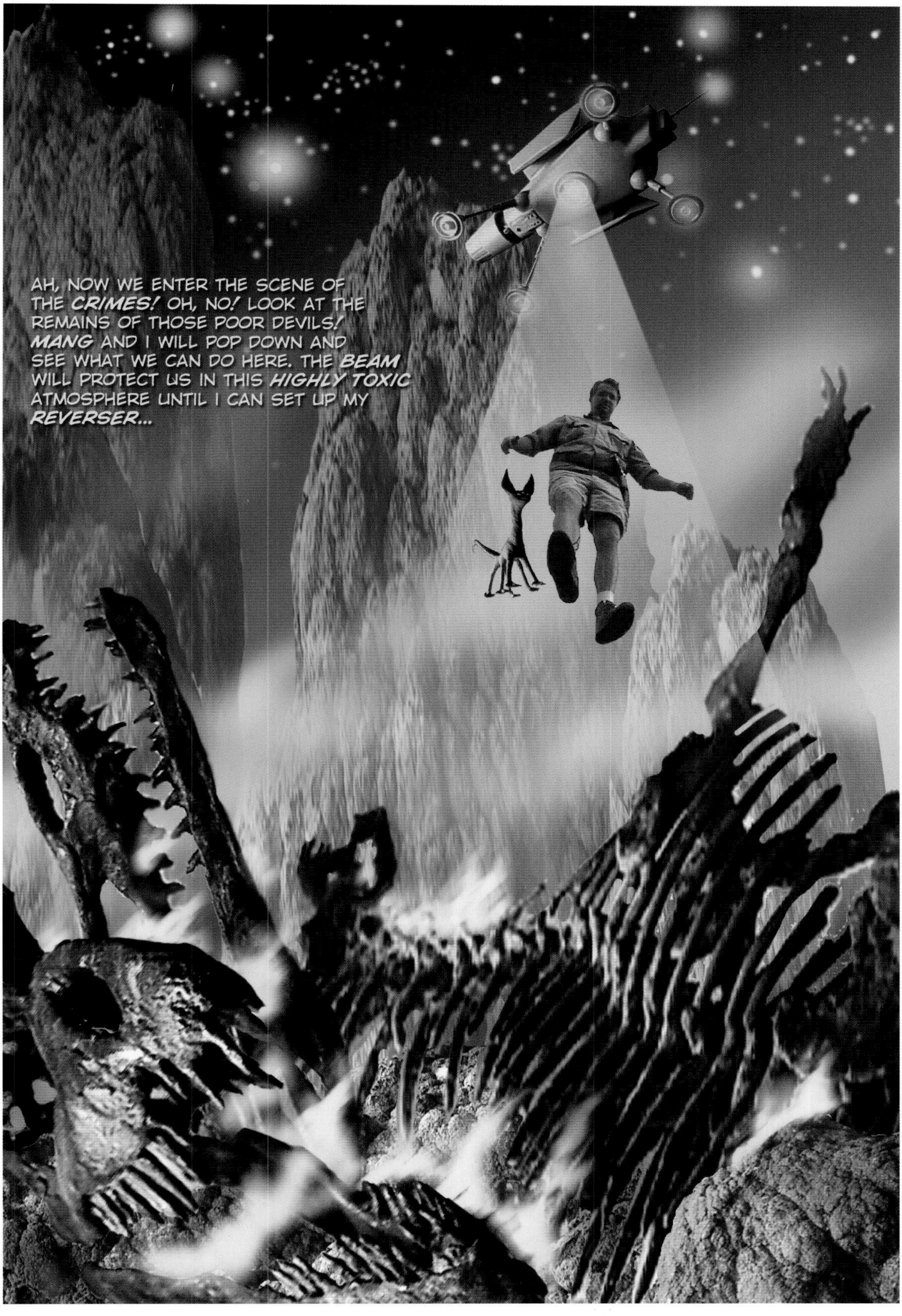
AH, NOW WE ENTER THE SCENE OF THE *CRIMES!* OH, NO! LOOK AT THE REMAINS OF THOSE POOR DEVILS! *MANG* AND I WILL POP DOWN AND SEE WHAT WE CAN DO HERE. THE *BEAM* WILL PROTECT US IN THIS *HIGHLY TOXIC* ATMOSPHERE UNTIL I CAN SET UP MY *REVERSER*...

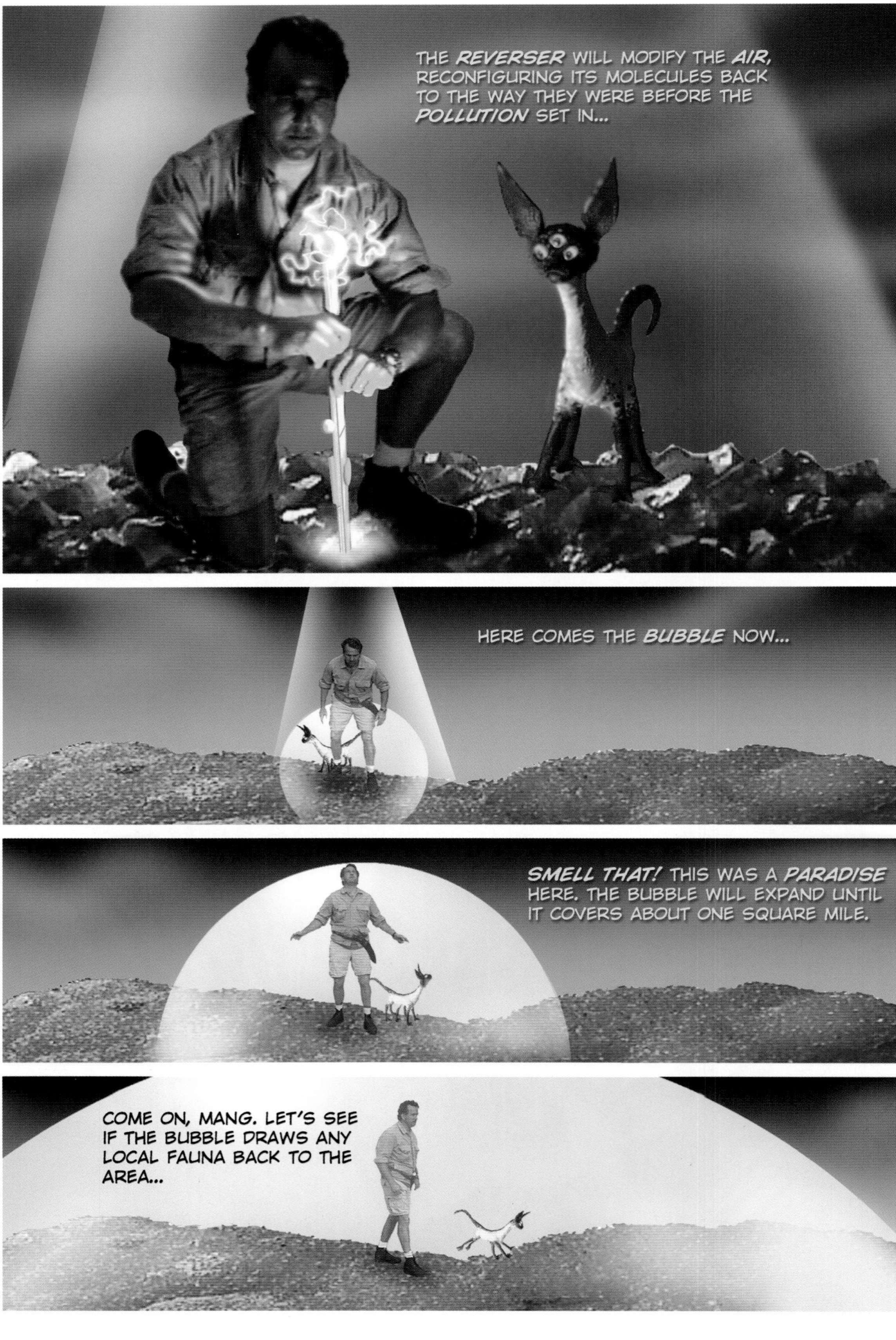
THE REVERSER WILL MODIFY THE AIR, RECONFIGURING ITS MOLECULES BACK TO THE WAY THEY WERE BEFORE THE POLLUTION SET IN...
HERE COMES THE BUBBLE NOW...
SMELL THAT! THIS WAS A PARADISE HERE. THE BUBBLE WILL EXPAND UNTIL IT COVERS ABOUT ONE SQUARE MILE.
COME ON, MANG. LET'S SEE IF THE BUBBLE DRAWS ANY LOCAL FAUNA BACK TO THE AREA...

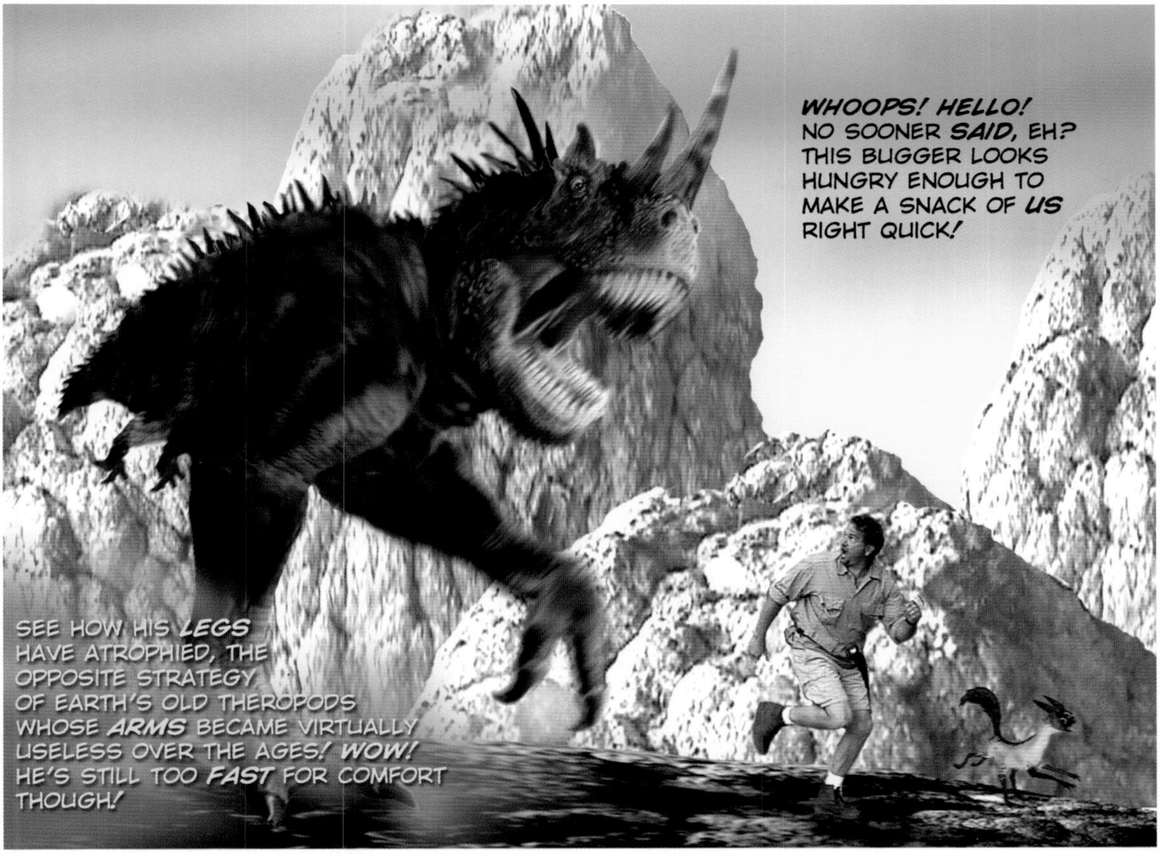
WHOOPS! HELLO! NO SOONER SAID, EH? THIS BUGGER LOOKS HUNGRY ENOUGH TO MAKE A SNACK OF US RIGHT QUICK!
SEE HOW HIS LEGS HAVE ATROPHIED, THE OPPOSITE STRATEGY OF EARTH'S OLD THEROPODS WHOSE ARMS BECAME VIRTUALLY USELESS OVER THE AGES! WOW! HE'S STILL TOO FAST FOR COMFORT THOUGH!

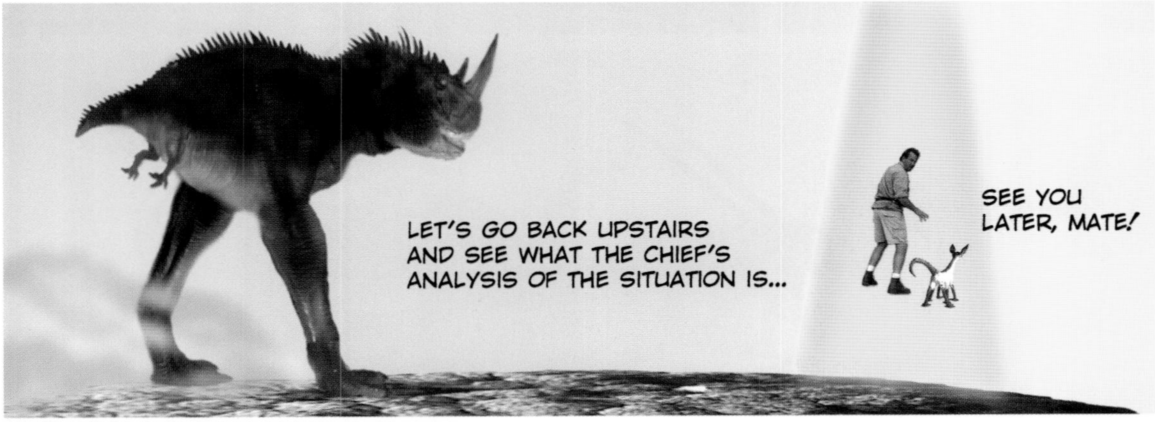
LET'S GO BACK UPSTAIRS AND SEE WHAT THE CHIEF'S ANALYSIS OF THE SITUATION IS...
SEE YOU LATER, MATE!

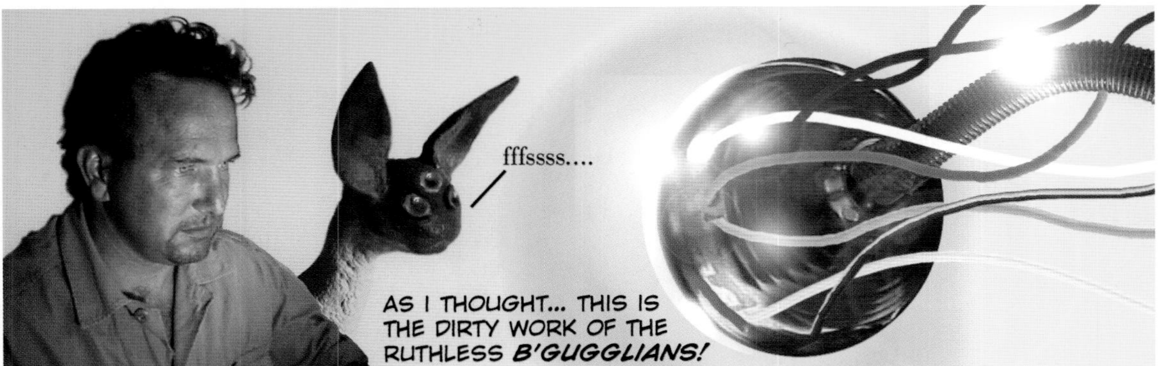
fffssss....
AS I THOUGHT... THIS IS THE DIRTY WORK OF THE RUTHLESS B'GUGGLIANS!

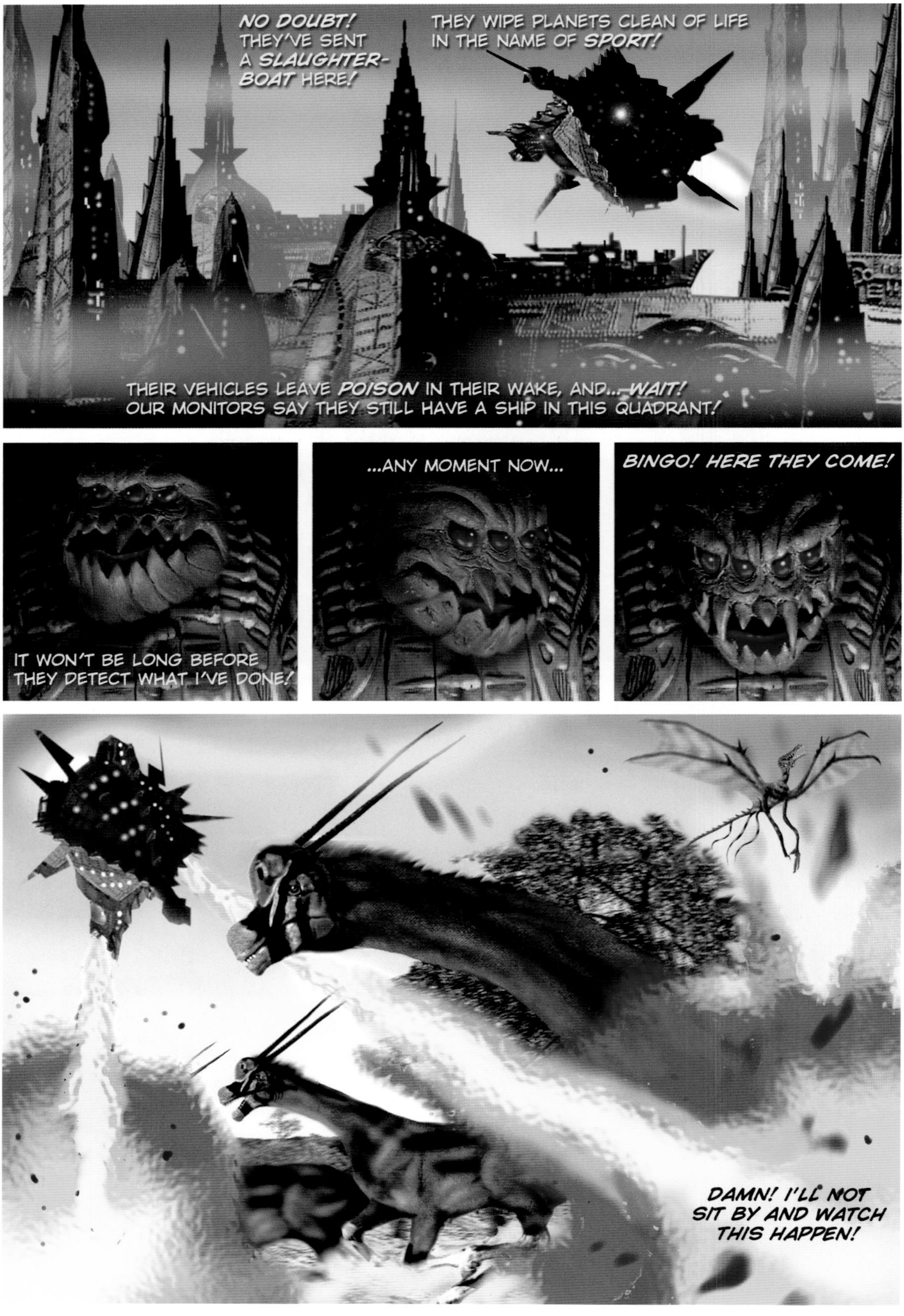
NO DOUBT! THEY'VE SENT A SLAUGHTER-BOAT HERE!
THEY WIPE PLANETS CLEAN OF LIFE IN THE NAME OF SPORT!
THEIR VEHICLES LEAVE POISON IN THEIR WAKE, AND... WAIT! OUR MONITORS SAY THEY STILL HAVE A SHIP IN THIS QUADRANT!
IT WON'T BE LONG BEFORE THEY DETECT WHAT I'VE DONE!
...ANY MOMENT NOW...
BINGO! HERE THEY COME!
DAMN! I'LL NOT SIT BY AND WATCH THIS HAPPEN!

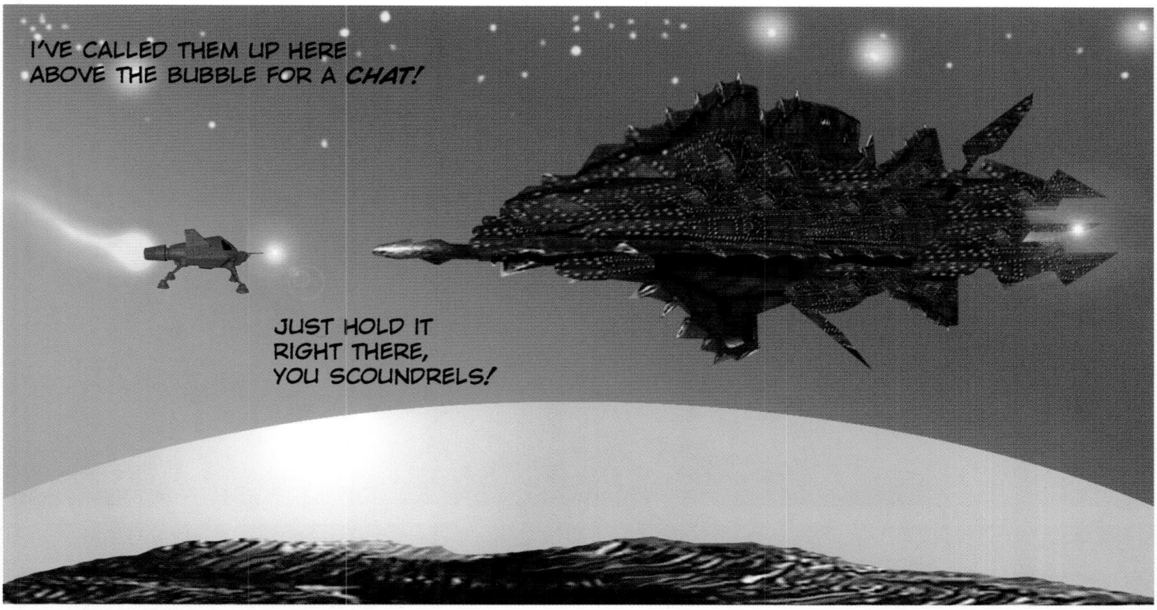
I'VE CALLED THEM UP HERE ABOVE THE BUBBLE FOR A *CHAT!*
JUST HOLD IT RIGHT THERE, YOU SCOUNDRELS!

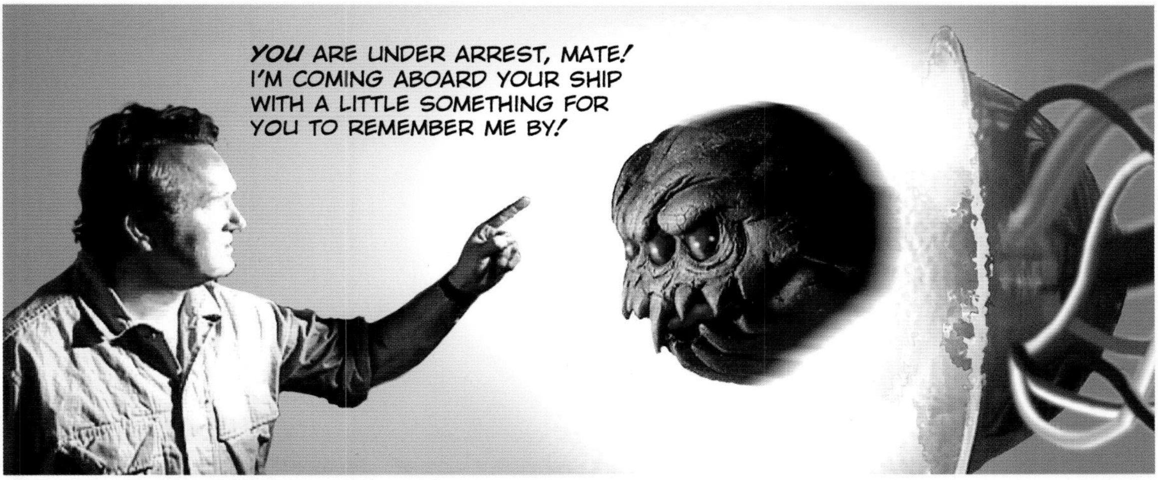
*YOU* ARE UNDER ARREST, MATE! I'M COMING ABOARD YOUR SHIP WITH A LITTLE SOMETHING FOR YOU TO REMEMBER ME BY!

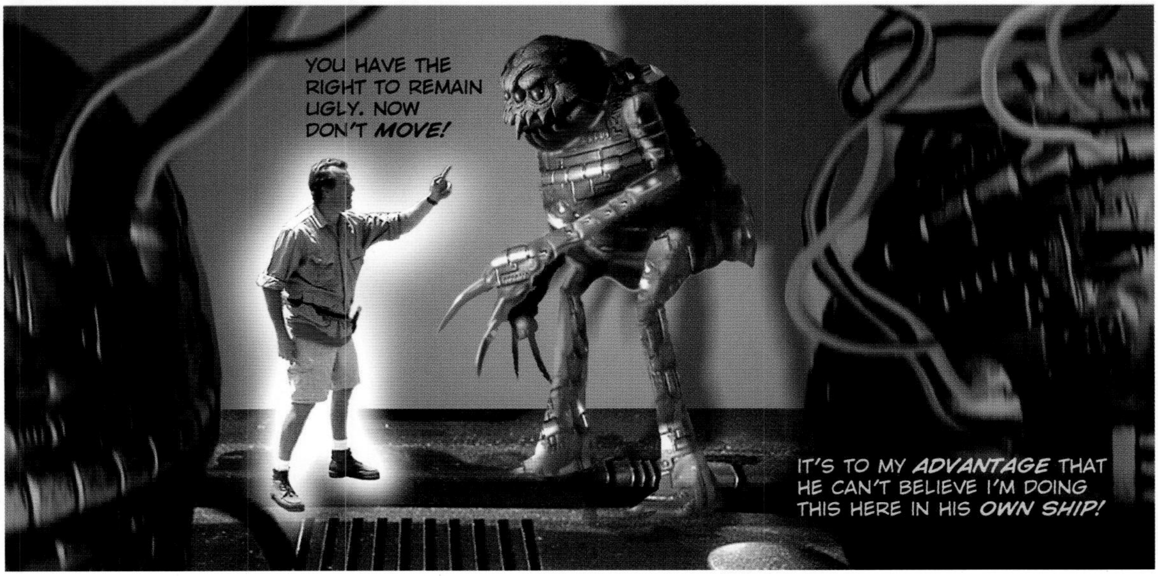
YOU HAVE THE RIGHT TO REMAIN UGLY. NOW DON'T *MOVE!*
IT'S TO MY *ADVANTAGE* THAT HE CAN'T BELIEVE I'M DOING THIS HERE IN HIS *OWN SHIP!*

TAG! YOU'RE IT! THIS ELECTRONIC STAMP CANNOT BE REMOVED!

SEE YOU IN *COURT!*

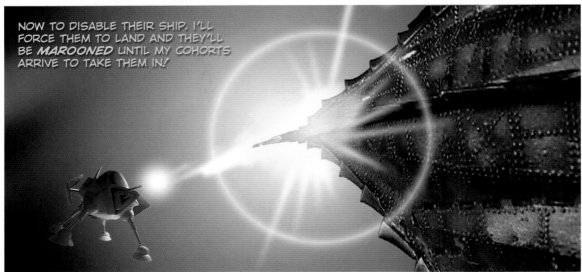

NOW TO DISABLE THEIR SHIP. I'LL FORCE THEM TO LAND AND THEY'LL BE *MAROONED* UNTIL MY COHORTS ARRIVE TO TAKE THEM IN!

THERE THEY GO...

HAPPY LANDINGS!

NOW TO CHECK WITH THE *CHIEF...*

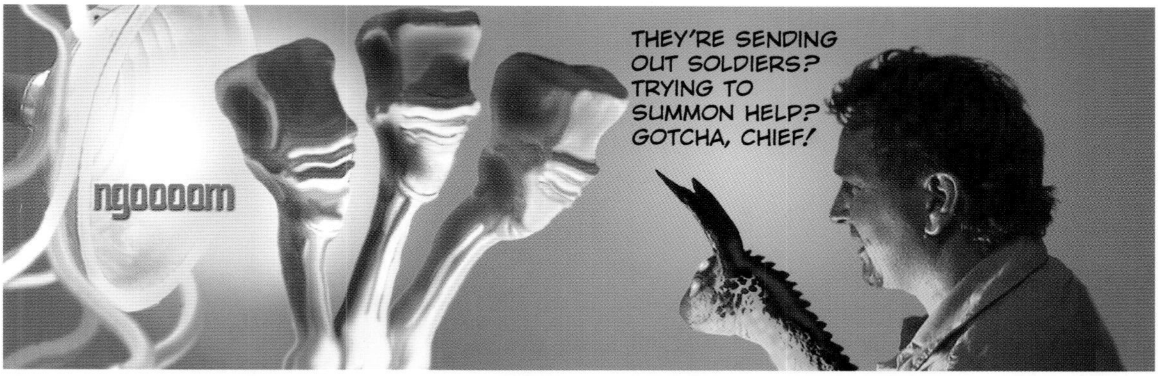
ngoooom
THEY'RE SENDING OUT SOLDIERS? TRYING TO SUMMON HELP? GOTCHA, CHIEF!

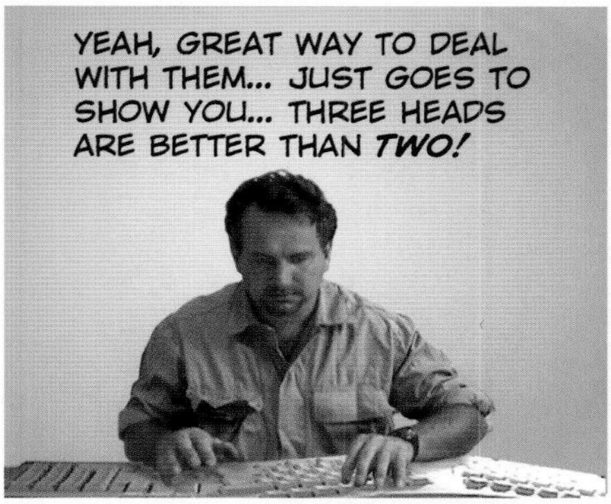
YEAH, GREAT WAY TO DEAL WITH THEM... JUST GOES TO SHOW YOU... THREE HEADS ARE BETTER THAN TWO!

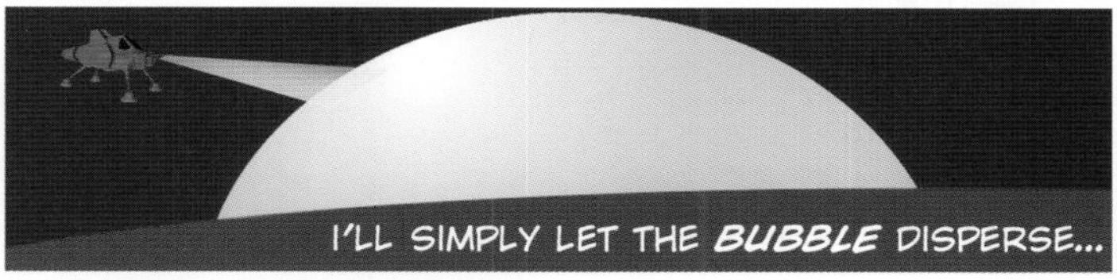
I'LL SIMPLY LET THE BUBBLE DISPERSE...

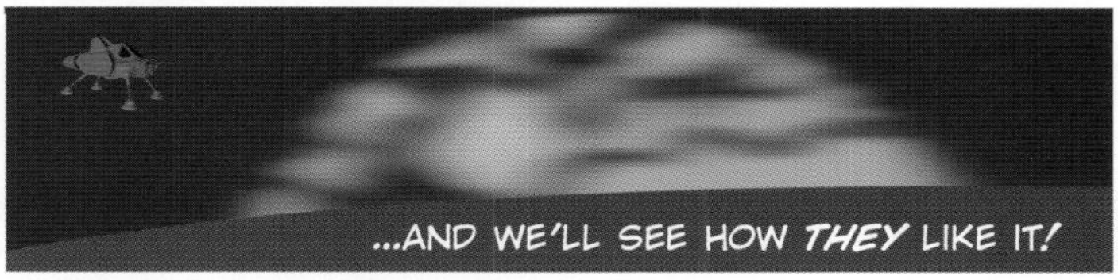
...AND WE'LL SEE HOW THEY LIKE IT!

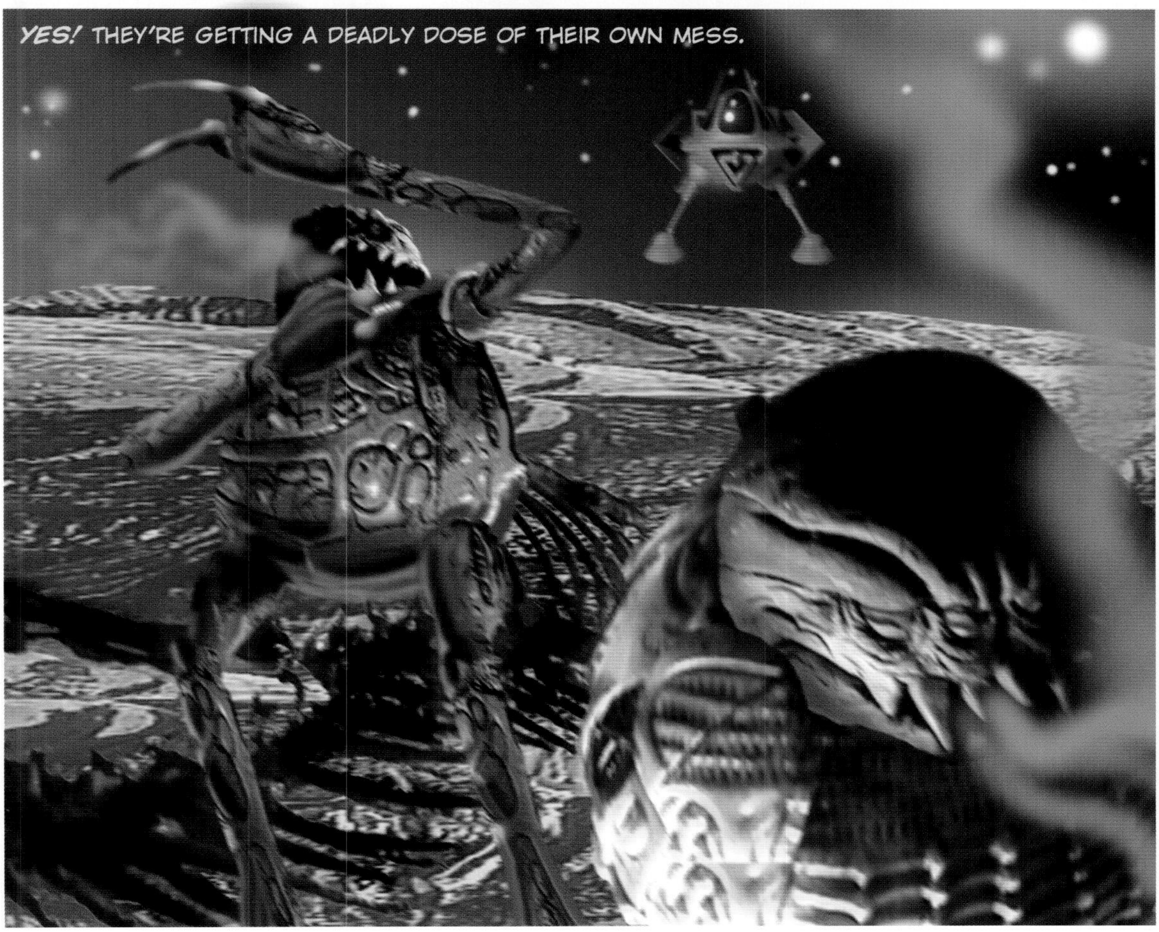
YES! THEY'RE GETTING A DEADLY DOSE OF THEIR OWN MESS.

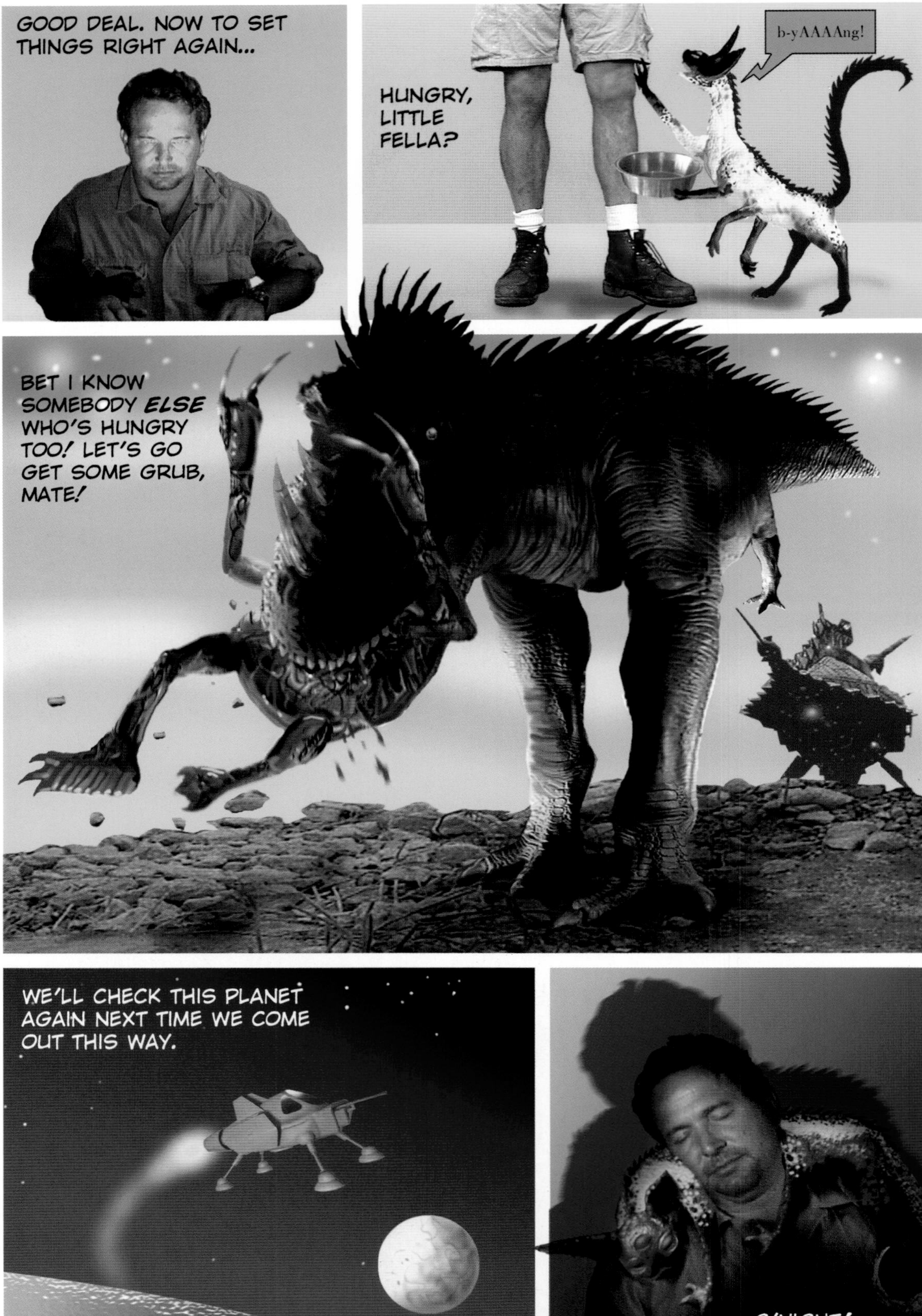
GOOD DEAL. NOW TO SET THINGS RIGHT AGAIN...
HUNGRY, LITTLE FELLA?
b-yAAAAng!
BET I KNOW SOMEBODY *ELSE* WHO'S HUNGRY TOO! LET'S GO GET SOME GRUB, MATE!
WE'LL CHECK THIS PLANET AGAIN NEXT TIME WE COME OUT THIS WAY.
G'NIGHT!

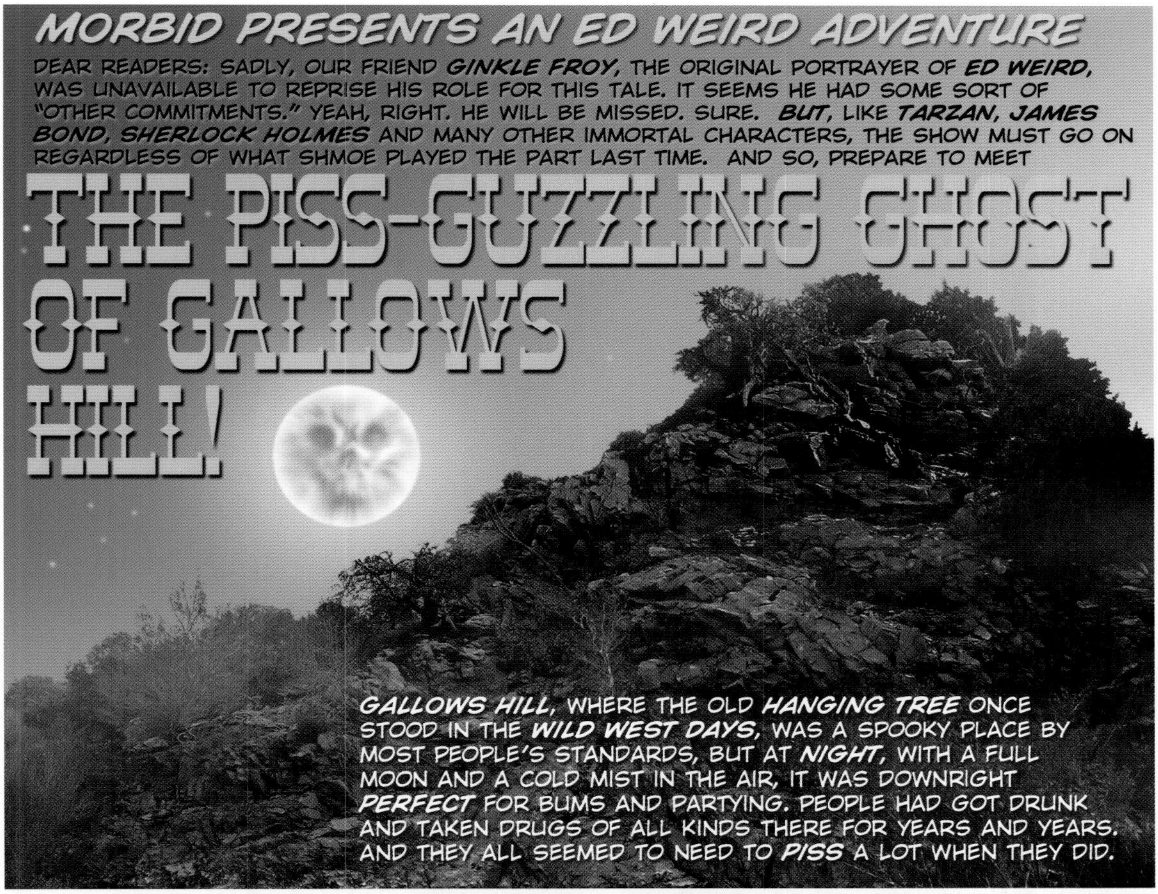
MORBID PRESENTS AN ED WEIRD ADVENTURE
DEAR READERS: SADLY, OUR FRIEND GINKLE FROY, THE ORIGINAL PORTRAYER OF ED WEIRD, WAS UNAVAILABLE TO REPRISE HIS ROLE FOR THIS TALE. IT SEEMS HE HAD SOME SORT OF "OTHER COMMITMENTS." YEAH, RIGHT. HE WILL BE MISSED. SURE. BUT, LIKE TARZAN, JAMES BOND, SHERLOCK HOLMES AND MANY OTHER IMMORTAL CHARACTERS, THE SHOW MUST GO ON REGARDLESS OF WHAT SHMOE PLAYED THE PART LAST TIME. AND SO, PREPARE TO MEET
THE PISS-GUZZLING GHOST OF GALLOWS HILL!
GALLOWS HILL, WHERE THE OLD HANGING TREE ONCE STOOD IN THE WILD WEST DAYS, WAS A SPOOKY PLACE BY MOST PEOPLE'S STANDARDS, BUT AT NIGHT, WITH A FULL MOON AND A COLD MIST IN THE AIR, IT WAS DOWNRIGHT PERFECT FOR BUMS AND PARTYING. PEOPLE HAD GOT DRUNK AND TAKEN DRUGS OF ALL KINDS THERE FOR YEARS AND YEARS. AND THEY ALL SEEMED TO NEED TO PISS A LOT WHEN THEY DID.

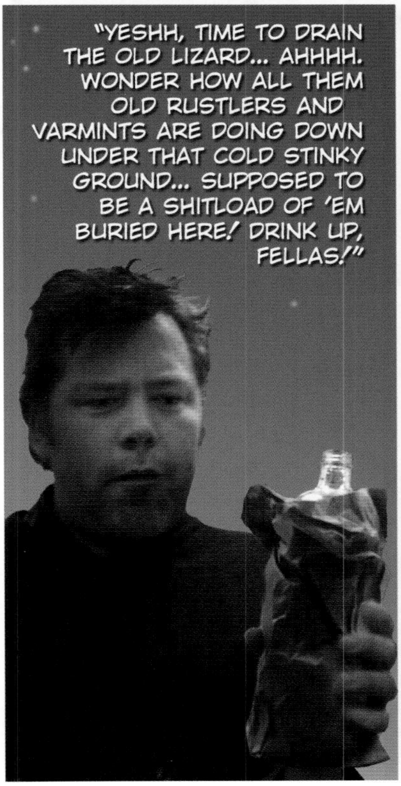
"YESHH, TIME TO DRAIN THE OLD LIZARD... AHHHH. WONDER HOW ALL THEM OLD RUSTLERS AND VARMINTS ARE DOING DOWN UNDER THAT COLD STINKY GROUND... SUPPOSED TO BE A SHITLOAD OF 'EM BURIED HERE! DRINK UP, FELLAS!"

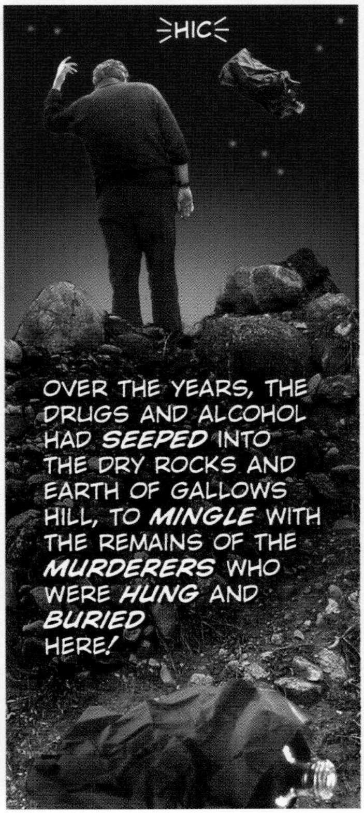
HIC
OVER THE YEARS, THE DRUGS AND ALCOHOL HAD SEEPED INTO THE DRY ROCKS AND EARTH OF GALLOWS HILL, TO MINGLE WITH THE REMAINS OF THE MURDERERS WHO WERE HUNG AND BURIED HERE!

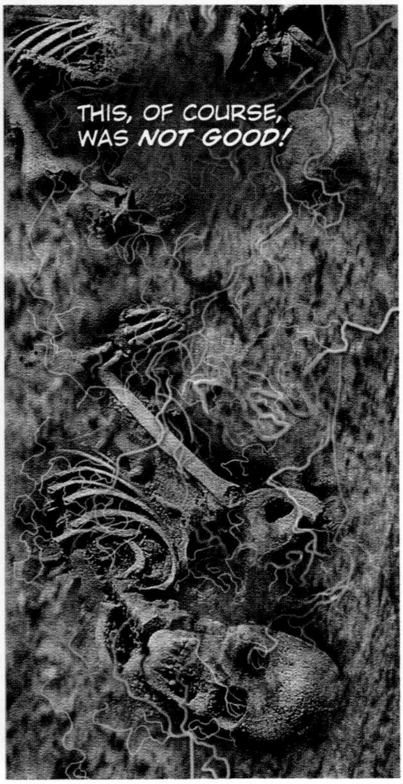
THIS, OF COURSE, WAS NOT GOOD!

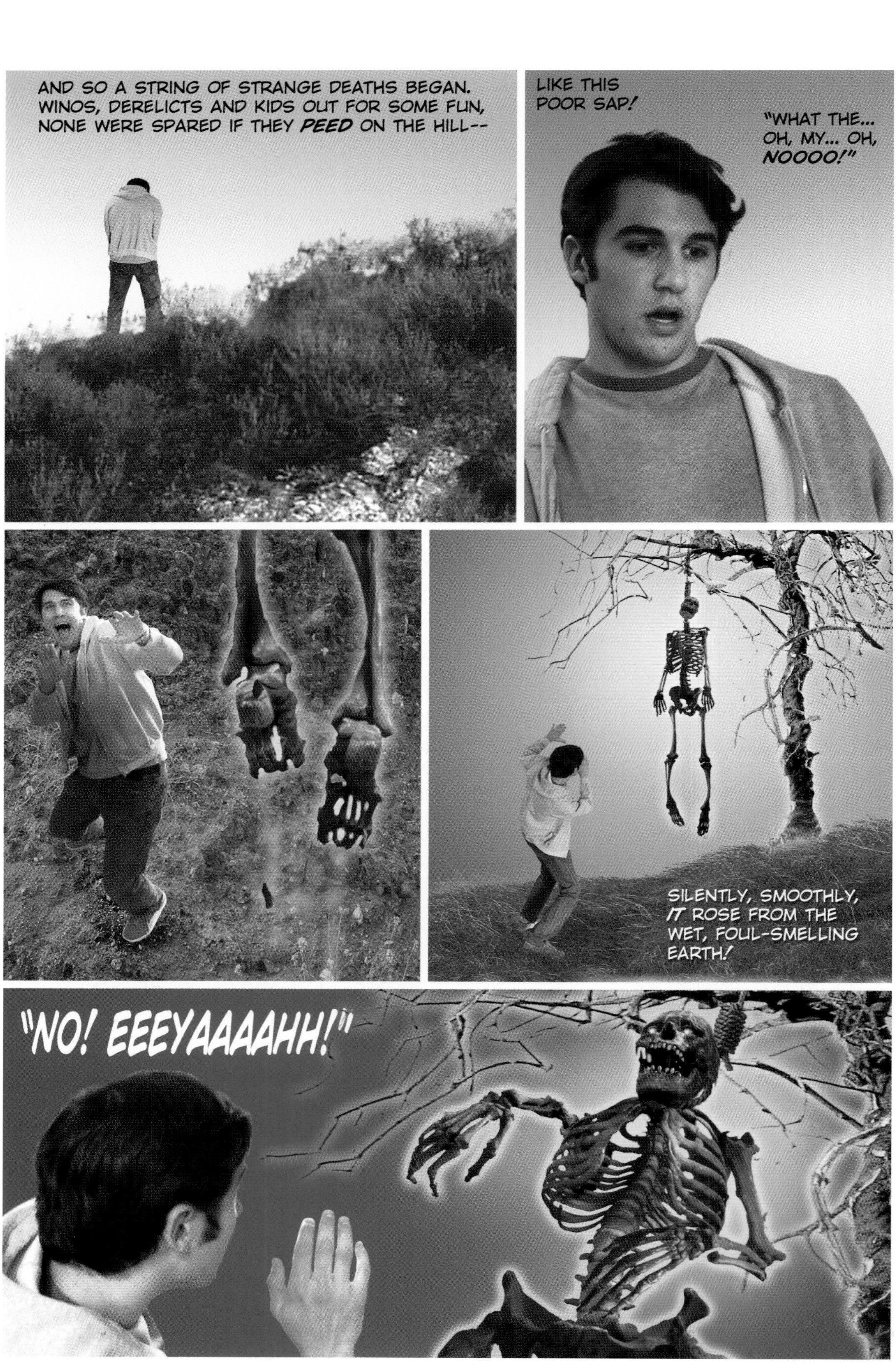
AND SO A STRING OF STRANGE DEATHS BEGAN. WINOS, DERELICTS AND KIDS OUT FOR SOME FUN, NONE WERE SPARED IF THEY PEED ON THE HILL--
LIKE THIS POOR SAP!
"WHAT THE... OH, MY... OH, NOOOO!"
SILENTLY, SMOOTHLY, IT ROSE FROM THE WET, FOUL-SMELLING EARTH!
"NO! EEEYAAAAHH!"

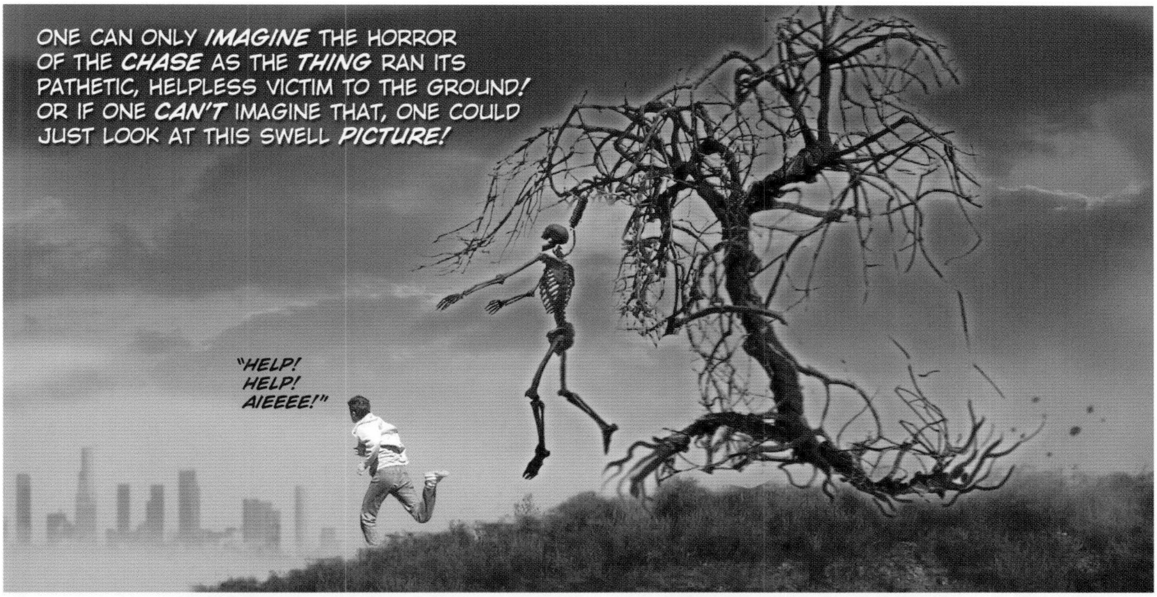
ONE CAN ONLY IMAGINE THE HORROR OF THE CHASE AS THE THING RAN ITS PATHETIC, HELPLESS VICTIM TO THE GROUND! OR IF ONE CAN'T IMAGINE THAT, ONE COULD JUST LOOK AT THIS SWELL PICTURE!
"HELP! HELP! AIEEEE!"

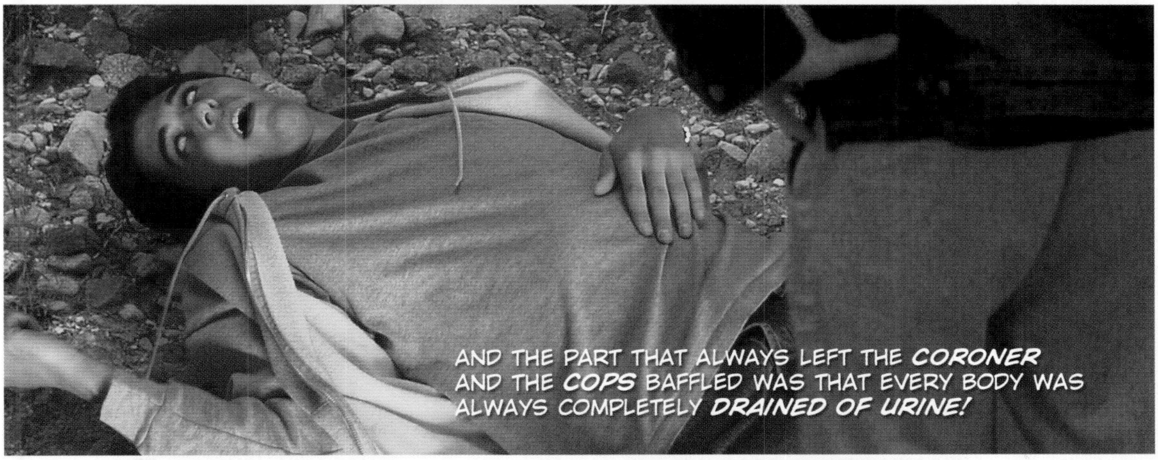
AND THE PART THAT ALWAYS LEFT THE CORONER AND THE COPS BAFFLED WAS THAT EVERY BODY WAS ALWAYS COMPLETELY DRAINED OF URINE!

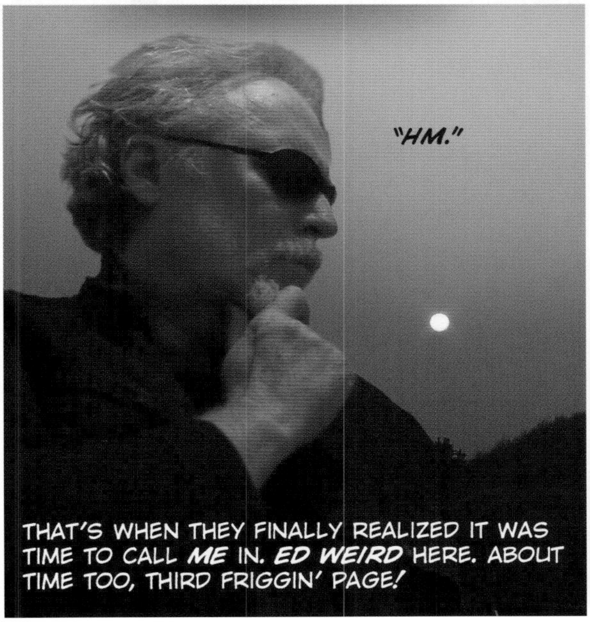
"HM."
THAT'S WHEN THEY FINALLY REALIZED IT WAS TIME TO CALL ME IN. ED WEIRD HERE. ABOUT TIME TOO, THIRD FRIGGIN' PAGE!

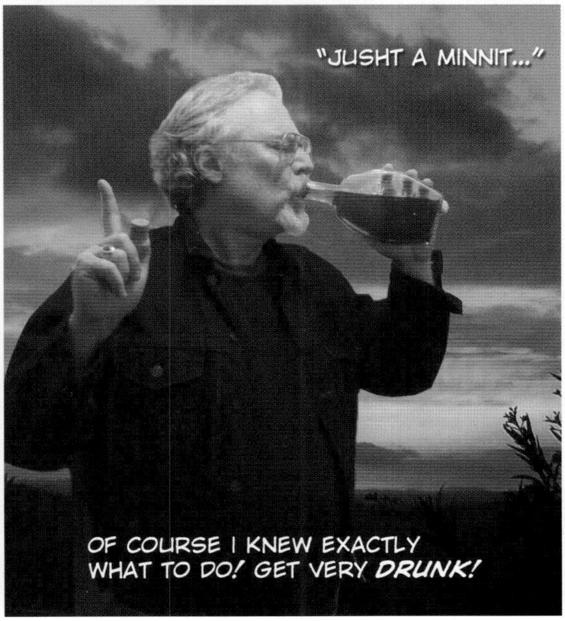
"JUSHT A MINNIT..."
OF COURSE I KNEW EXACTLY WHAT TO DO! GET VERY DRUNK!

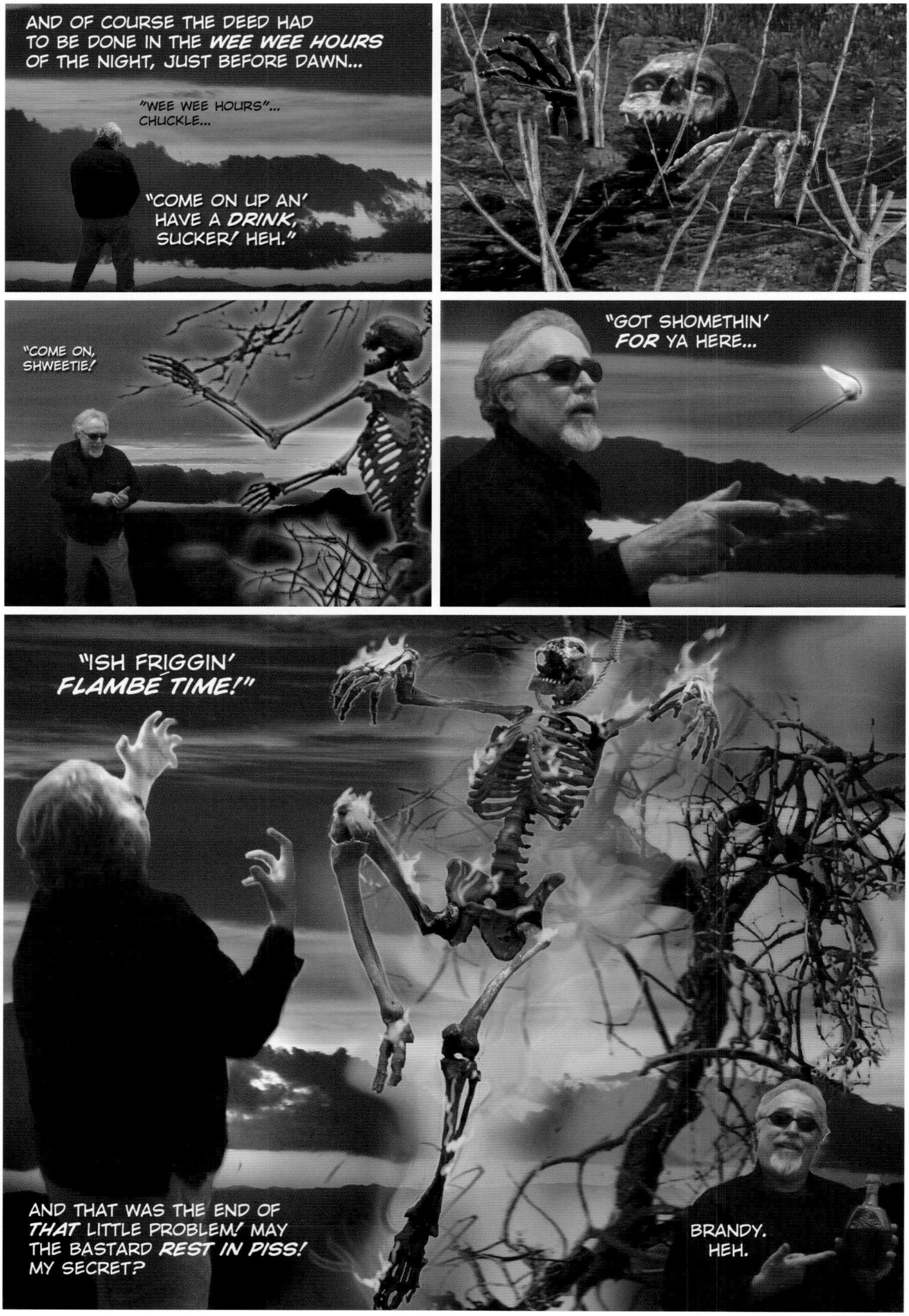
AND OF COURSE THE DEED HAD TO BE DONE IN THE *WEE WEE HOURS* OF THE NIGHT, JUST BEFORE DAWN...
"WEE WEE HOURS"... CHUCKLE...
"COME ON UP AN' HAVE A *DRINK*, SUCKER! HEH."
"COME ON, SHWEETIE!
"GOT SHOMETHIN' *FOR* YA HERE...
"ISH FRIGGIN' *FLAMBÉ TIME!*"
AND THAT WAS THE END OF *THAT* LITTLE PROBLEM! MAY THE BASTARD *REST IN PISS!* MY SECRET?
BRANDY. HEH.

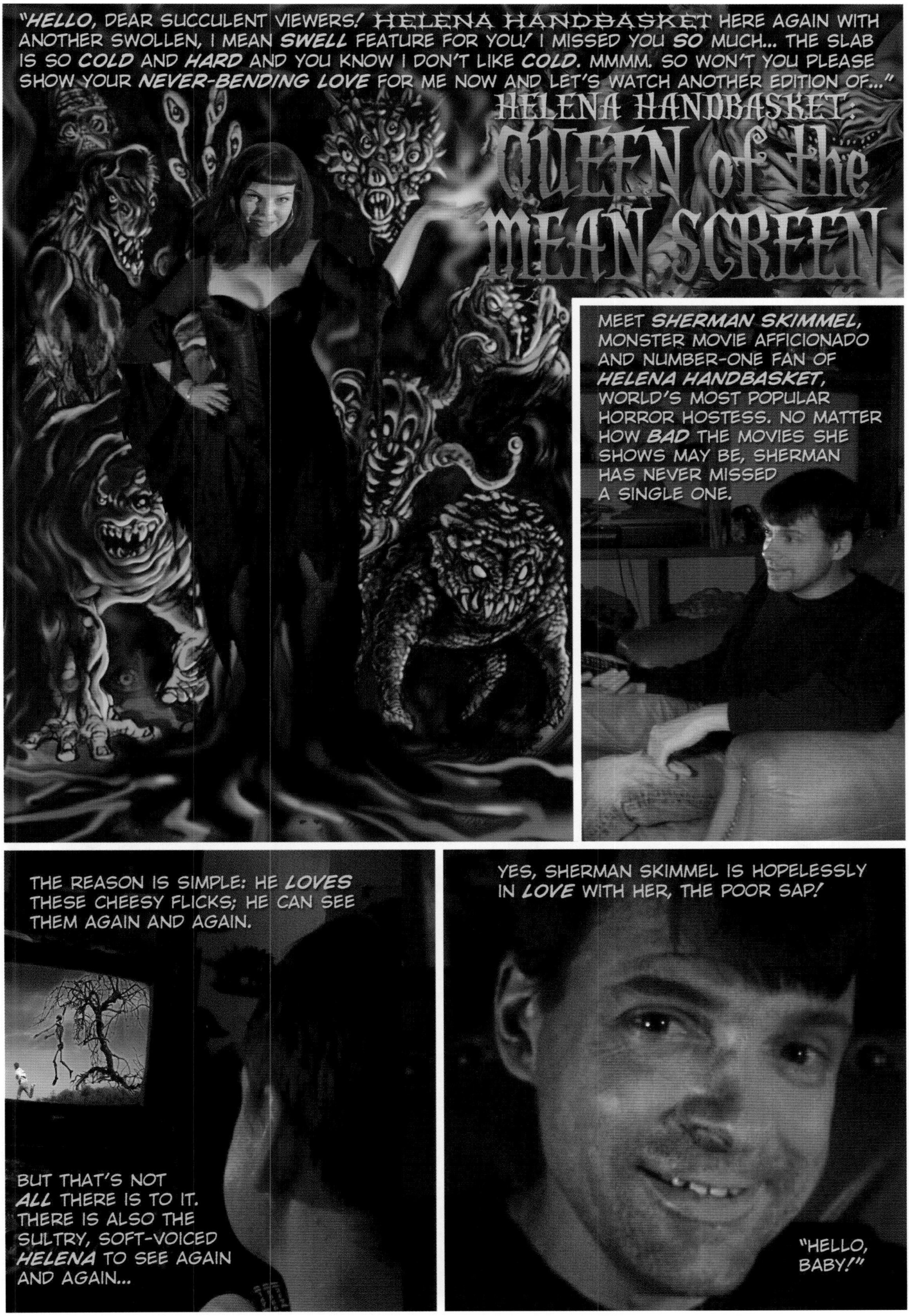
"HELLO, DEAR SUCCULENT VIEWERS! HELENA HANDBASKET HERE AGAIN WITH ANOTHER SWOLLEN, I MEAN SWELL FEATURE FOR YOU! I MISSED YOU SO MUCH... THE SLAB IS SO COLD AND HARD AND YOU KNOW I DON'T LIKE COLD. MMMM. SO WON'T YOU PLEASE SHOW YOUR NEVER-BENDING LOVE FOR ME NOW AND LET'S WATCH ANOTHER EDITION OF..."
HELENA HANDBASKET:
QUEEN of the MEAN SCREEN
MEET SHERMAN SKIMMEL, MONSTER MOVIE AFFICIONADO AND NUMBER-ONE FAN OF HELENA HANDBASKET, WORLD'S MOST POPULAR HORROR HOSTESS. NO MATTER HOW BAD THE MOVIES SHE SHOWS MAY BE, SHERMAN HAS NEVER MISSED A SINGLE ONE.
THE REASON IS SIMPLE: HE LOVES THESE CHEESY FLICKS; HE CAN SEE THEM AGAIN AND AGAIN.
BUT THAT'S NOT ALL THERE IS TO IT. THERE IS ALSO THE SULTRY, SOFT-VOICED HELENA TO SEE AGAIN AND AGAIN...
YES, SHERMAN SKIMMEL IS HOPELESSLY IN LOVE WITH HER, THE POOR SAP!
"HELLO, BABY!"

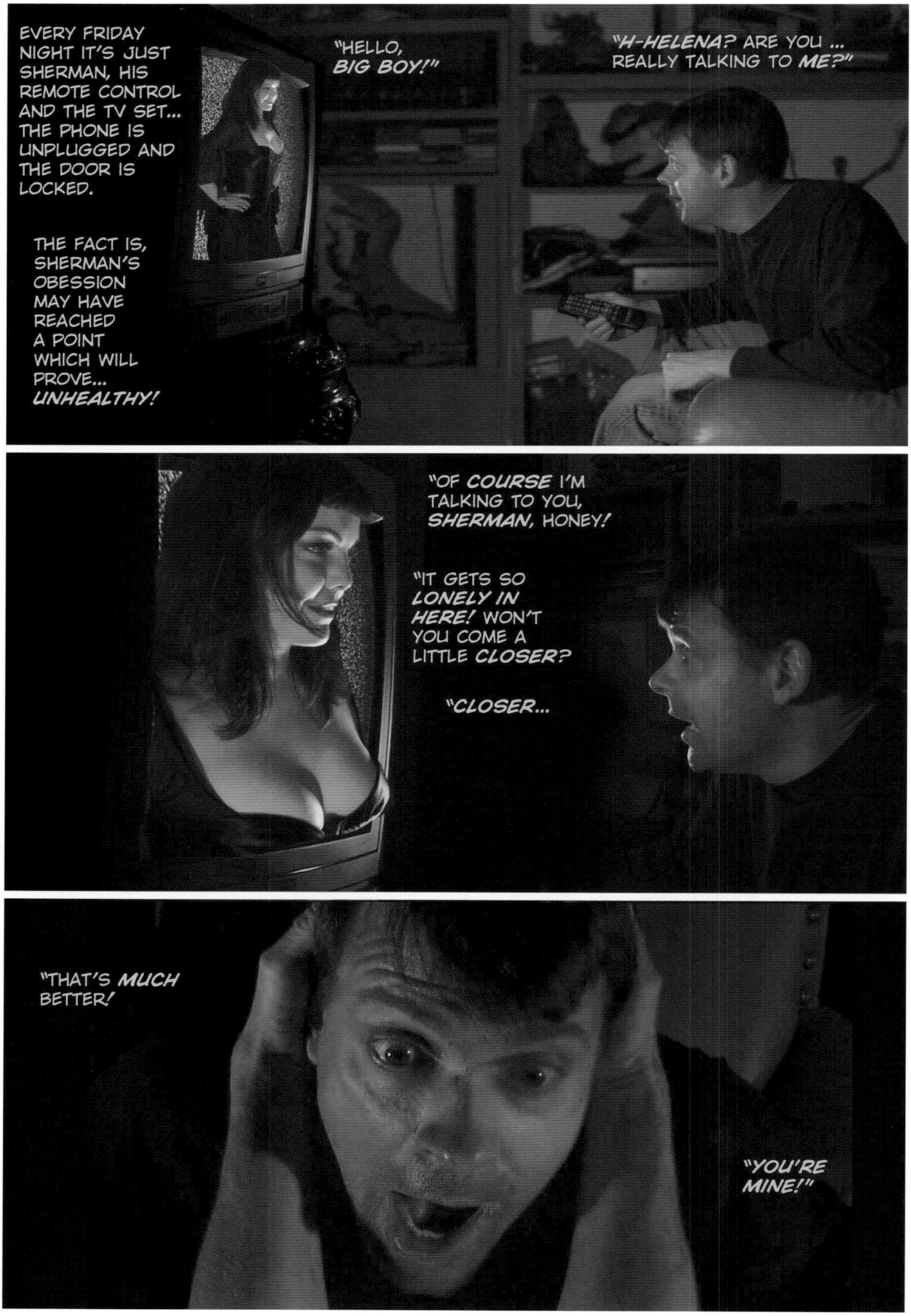
EVERY FRIDAY NIGHT IT'S JUST SHERMAN, HIS REMOTE CONTROL AND THE TV SET... THE PHONE IS UNPLUGGED AND THE DOOR IS LOCKED.
THE FACT IS, SHERMAN'S OBESSION MAY HAVE REACHED A POINT WHICH WILL PROVE... UNHEALTHY!
"HELLO, BIG BOY!"
"H-HELENA? ARE YOU ... REALLY TALKING TO ME?"
"OF COURSE I'M TALKING TO YOU, SHERMAN, HONEY!
"IT GETS SO LONELY IN HERE! WON'T YOU COME A LITTLE CLOSER?
"CLOSER...
"THAT'S MUCH BETTER!
"YOU'RE MINE!"

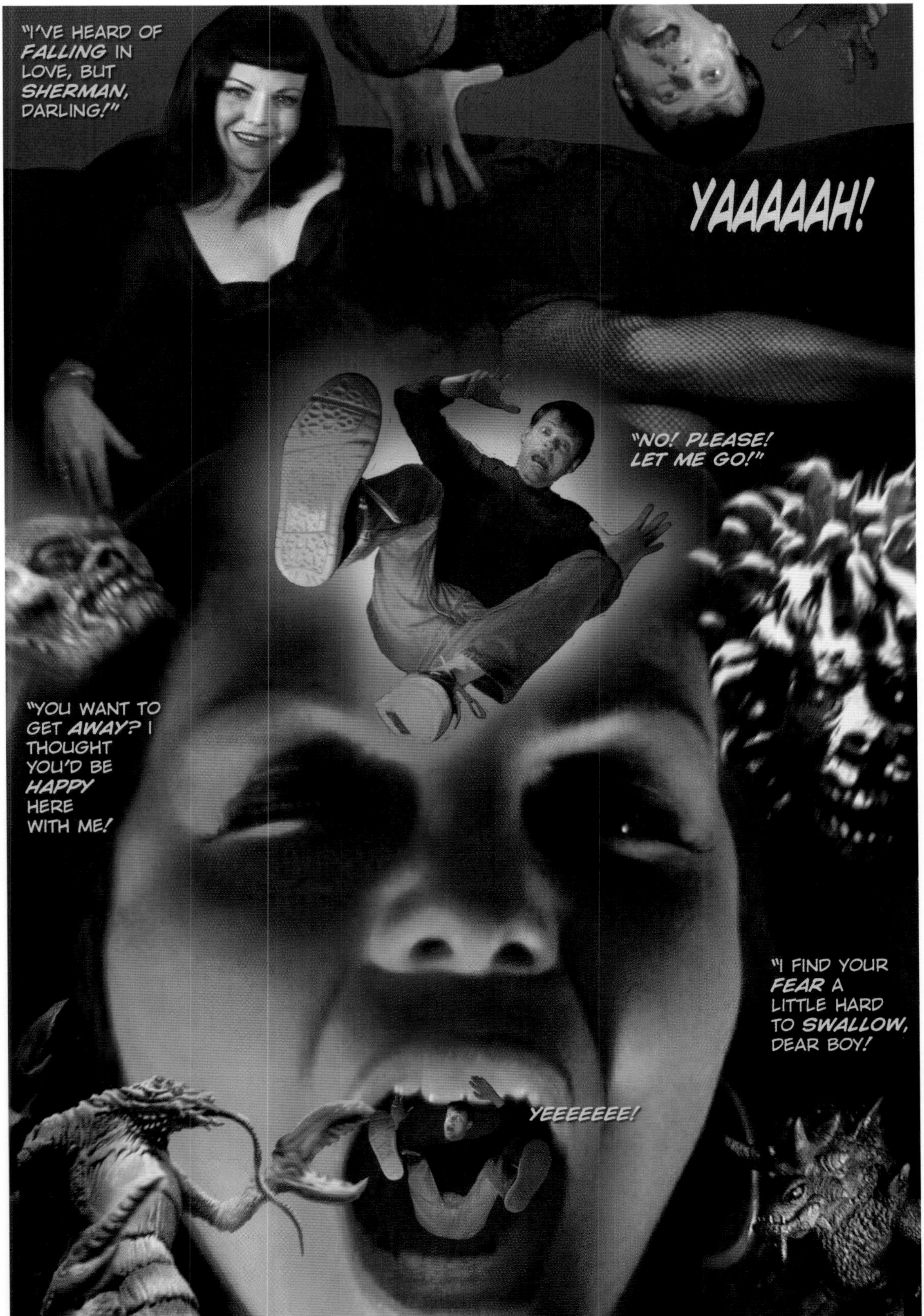
"I'VE HEARD OF FALLING IN LOVE, BUT SHERMAN, DARLING!"
YAAAAAH!
"NO! PLEASE! LET ME GO!"
"YOU WANT TO GET AWAY? I THOUGHT YOU'D BE HAPPY HERE WITH ME!
"I FIND YOUR FEAR A LITTLE HARD TO SWALLOW, DEAR BOY!
YEEEEEEE!

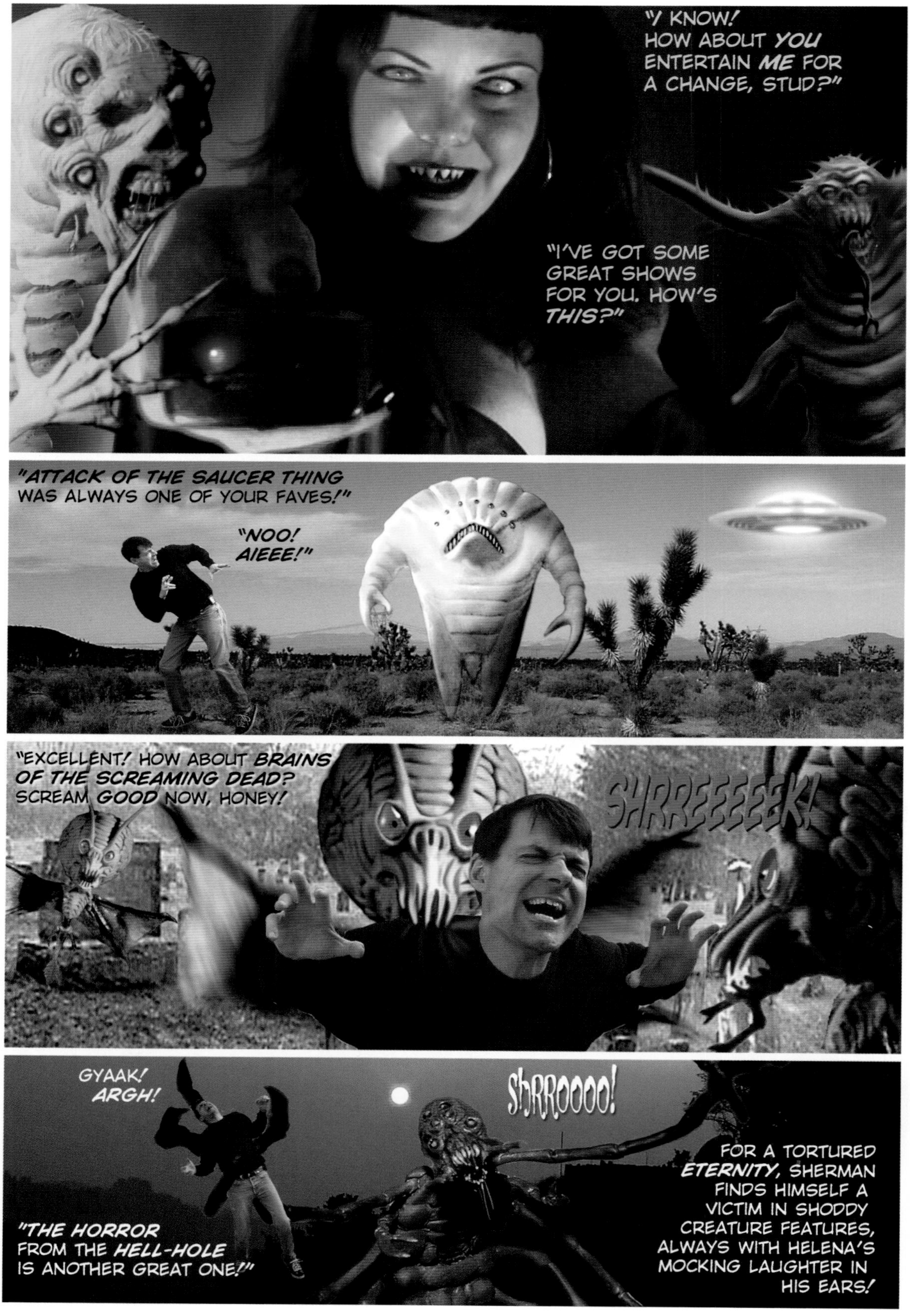
"I KNOW! HOW ABOUT *YOU* ENTERTAIN *ME* FOR A CHANGE, STUD?"
"I'VE GOT SOME GREAT SHOWS FOR YOU. HOW'S *THIS?*"
*"ATTACK OF THE SAUCER THING* WAS ALWAYS ONE OF YOUR FAVES!"
*"NOO! AIEEE!"*
"EXCELLENT! HOW ABOUT *BRAINS OF THE SCREAMING DEAD?* SCREAM *GOOD* NOW, HONEY!
SHRREEEEEK!
GYAAK! *ARGH!*
SHRROOOO!
*"THE HORROR* FROM THE *HELL-HOLE* IS ANOTHER GREAT ONE!"
FOR A TORTURED *ETERNITY,* SHERMAN FINDS HIMSELF A VICTIM IN SHODDY CREATURE FEATURES, ALWAYS WITH HELENA'S MOCKING LAUGHTER IN HIS EARS!

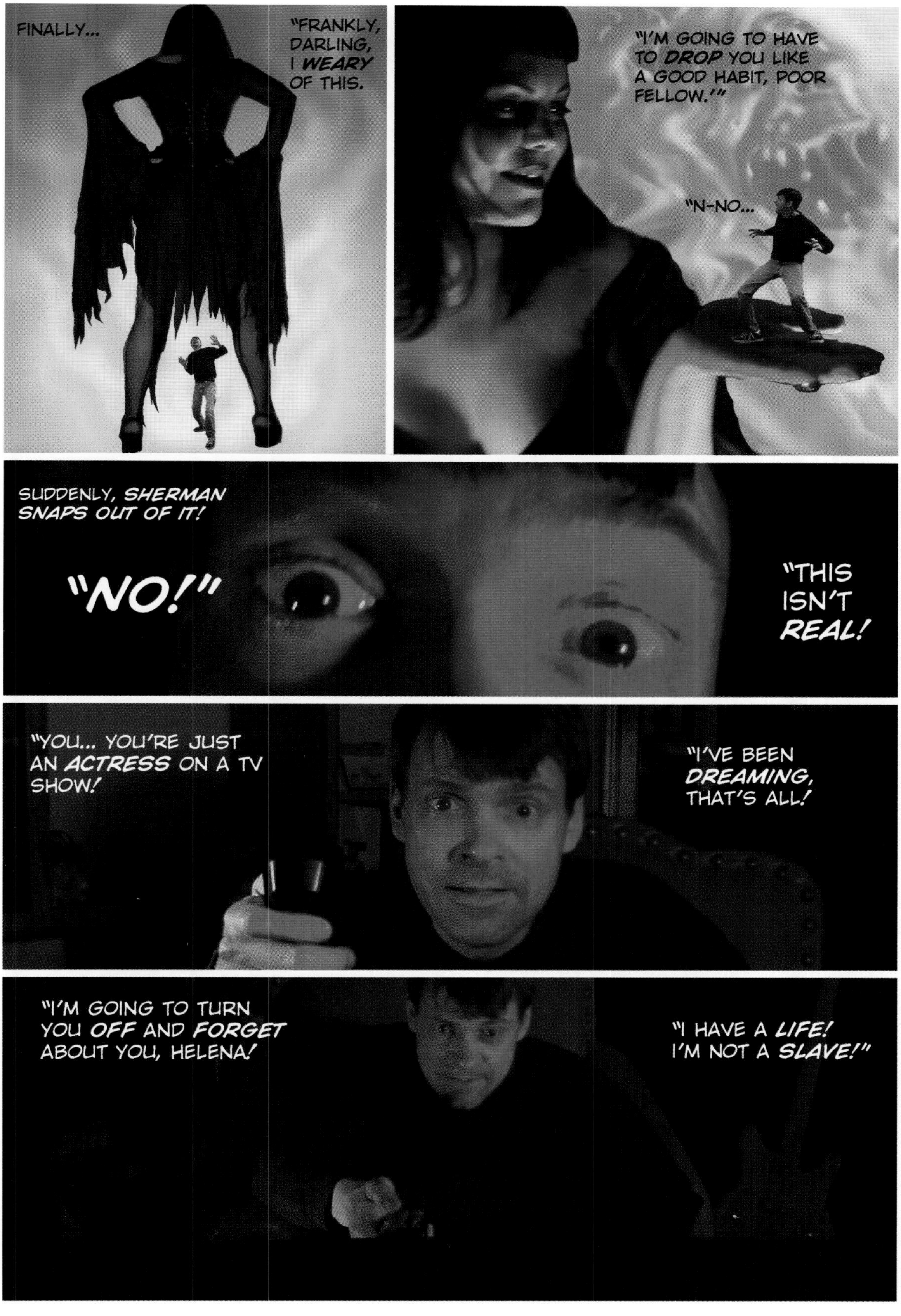
FINALLY...
"FRANKLY, DARLING, I WEARY OF THIS.
"I'M GOING TO HAVE TO DROP YOU LIKE A GOOD HABIT, POOR FELLOW.'"
"N-NO...
SUDDENLY, SHERMAN SNAPS OUT OF IT!
"NO!"
"THIS ISN'T REAL!
"YOU... YOU'RE JUST AN ACTRESS ON A TV SHOW!
"I'VE BEEN DREAMING, THAT'S ALL!
"I'M GOING TO TURN YOU OFF AND FORGET ABOUT YOU, HELENA!
"I HAVE A LIFE! I'M NOT A SLAVE!"

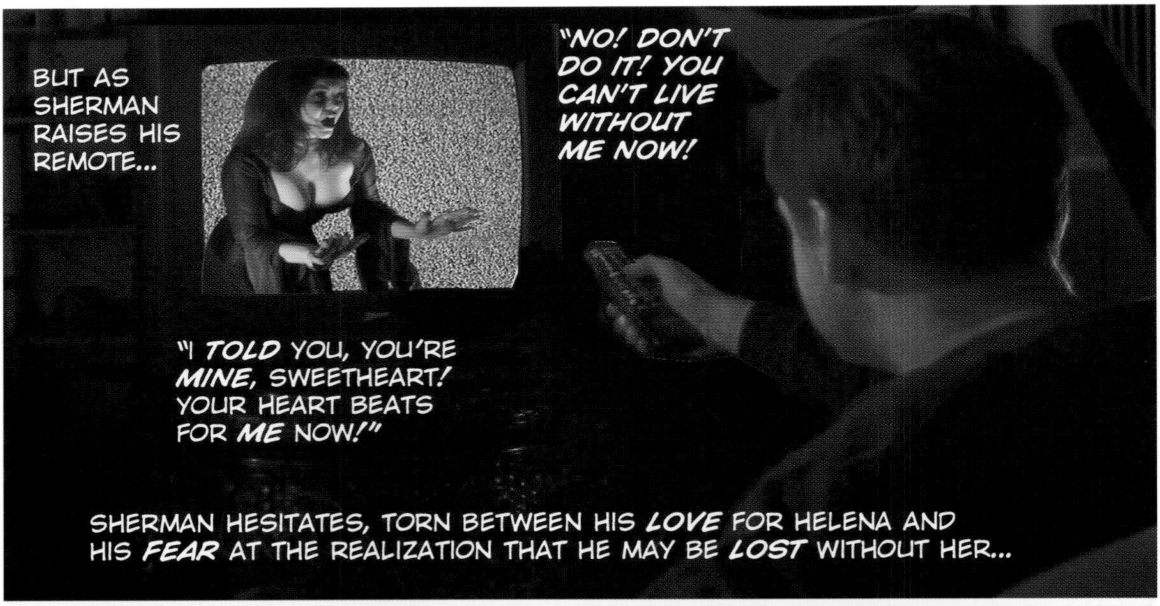
BUT AS SHERMAN RAISES HIS REMOTE...
"NO! DON'T DO IT! YOU CAN'T LIVE WITHOUT ME NOW!
"I TOLD YOU, YOU'RE MINE, SWEETHEART! YOUR HEART BEATS FOR ME NOW!"
SHERMAN HESITATES, TORN BETWEEN HIS LOVE FOR HELENA AND HIS FEAR AT THE REALIZATION THAT HE MAY BE LOST WITHOUT HER...

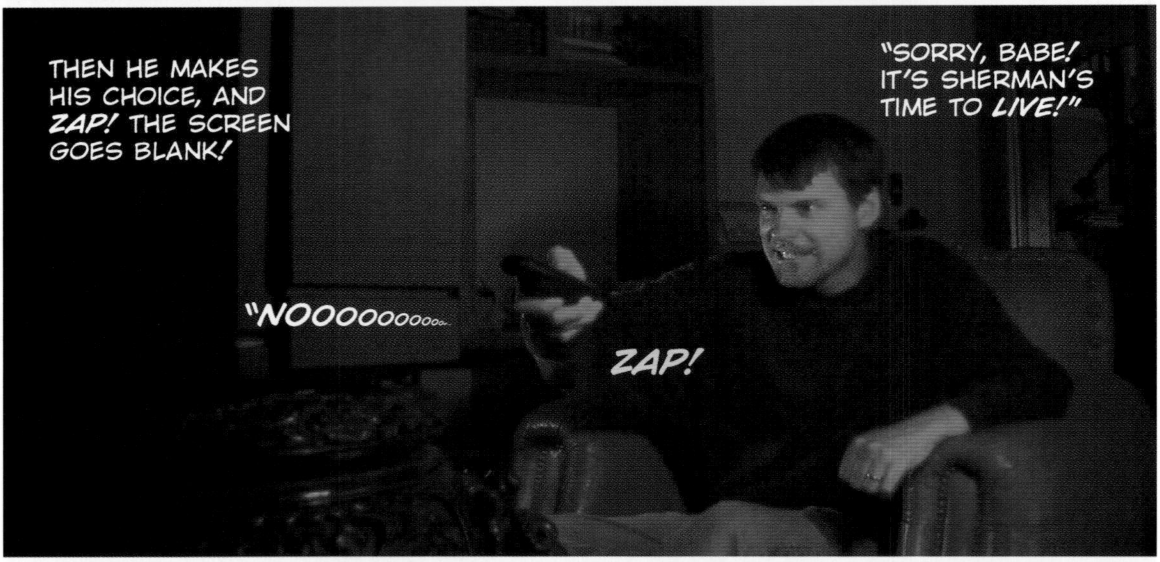
THEN HE MAKES HIS CHOICE, AND ZAP! THE SCREEN GOES BLANK!
"SORRY, BABE! IT'S SHERMAN'S TIME TO LIVE!"
"NOOOOOOOOOO...
ZAP!

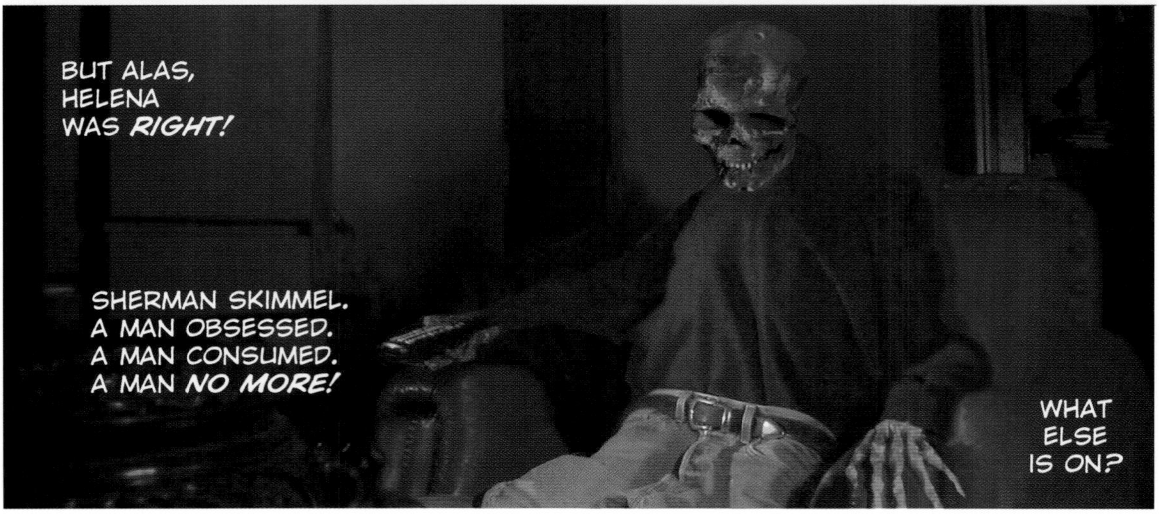
BUT ALAS, HELENA WAS RIGHT!
SHERMAN SKIMMEL. A MAN OBSESSED. A MAN CONSUMED. A MAN NO MORE!
WHAT ELSE IS ON?

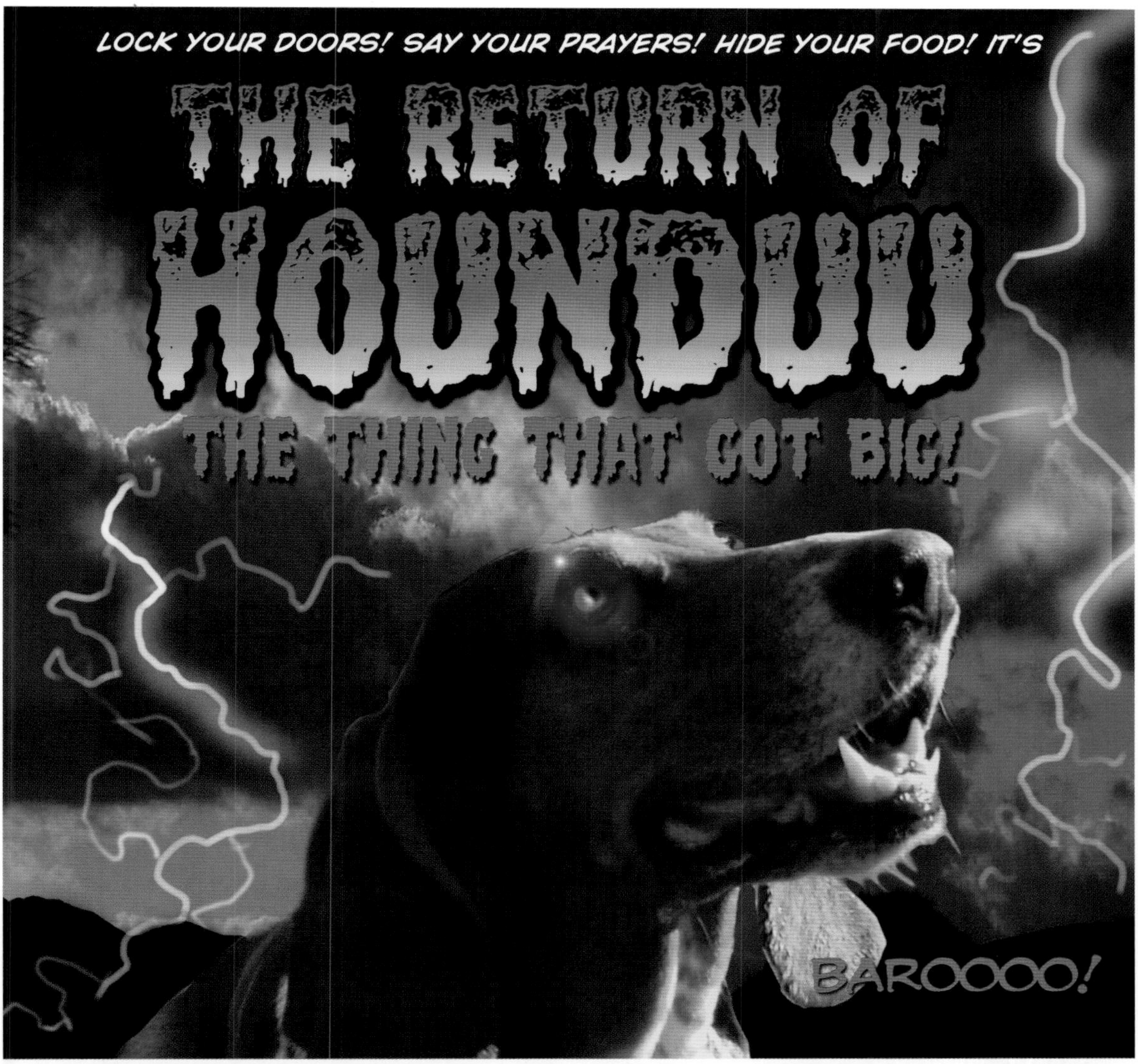
LOCK YOUR DOORS! SAY YOUR PRAYERS! HIDE YOUR FOOD! IT'S
THE RETURN OF
HOUNDUU
THE THING THAT GOT BIG!
BAROOOO!

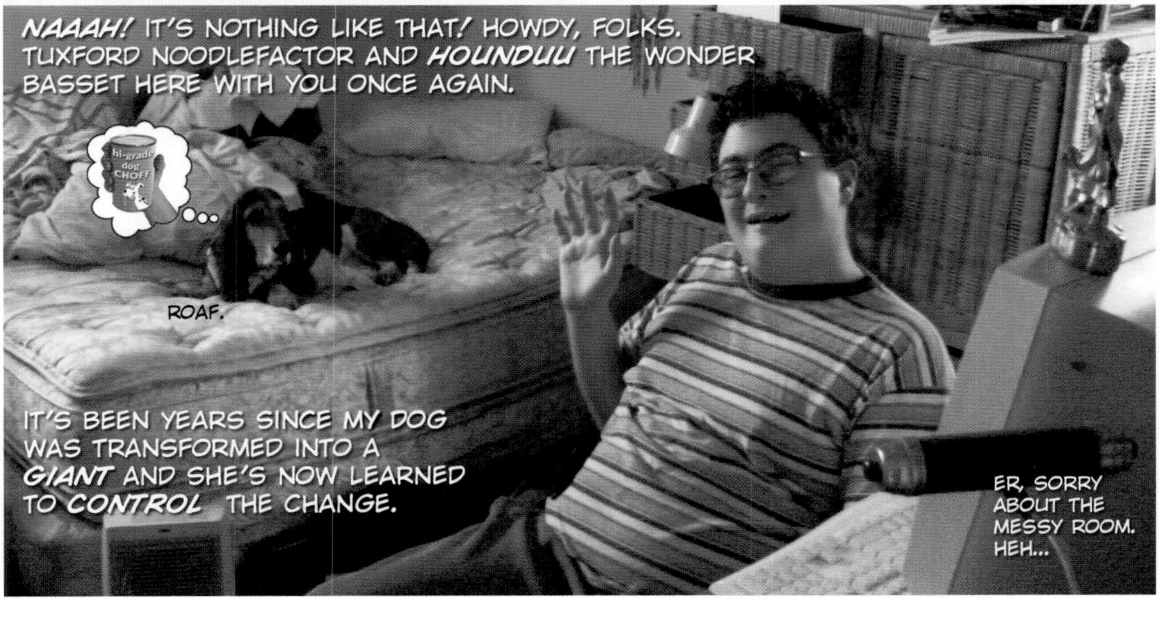
NAAAH! IT'S NOTHING LIKE THAT! HOWDY, FOLKS. TUXFORD NOODLEFACTOR AND HOUNDUU THE WONDER BASSET HERE WITH YOU ONCE AGAIN.
hi-grade dog CHOFF
...
ROAF.
IT'S BEEN YEARS SINCE MY DOG WAS TRANSFORMED INTO A GIANT AND SHE'S NOW LEARNED TO CONTROL THE CHANGE.
ER, SORRY ABOUT THE MESSY ROOM. HEH...

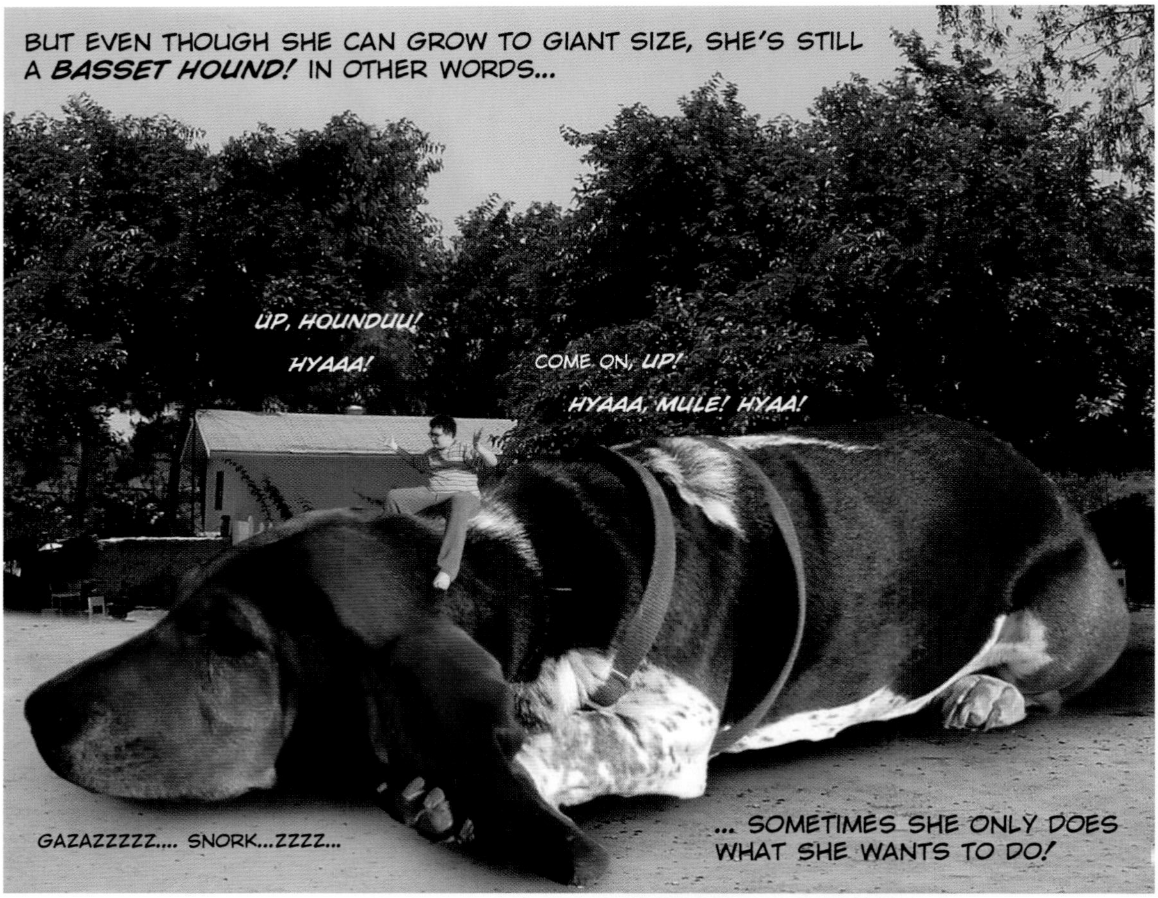
BUT EVEN THOUGH SHE CAN GROW TO GIANT SIZE, SHE'S STILL A *BASSET HOUND!* IN OTHER WORDS...
UP, HOUNDUU!
HYAAA!
COME ON, UP!
HYAAA, MULE! HYAA!
GAZAZZZZZ.... SNORK...ZZZZ...
... SOMETIMES SHE ONLY DOES WHAT SHE WANTS TO DO!

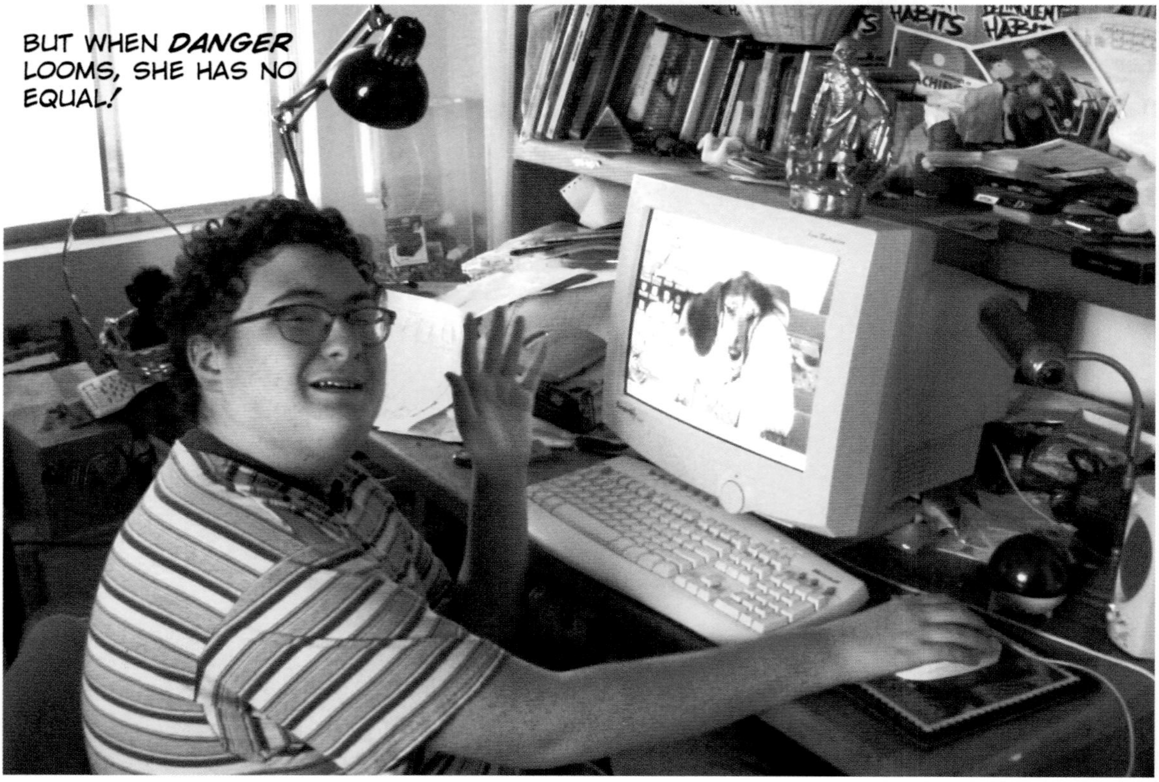
BUT WHEN *DANGER* LOOMS, SHE HAS NO EQUAL!

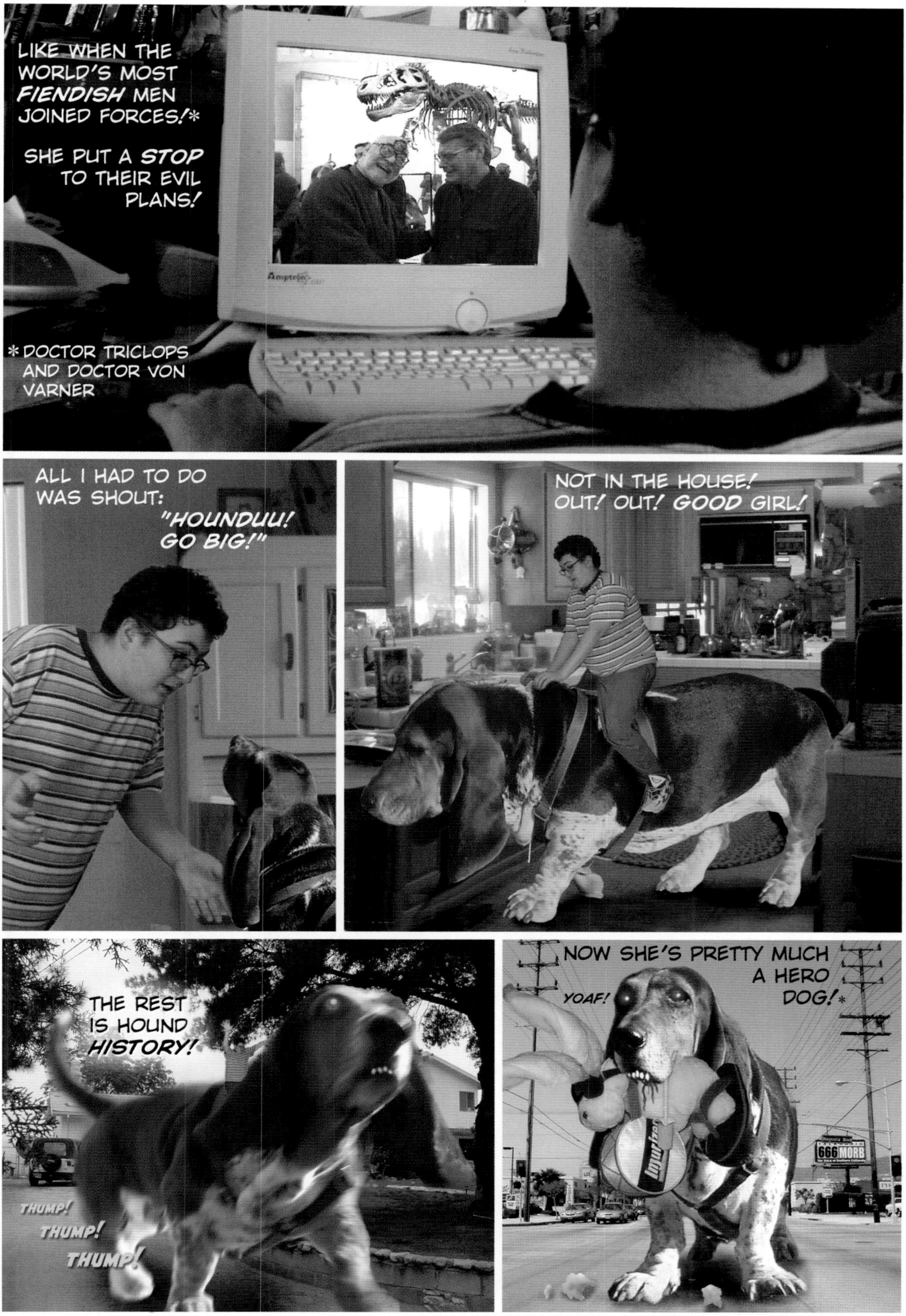
LIKE WHEN THE WORLD'S MOST *FIENDISH* MEN JOINED FORCES!*
SHE PUT A *STOP* TO THEIR EVIL PLANS!
*DOCTOR TRICLOPS AND DOCTOR VON VARNER
ALL I HAD TO DO WAS SHOUT:
*"HOUNDUU! GO BIG!"*
NOT IN THE HOUSE! OUT! OUT! *GOOD* GIRL!
THE REST IS HOUND *HISTORY!*
THUMP!
THUMP!
THUMP!
NOW SHE'S PRETTY MUCH A HERO DOG!*
YOAF!
666MORB

*SEE ***"NIGHT OF THE ELECTRO-LEPUS,"*** AKA "SCOURGE OF THE ***INJURIZER BUNNY."***

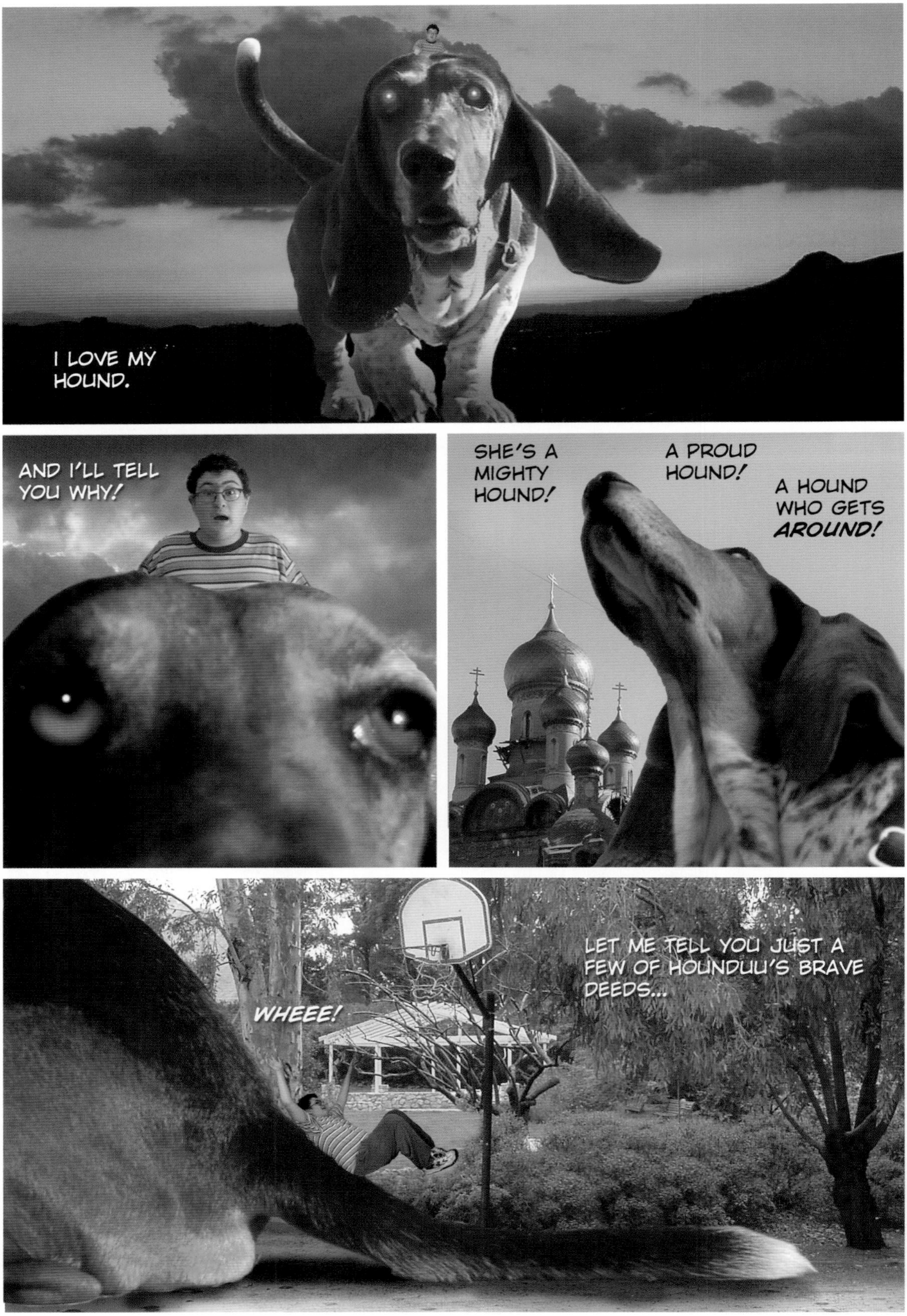
I LOVE MY HOUND.
AND I'LL TELL YOU WHY!
SHE'S A MIGHTY HOUND!
A PROUD HOUND!
A HOUND WHO GETS AROUND!
LET ME TELL YOU JUST A FEW OF HOUNDUU'S BRAVE DEEDS...
WHEEE!

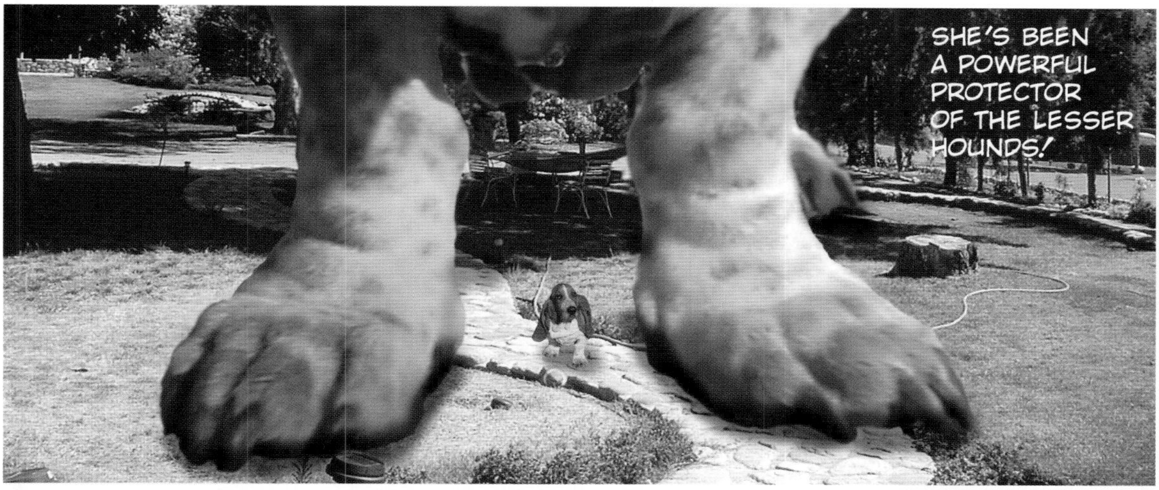
SHE'S BEEN A POWERFUL PROTECTOR OF THE LESSER HOUNDS!

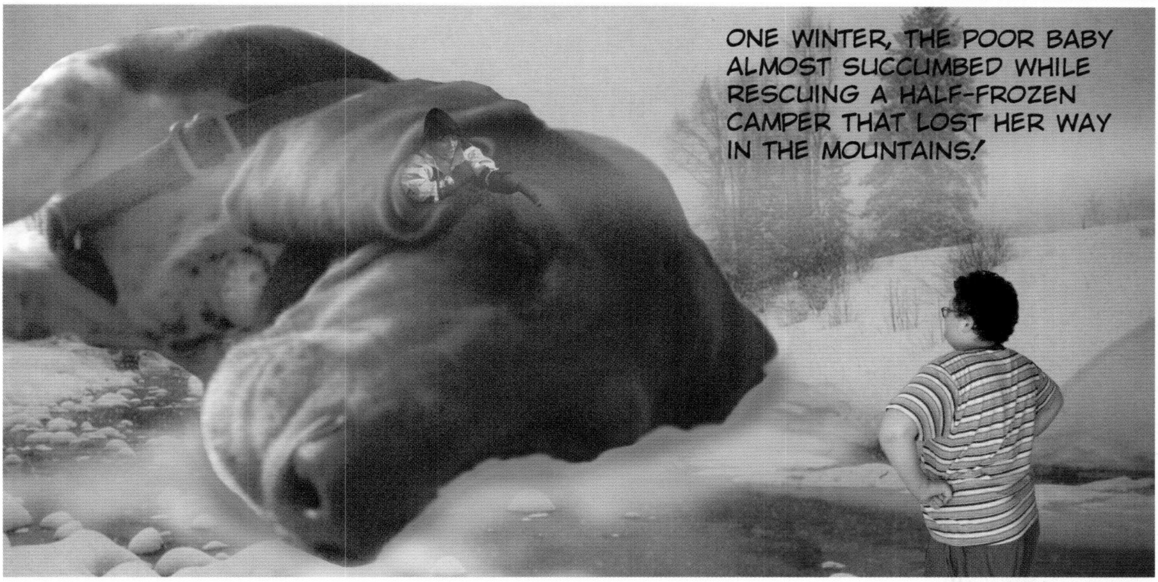
ONE WINTER, THE POOR BABY ALMOST SUCCUMBED WHILE RESCUING A HALF-FROZEN CAMPER THAT LOST HER WAY IN THE MOUNTAINS!

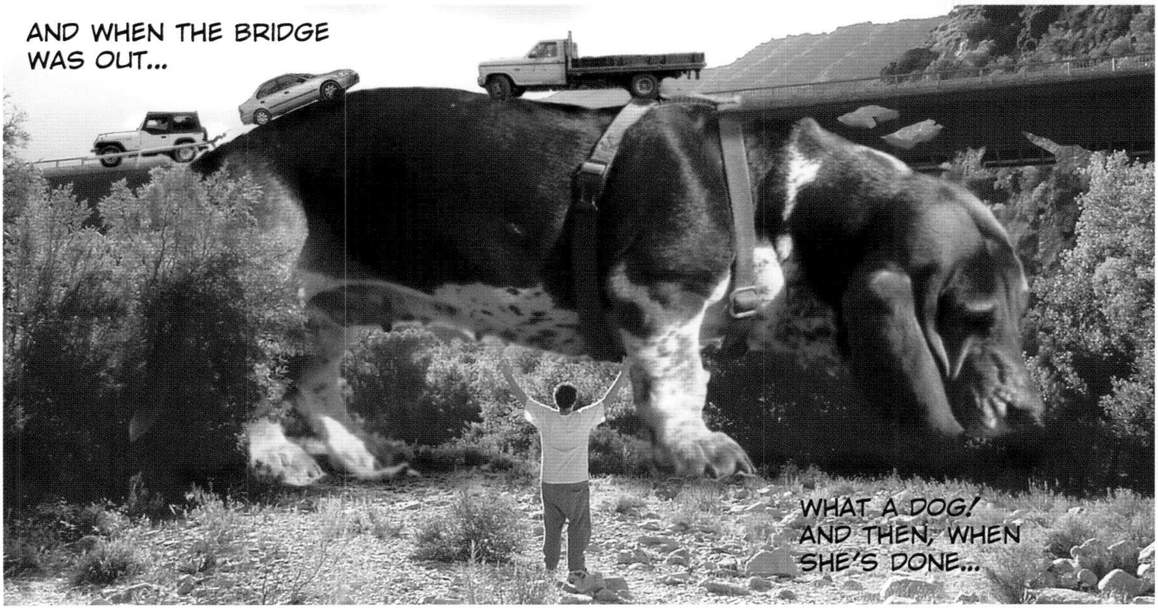
AND WHEN THE BRIDGE WAS OUT...
WHAT A DOG! AND THEN, WHEN SHE'S DONE...

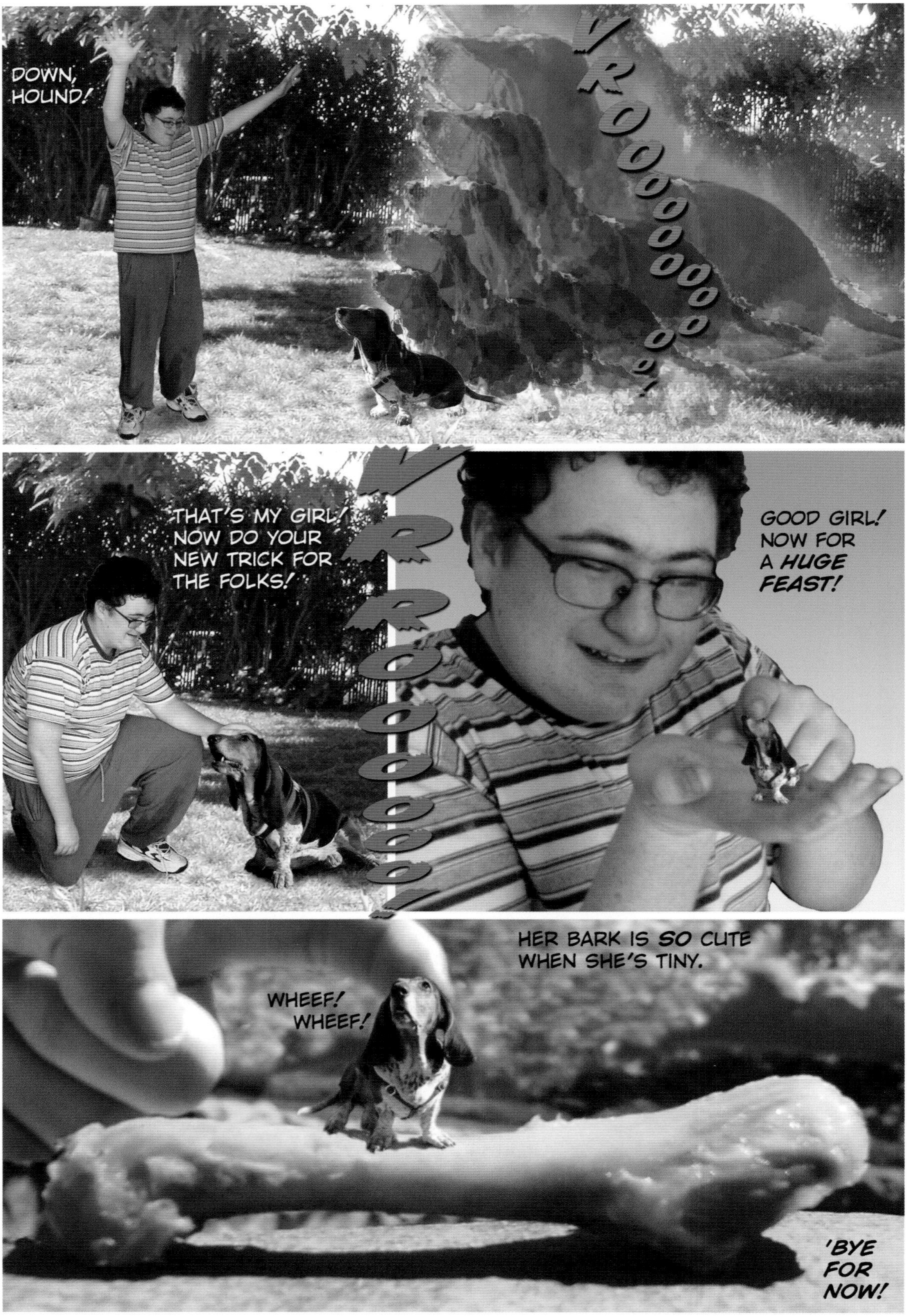
DOWN, HOUND!
VROOOOOOOOOOOO!
THAT'S MY GIRL! NOW DO YOUR NEW TRICK FOR THE FOLKS!
VRROOOOOOO!
GOOD GIRL! NOW FOR A *HUGE FEAST!*
HER BARK IS *SO* CUTE WHEN SHE'S TINY.
WHEEF! WHEEF!
*'BYE FOR NOW!*

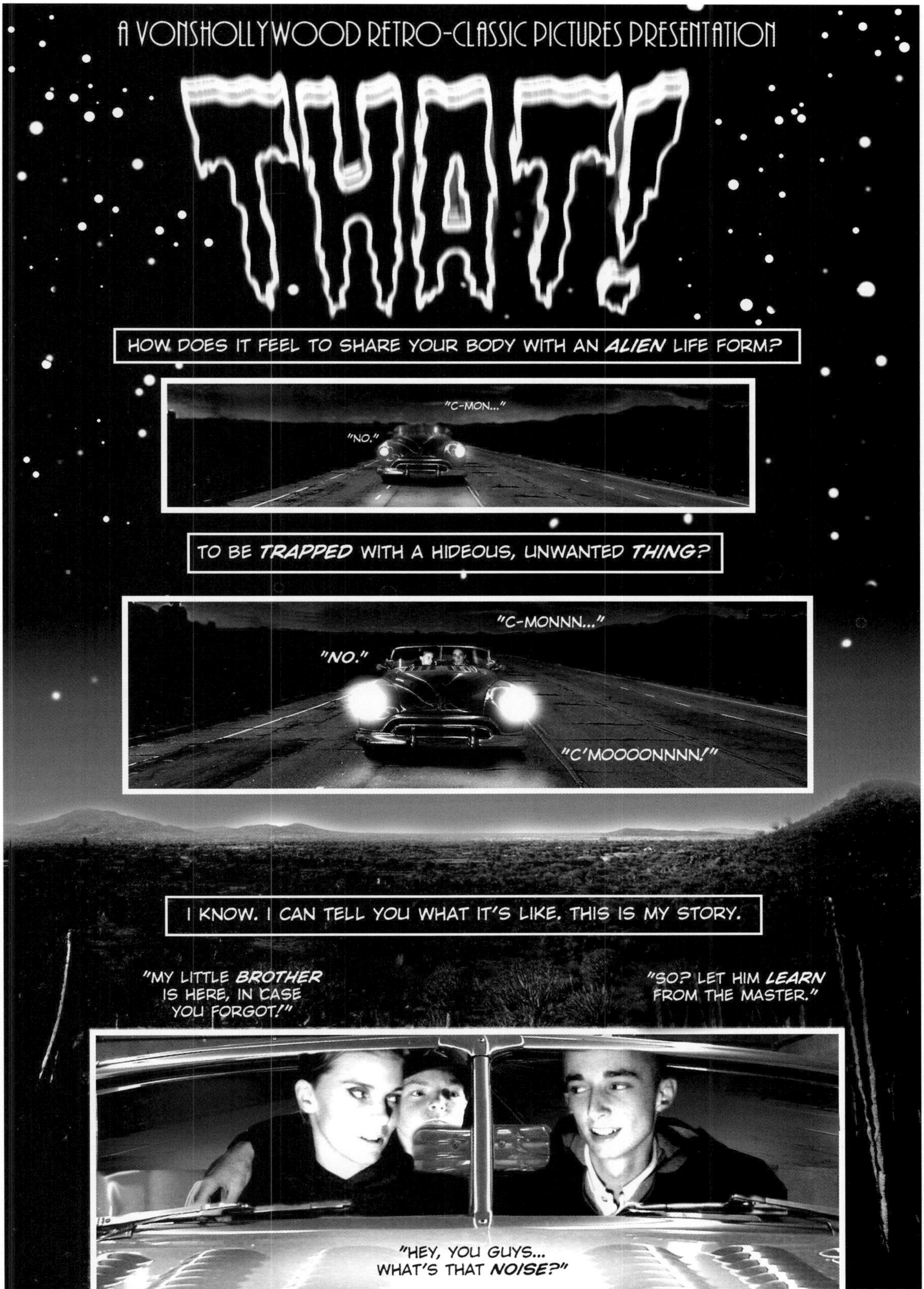
A VONSHOLLYWOOD RETRO-CLASSIC PICTURES PRESENTATION
THAT!
HOW DOES IT FEEL TO SHARE YOUR BODY WITH AN ALIEN LIFE FORM?
"C-MON..."
"NO."
TO BE TRAPPED WITH A HIDEOUS, UNWANTED THING?
"C-MONNN..."
"NO."
"C'MOOOONNNN!"
I KNOW. I CAN TELL YOU WHAT IT'S LIKE. THIS IS MY STORY.
"MY LITTLE BROTHER IS HERE, IN CASE YOU FORGOT!"
"SO? LET HIM LEARN FROM THE MASTER."
"HEY, YOU GUYS... WHAT'S THAT NOISE?"
OOEEEEOOOEEEEOEOOOOEEEEEEEEOOOOOOOOOEEEEEEEE

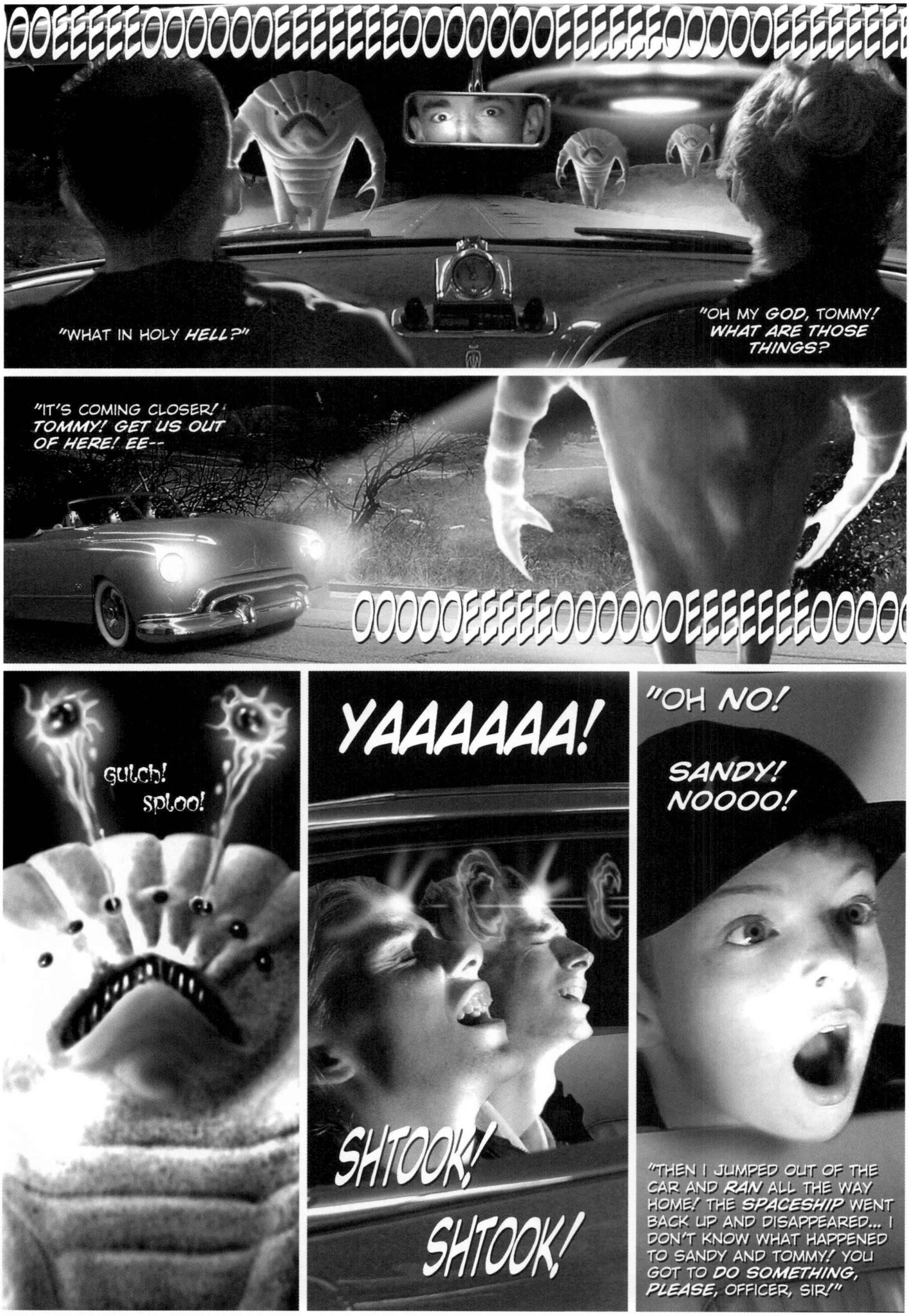
OOEEEEEEOOOOOOOEEEEEEEEOOOOOOOOEEEEEOOOOOOEEEEEEE
"WHAT IN HOLY *HELL?*"
"OH MY *GOD*, TOMMY! *WHAT ARE THOSE THINGS?*
"IT'S COMING CLOSER! *TOMMY! GET US OUT OF HERE! EE--*
OOOOOEEEEEOOOOOOOEEEEEEEOOOOO
Gulch! Sploo!
YAAAAAA!
SHTOOK! SHTOOK!
"OH *NO!*
*SANDY! NOOOO!*
"THEN I JUMPED OUT OF THE CAR AND *RAN* ALL THE WAY HOME! THE *SPACESHIP* WENT BACK UP AND DISAPPEARED... I DON'T KNOW WHAT HAPPENED TO SANDY AND TOMMY! YOU GOT TO *DO SOMETHING, PLEASE,* OFFICER, SIR!"

"TAKE IT EASY, *DAVEY!* OFFICER TIM'S ON *OUR* SIDE! YOUR MOTHER AND I ARE JUST AS WORRIED ABOUT THEM AS YOU ARE."

"BUT THERE WERE MONSTERS! REAL HONEST-TO-GOD MONSTERS!"

"MY MEN AND I WILL INVESTIGATE, DAVEY. WE'LL GET TO THE BOTTOM OF THIS, SON. DON'T WORRY."

"BUT WHAT IF THE MONSTERS TOOK THEM AWAY TO ANOTHER PLANET IN THEIR SHIP?"

"WHAT ARE YOU *TALKING* ABOUT, DAVEY?

"YOUR SISTER AND I ARE JUST *FINE.*"

"SEE?

"DON'T RUN *OFF* LIKE THAT AGAIN, KID! YOU GOT EVERYBODY *UPSET.*

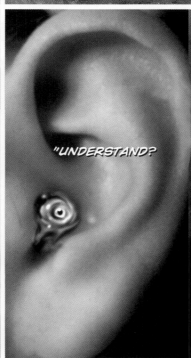

"UNDERSTAND?

"IT'S JUST YOUR *IMAGINATION!*"

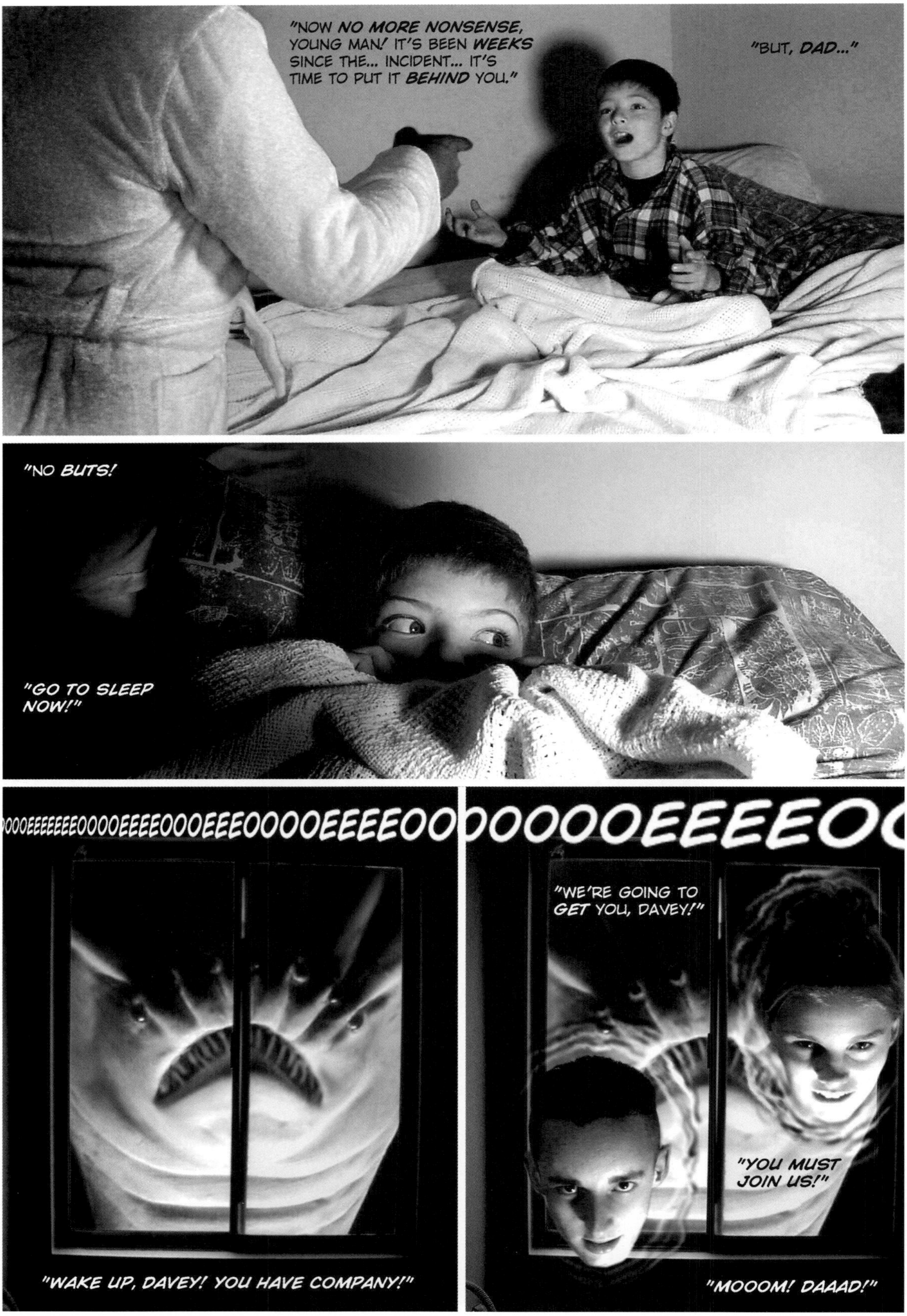
"NOW NO MORE NONSENSE, YOUNG MAN! IT'S BEEN WEEKS SINCE THE... INCIDENT... IT'S TIME TO PUT IT BEHIND YOU."
"BUT, DAD..."
"NO BUTS!
"GO TO SLEEP NOW!"
OOOEEEEEEEEOOOOEEEEOOOEEEOOOOEEEEOO
OOOOOOEEEEEEOO
"WAKE UP, DAVEY! YOU HAVE COMPANY!"
"WE'RE GOING TO GET YOU, DAVEY!"
"YOU MUST JOIN US!"
"MOOOM! DAAAD!"

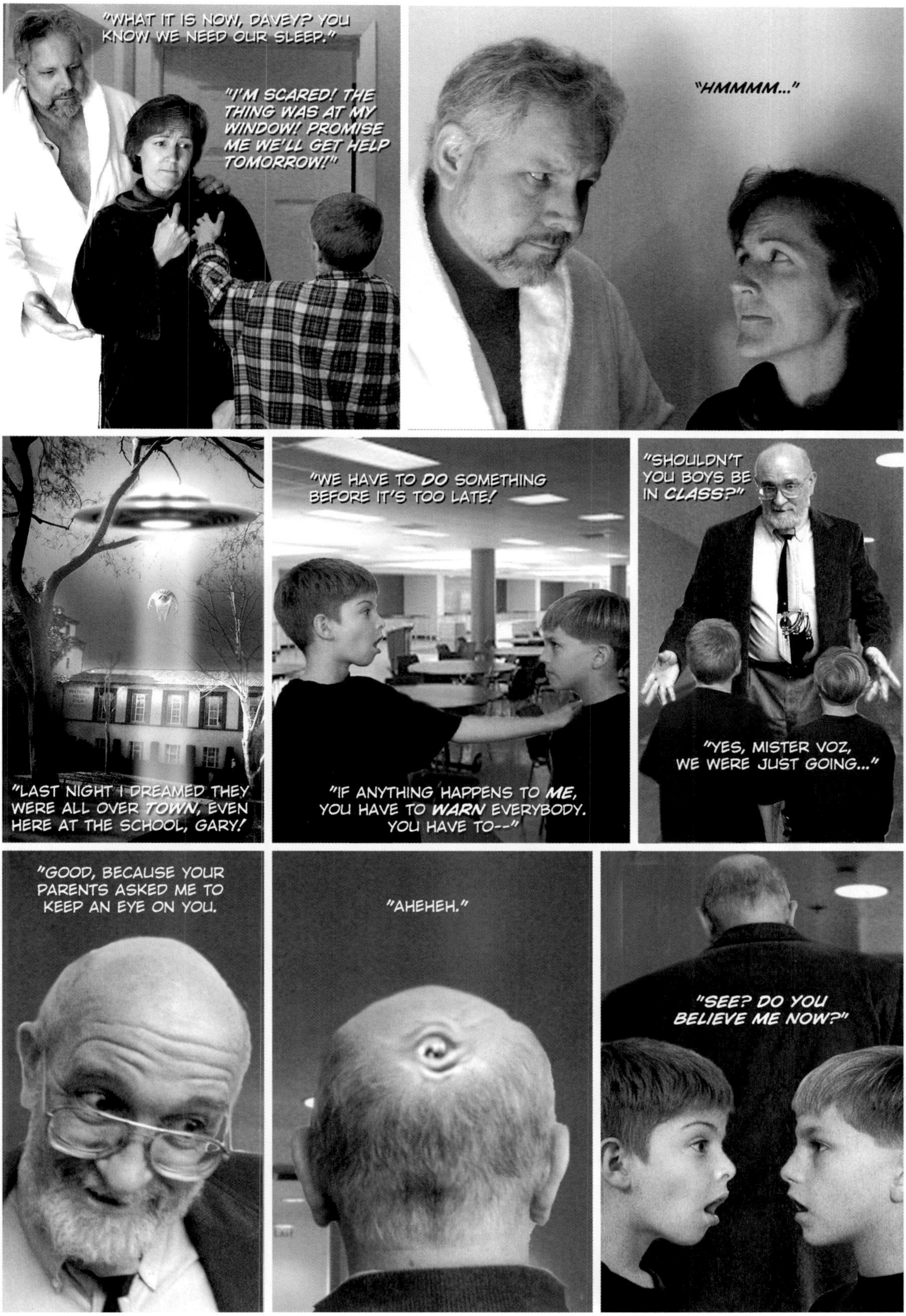
"WHAT IT IS NOW, DAVEY? YOU KNOW WE NEED OUR SLEEP."
"I'M SCARED! THE THING WAS AT MY WINDOW! PROMISE ME WE'LL GET HELP TOMORROW!"
"HMMMM..."
"LAST NIGHT I DREAMED THEY WERE ALL OVER TOWN, EVEN HERE AT THE SCHOOL, GARY!
"WE HAVE TO DO SOMETHING BEFORE IT'S TOO LATE!
"IF ANYTHING HAPPENS TO ME, YOU HAVE TO WARN EVERYBODY. YOU HAVE TO--"
"SHOULDN'T YOU BOYS BE IN CLASS?"
"YES, MISTER VOZ, WE WERE JUST GOING..."
"GOOD, BECAUSE YOUR PARENTS ASKED ME TO KEEP AN EYE ON YOU.
"AHEHEH."
"SEE? DO YOU BELIEVE ME NOW?"

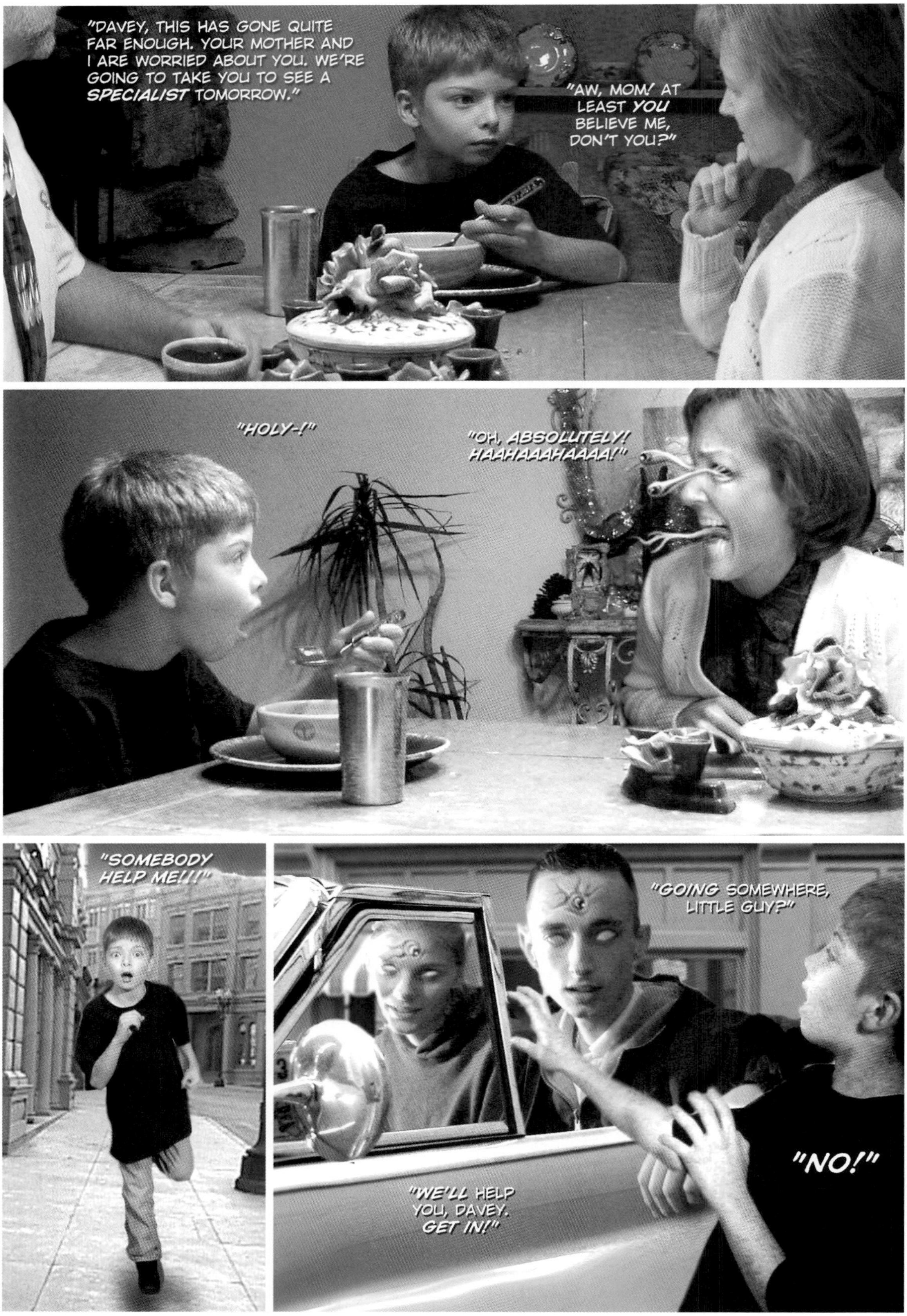
"DAVEY, THIS HAS GONE QUITE FAR ENOUGH. YOUR MOTHER AND I ARE WORRIED ABOUT YOU. WE'RE GOING TO TAKE YOU TO SEE A SPECIALIST TOMORROW."
"AW, MOM! AT LEAST YOU BELIEVE ME, DON'T YOU?"
"HOLY-!"
"OH, ABSOLUTELY! HAAHAAAHAAAA!"
"SOMEBODY HELP ME!!!"
"GOING SOMEWHERE, LITTLE GUY?"
"WE'LL HELP YOU, DAVEY. GET IN!"
"NO!"

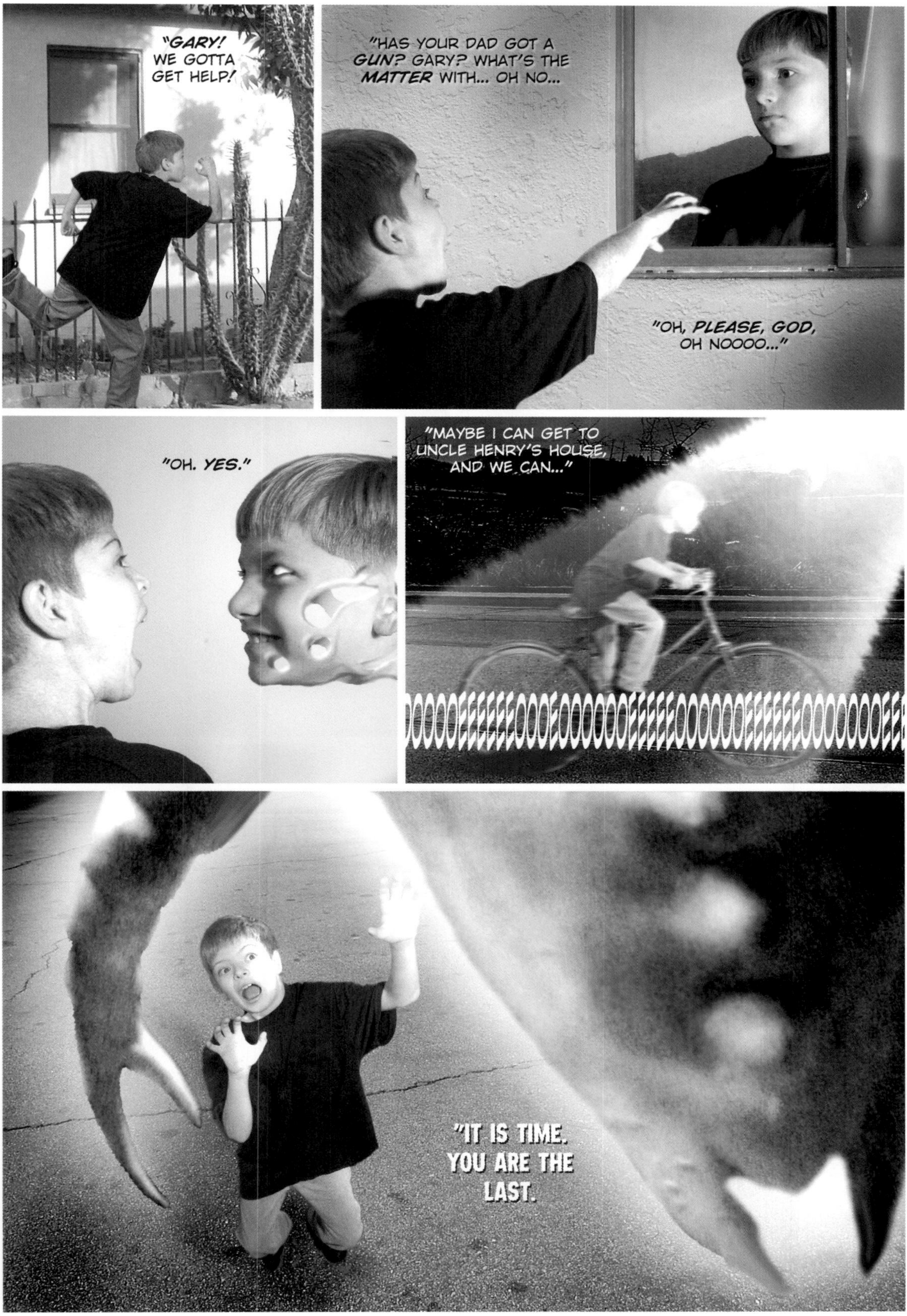
"GARY! WE GOTTA GET HELP!
"HAS YOUR DAD GOT A GUN? GARY? WHAT'S THE MATTER WITH... OH NO...
"OH, PLEASE, GOD, OH NOOOO..."
"OH. YES."
"MAYBE I CAN GET TO UNCLE HENRY'S HOUSE, AND WE CAN..."
"IT IS TIME. YOU ARE THE LAST.

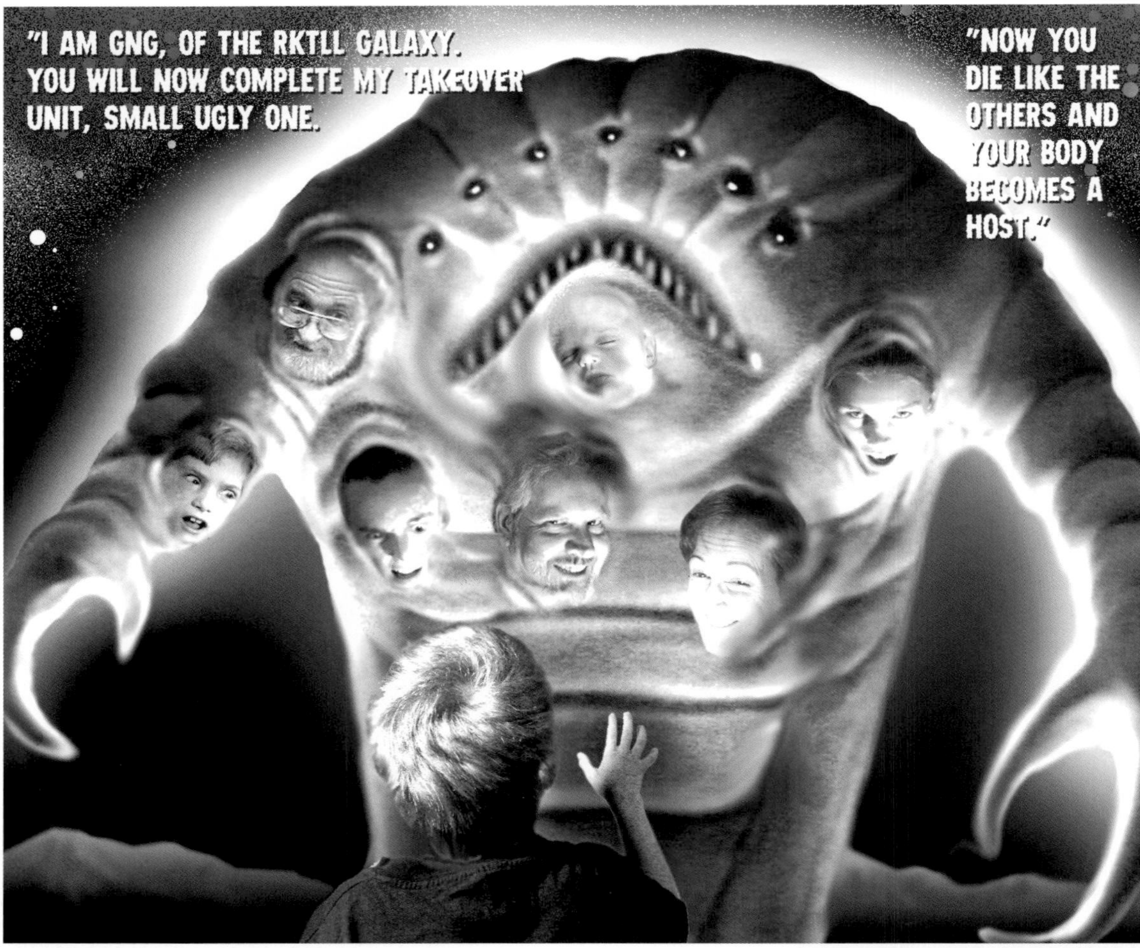
"I AM GNG, OF THE RKTLL GALAXY. YOU WILL NOW COMPLETE MY TAKEOVER UNIT, SMALL UGLY ONE.
"NOW YOU DIE LIKE THE OTHERS AND YOUR BODY BECOMES A HOST."

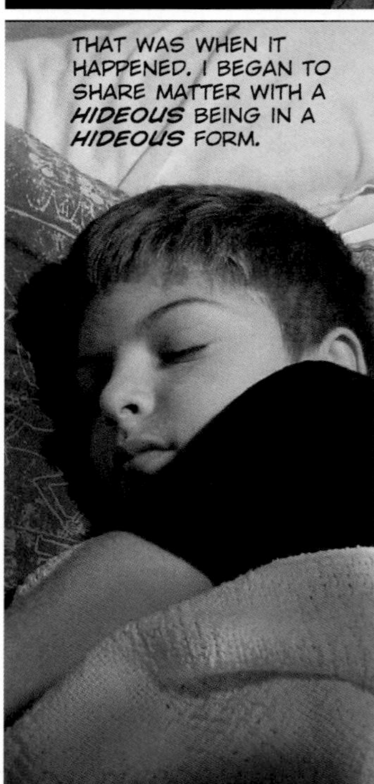
THAT WAS WHEN IT HAPPENED. I BEGAN TO SHARE MATTER WITH A *HIDEOUS* BEING IN A *HIDEOUS* FORM.

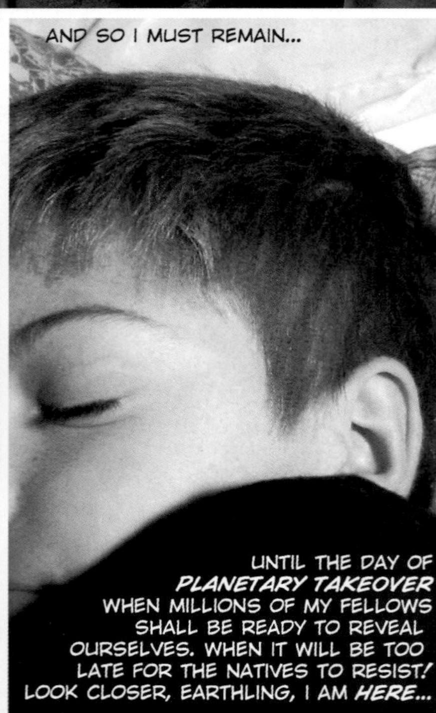
AND SO I MUST REMAIN...
UNTIL THE DAY OF *PLANETARY TAKEOVER* WHEN MILLIONS OF MY FELLOWS SHALL BE READY TO REVEAL OURSELVES. WHEN IT WILL BE TOO LATE FOR THE NATIVES TO RESIST! LOOK CLOSER, EARTHLING, I AM *HERE*...

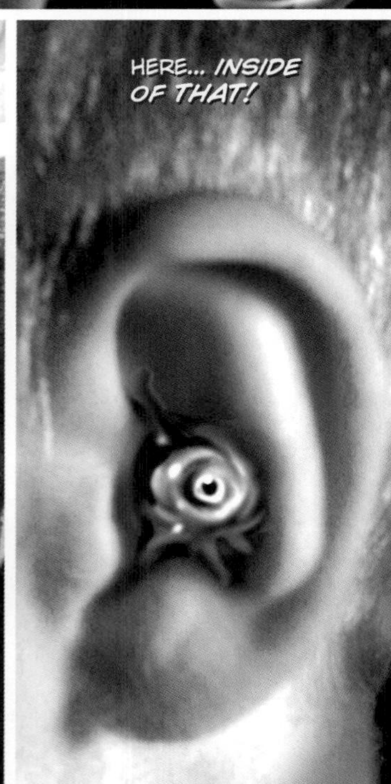
HERE... *INSIDE OF THAT!*

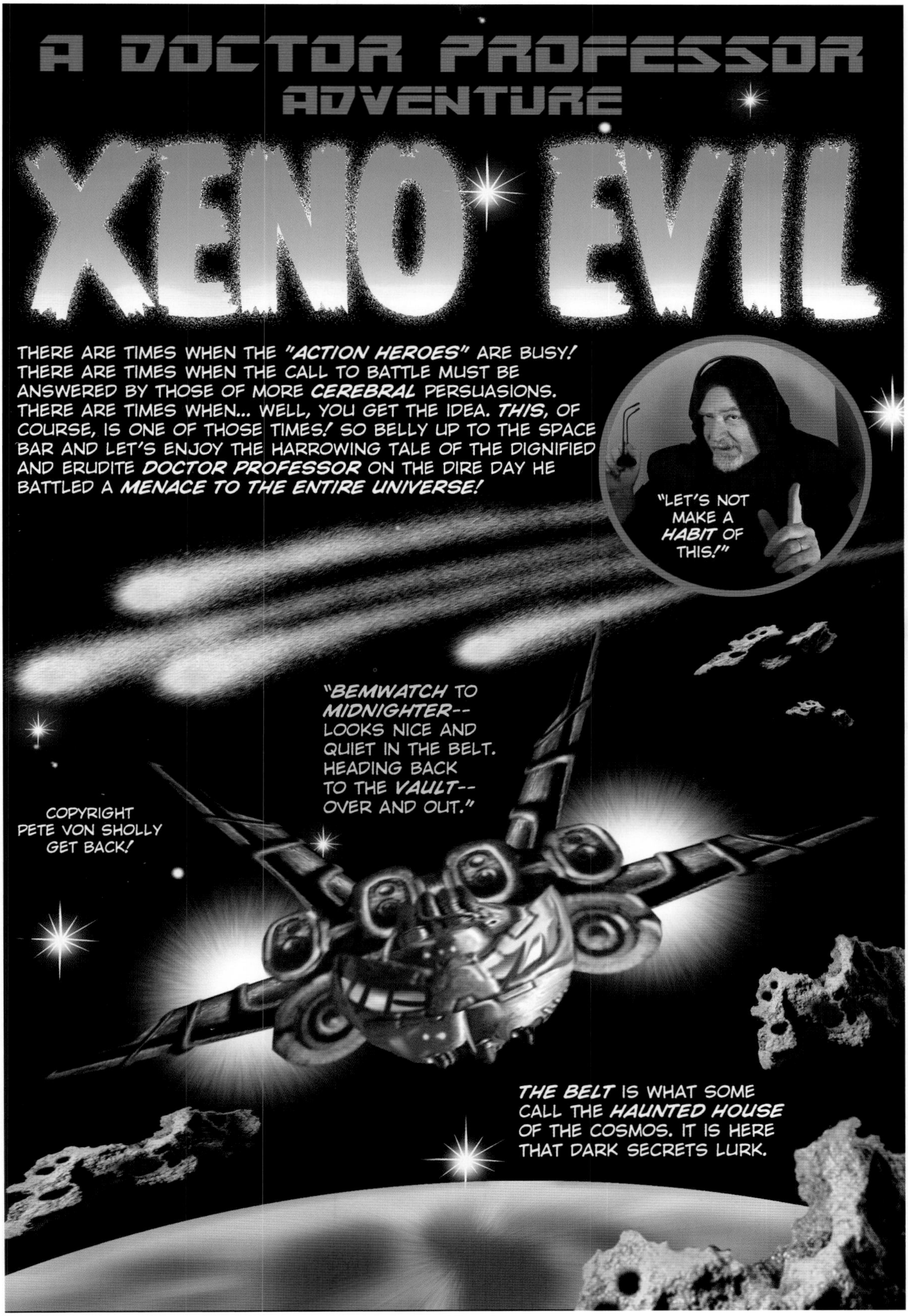
A DOCTOR PROFESSOR ADVENTURE
XENO EVIL
THERE ARE TIMES WHEN THE "ACTION HEROES" ARE BUSY! THERE ARE TIMES WHEN THE CALL TO BATTLE MUST BE ANSWERED BY THOSE OF MORE CEREBRAL PERSUASIONS. THERE ARE TIMES WHEN... WELL, YOU GET THE IDEA. THIS, OF COURSE, IS ONE OF THOSE TIMES! SO BELLY UP TO THE SPACE BAR AND LET'S ENJOY THE HARROWING TALE OF THE DIGNIFIED AND ERUDITE DOCTOR PROFESSOR ON THE DIRE DAY HE BATTLED A MENACE TO THE ENTIRE UNIVERSE!
"LET'S NOT MAKE A HABIT OF THIS!"
"BEMWATCH TO MIDNIGHTER-- LOOKS NICE AND QUIET IN THE BELT. HEADING BACK TO THE VAULT-- OVER AND OUT."
COPYRIGHT PETE VON SHOLLY GET BACK!
THE BELT IS WHAT SOME CALL THE HAUNTED HOUSE OF THE COSMOS. IT IS HERE THAT DARK SECRETS LURK.

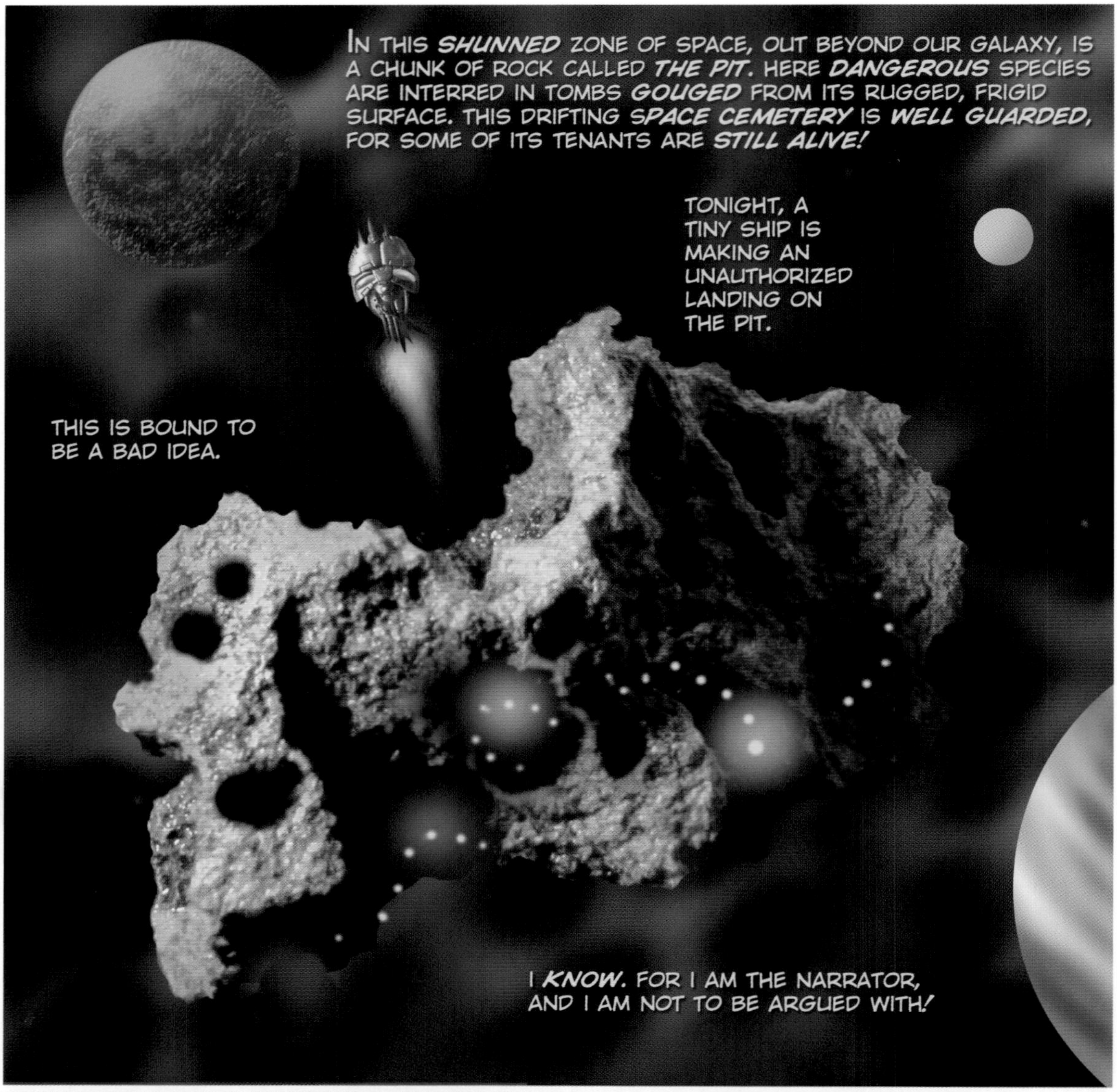

IN THIS SHUNNED ZONE OF SPACE, OUT BEYOND OUR GALAXY, IS A CHUNK OF ROCK CALLED THE PIT. HERE DANGEROUS SPECIES ARE INTERRED IN TOMBS GOUGED FROM ITS RUGGED, FRIGID SURFACE. THIS DRIFTING SPACE CEMETERY IS WELL GUARDED, FOR SOME OF ITS TENANTS ARE STILL ALIVE!
TONIGHT, A TINY SHIP IS MAKING AN UNAUTHORIZED LANDING ON THE PIT.
THIS IS BOUND TO BE A BAD IDEA.
I KNOW. FOR I AM THE NARRATOR, AND I AM NOT TO BE ARGUED WITH!


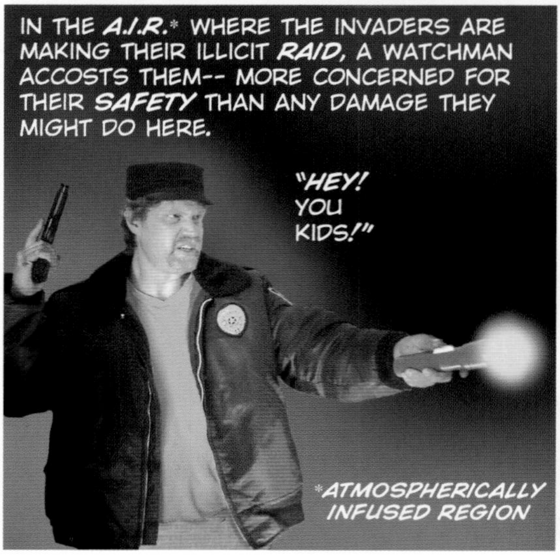

IN THE A.I.R.* WHERE THE INVADERS ARE MAKING THEIR ILLICIT RAID, A WATCHMAN ACCOSTS THEM-- MORE CONCERNED FOR THEIR SAFETY THAN ANY DAMAGE THEY MIGHT DO HERE.
"HEY! YOU KIDS!"
*ATMOSPHERICALLY INFUSED REGION


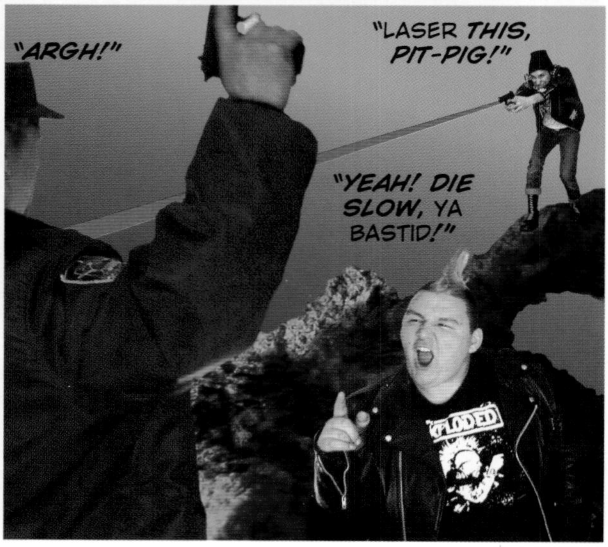

"ARGH!"
"LASER THIS, PIT-PIG!"
"YEAH! DIE SLOW, YA BASTID!"

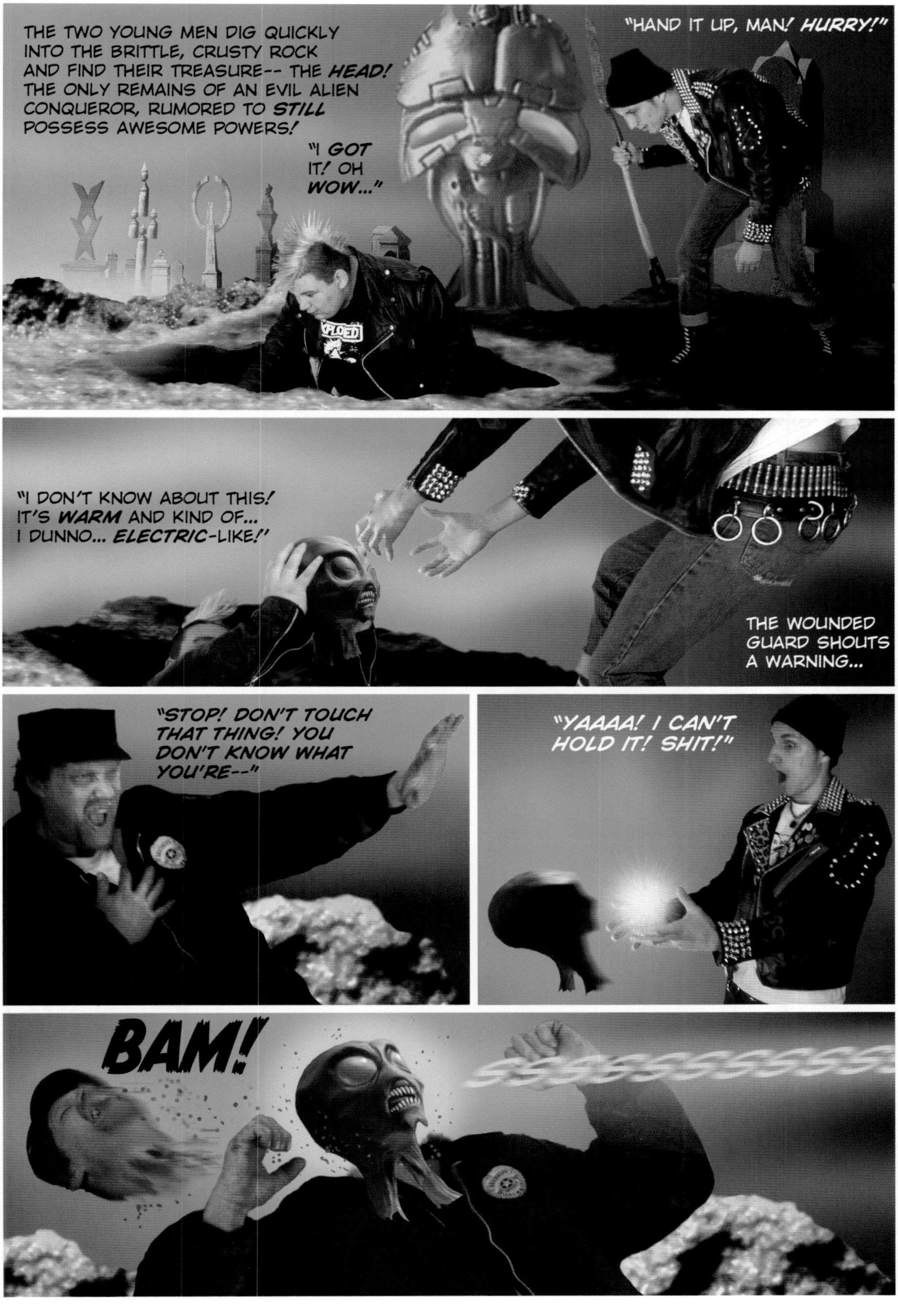
THE TWO YOUNG MEN DIG QUICKLY INTO THE BRITTLE, CRUSTY ROCK AND FIND THEIR TREASURE-- THE *HEAD!* THE ONLY REMAINS OF AN EVIL ALIEN CONQUEROR, RUMORED TO *STILL* POSSESS AWESOME POWERS!
"HAND IT UP, MAN! *HURRY!*"
"I *GOT* IT! OH *WOW*..."
"I DON'T KNOW ABOUT THIS! IT'S *WARM* AND KIND OF... I DUNNO... *ELECTRIC*-LIKE!"
THE WOUNDED GUARD SHOUTS A WARNING...
"STOP! DON'T TOUCH THAT THING! YOU DON'T KNOW WHAT YOU'RE--"
"YAAAA! I CAN'T HOLD IT! SHIT!"
BAM!

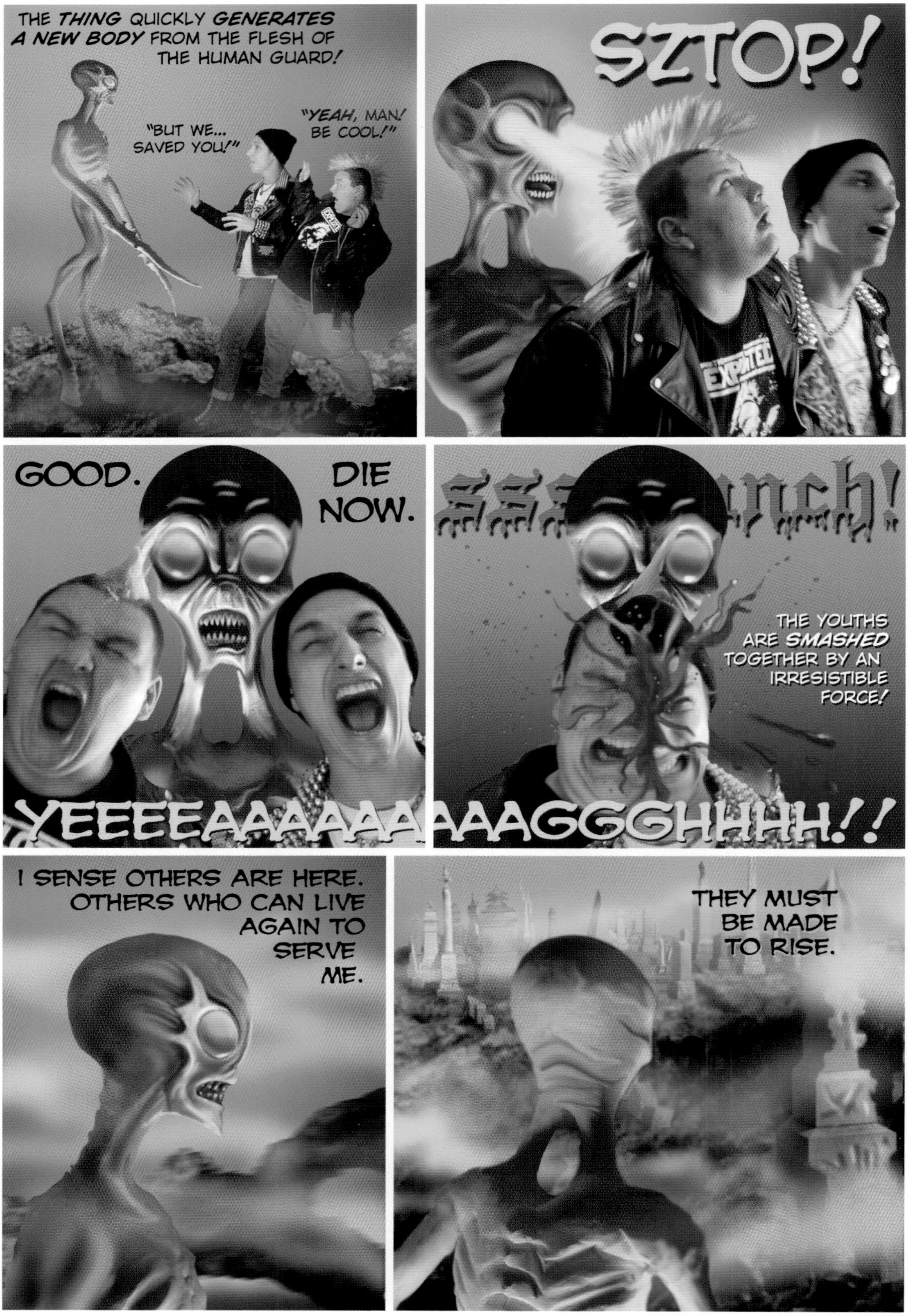
THE THING QUICKLY GENERATES A NEW BODY FROM THE FLESH OF THE HUMAN GUARD!
"BUT WE... SAVED YOU!"
"YEAH, MAN! BE COOL!"
SZTOP!
GOOD.
DIE NOW.
THE YOUTHS ARE SMASHED TOGETHER BY AN IRRESISTIBLE FORCE!
YEEEEAAAAAAAAAGGGHHHH!!
I SENSE OTHERS ARE HERE. OTHERS WHO CAN LIVE AGAIN TO SERVE ME.
THEY MUST BE MADE TO RISE.

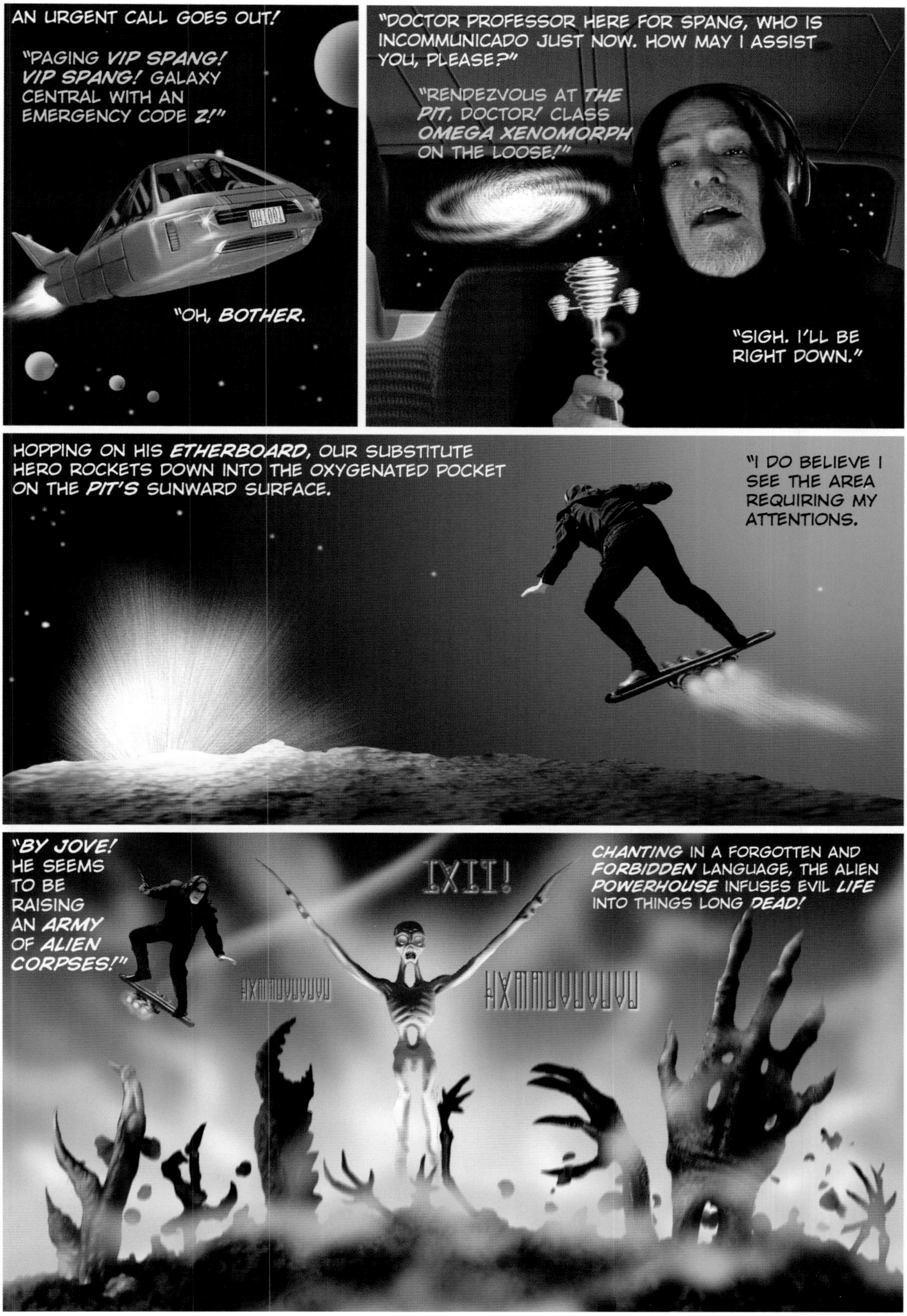
AN URGENT CALL GOES OUT!
"PAGING VIP SPANG! VIP SPANG! GALAXY CENTRAL WITH AN EMERGENCY CODE Z!"
HAL001
"OH, BOTHER.
"DOCTOR PROFESSOR HERE FOR SPANG, WHO IS INCOMMUNICADO JUST NOW. HOW MAY I ASSIST YOU, PLEASE?"
"RENDEZVOUS AT THE PIT, DOCTOR! CLASS OMEGA XENOMORPH ON THE LOOSE!"
"SIGH. I'LL BE RIGHT DOWN."
HOPPING ON HIS ETHERBOARD, OUR SUBSTITUTE HERO ROCKETS DOWN INTO THE OXYGENATED POCKET ON THE PIT'S SUNWARD SURFACE.
"I DO BELIEVE I SEE THE AREA REQUIRING MY ATTENTIONS.
"BY JOVE! HE SEEMS TO BE RAISING AN ARMY OF ALIEN CORPSES!"
IXIT!
CHANTING IN A FORGOTTEN AND FORBIDDEN LANGUAGE, THE ALIEN POWERHOUSE INFUSES EVIL LIFE INTO THINGS LONG DEAD!

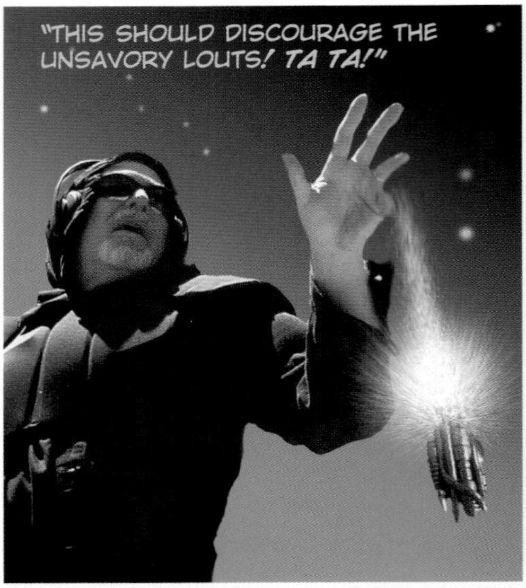
"THIS SHOULD DISCOURAGE THE UNSAVORY LOUTS! TA TA!"

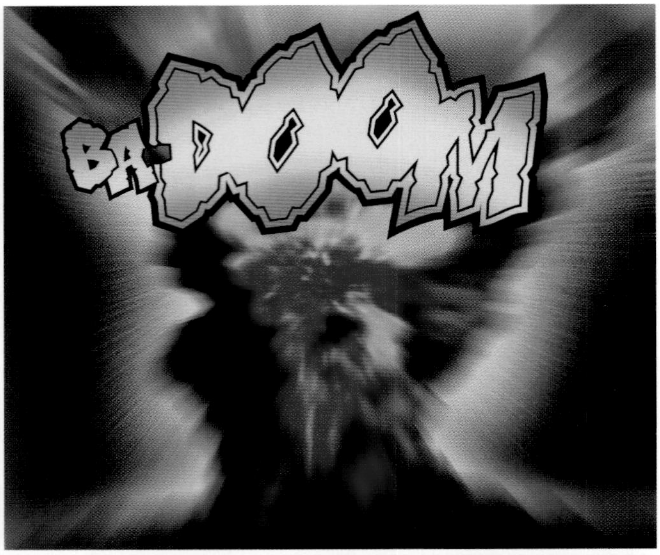
BA-DOOM

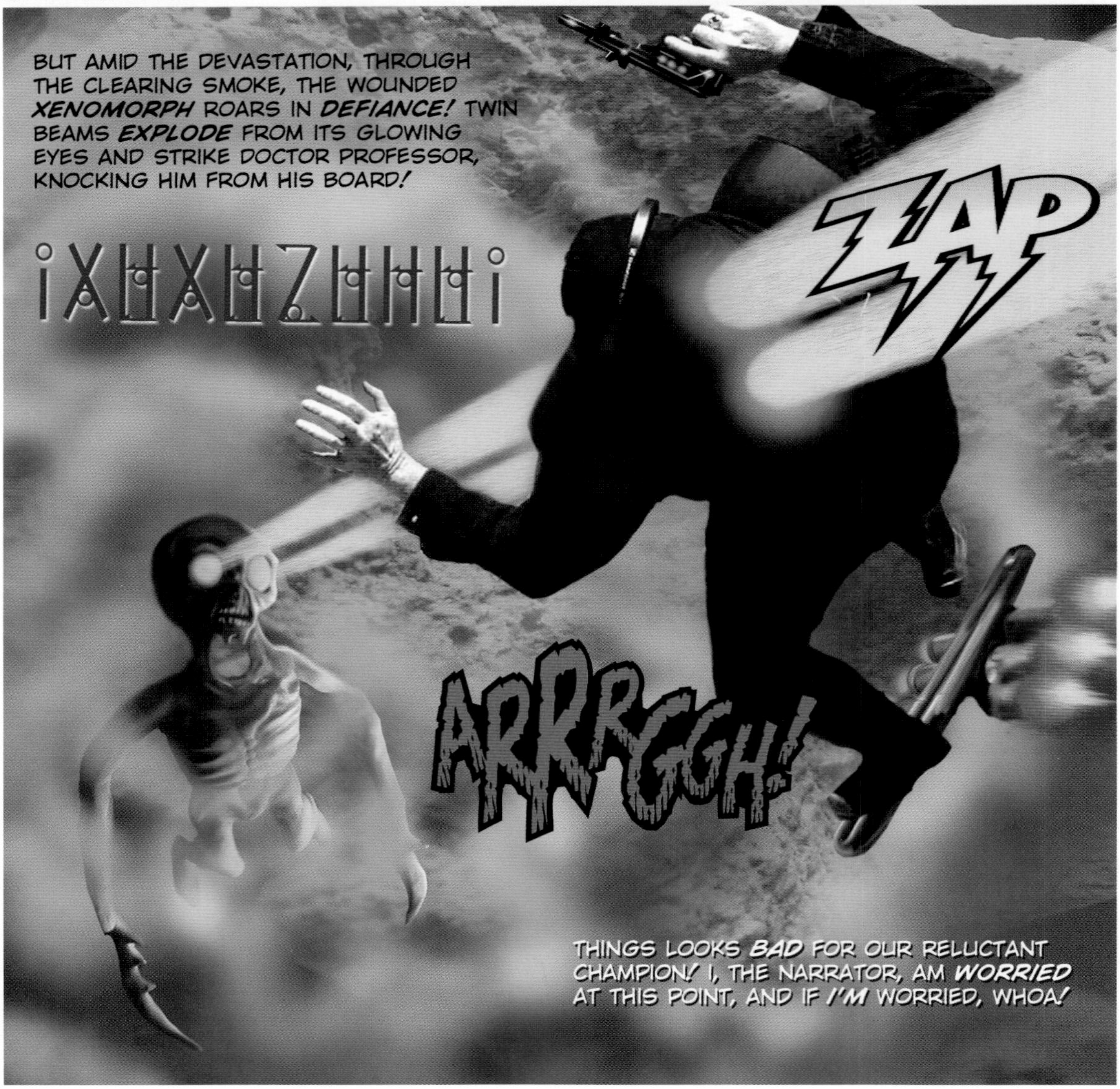
BUT AMID THE DEVASTATION, THROUGH THE CLEARING SMOKE, THE WOUNDED XENOMORPH ROARS IN DEFIANCE! TWIN BEAMS EXPLODE FROM ITS GLOWING EYES AND STRIKE DOCTOR PROFESSOR, KNOCKING HIM FROM HIS BOARD!
ZAP
ARRRGGH!
THINGS LOOKS BAD FOR OUR RELUCTANT CHAMPION! I, THE NARRATOR, AM WORRIED AT THIS POINT, AND IF I'M WORRIED, WHOA!

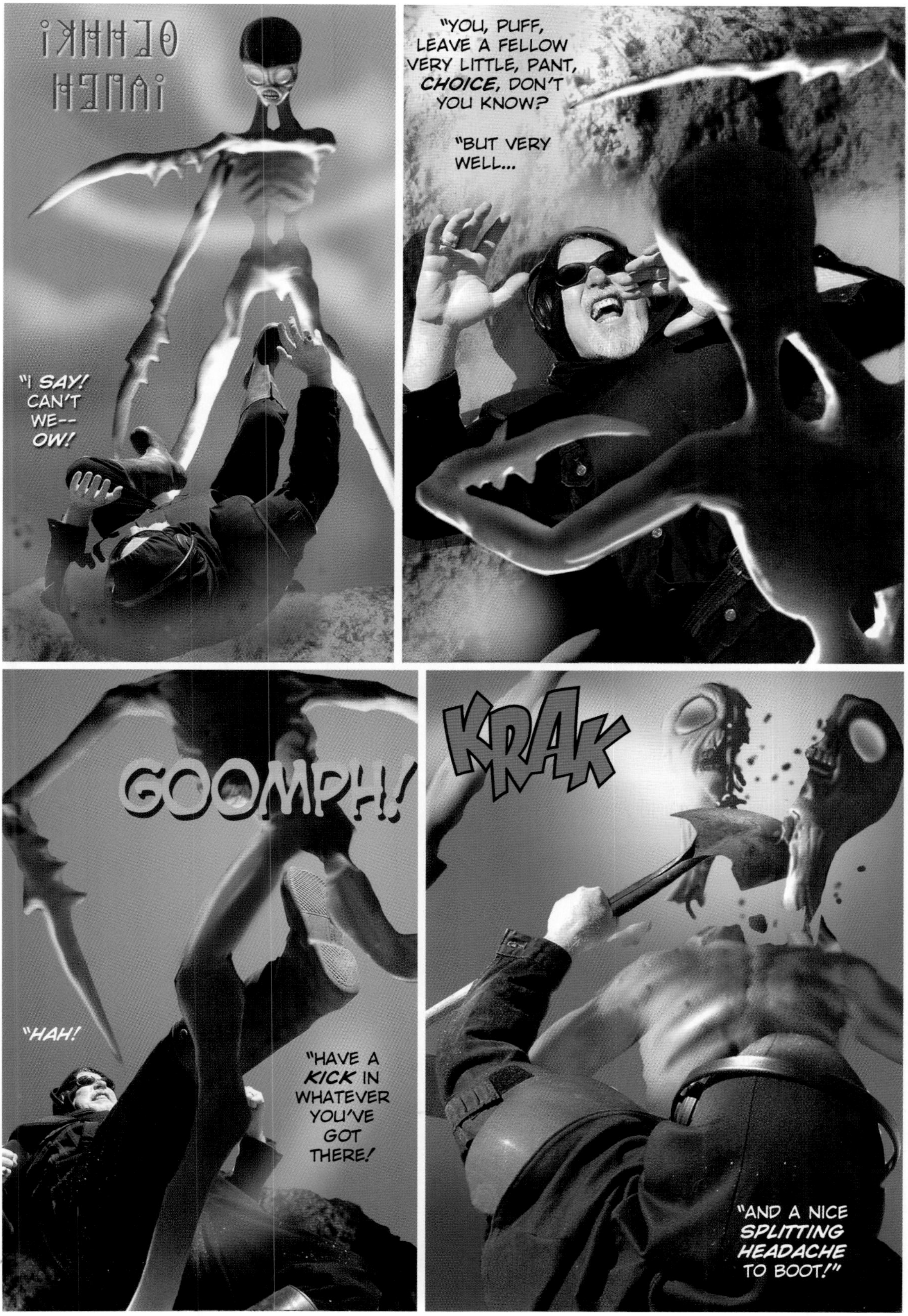
"I SAY! CAN'T WE-- OW!
"YOU, PUFF, LEAVE A FELLOW VERY LITTLE, PANT, CHOICE, DON'T YOU KNOW?
"BUT VERY WELL...
GOOMPH!
"HAH!
"HAVE A KICK IN WHATEVER YOU'VE GOT THERE!
KRAK
"AND A NICE SPLITTING HEADACHE TO BOOT!"

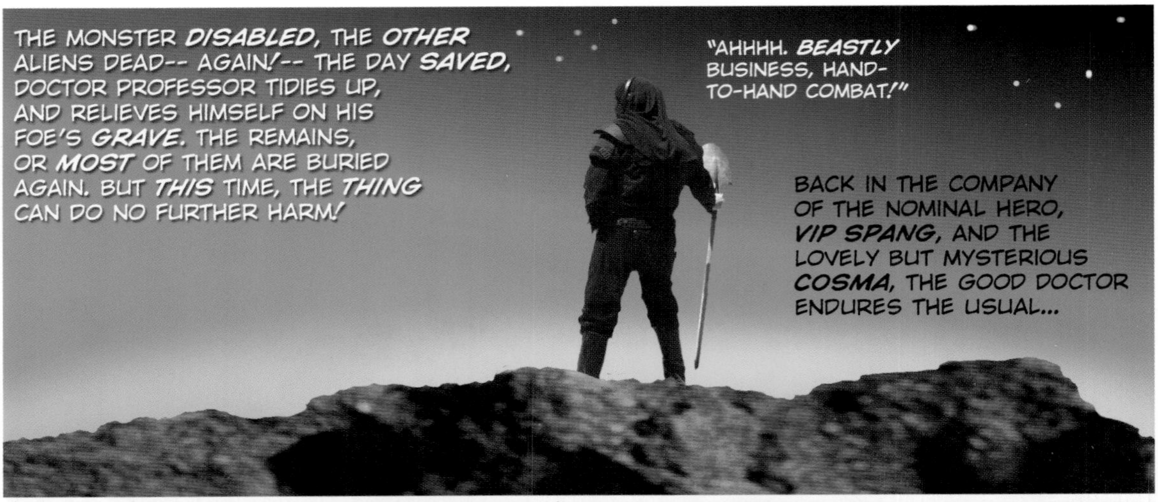
THE MONSTER DISABLED, THE OTHER ALIENS DEAD-- AGAIN!-- THE DAY SAVED, DOCTOR PROFESSOR TIDIES UP, AND RELIEVES HIMSELF ON HIS FOE'S GRAVE. THE REMAINS, OR MOST OF THEM ARE BURIED AGAIN. BUT THIS TIME, THE THING CAN DO NO FURTHER HARM!
"AHHHH. BEASTLY BUSINESS, HAND-TO-HAND COMBAT!"
BACK IN THE COMPANY OF THE NOMINAL HERO, VIP SPANG, AND THE LOVELY BUT MYSTERIOUS COSMA, THE GOOD DOCTOR ENDURES THE USUAL...

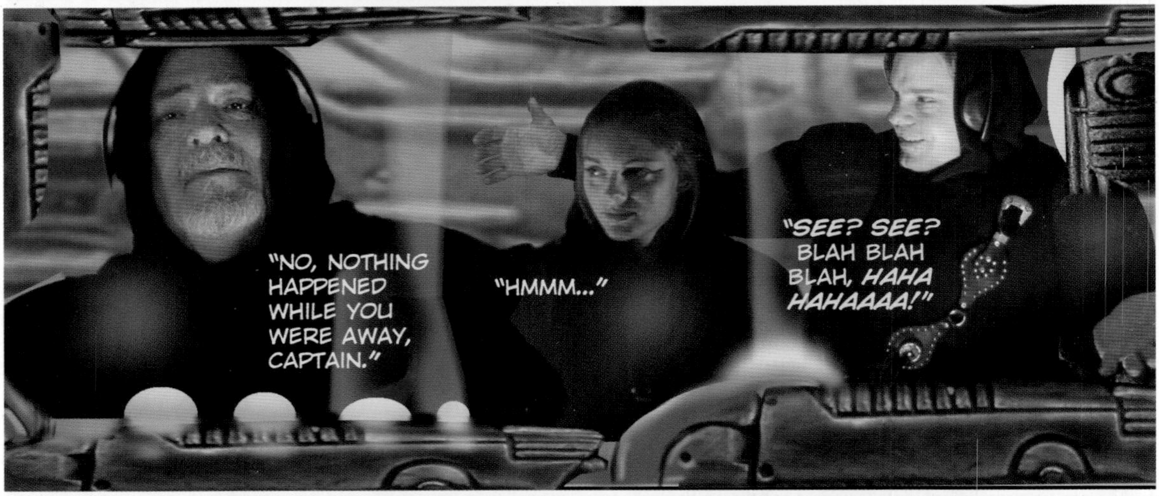
"SEE? SEE? BLAH BLAH BLAH, HAHA HAHAAAA!"
"HMMM..."
"NO, NOTHING HAPPENED WHILE YOU WERE AWAY, CAPTAIN."

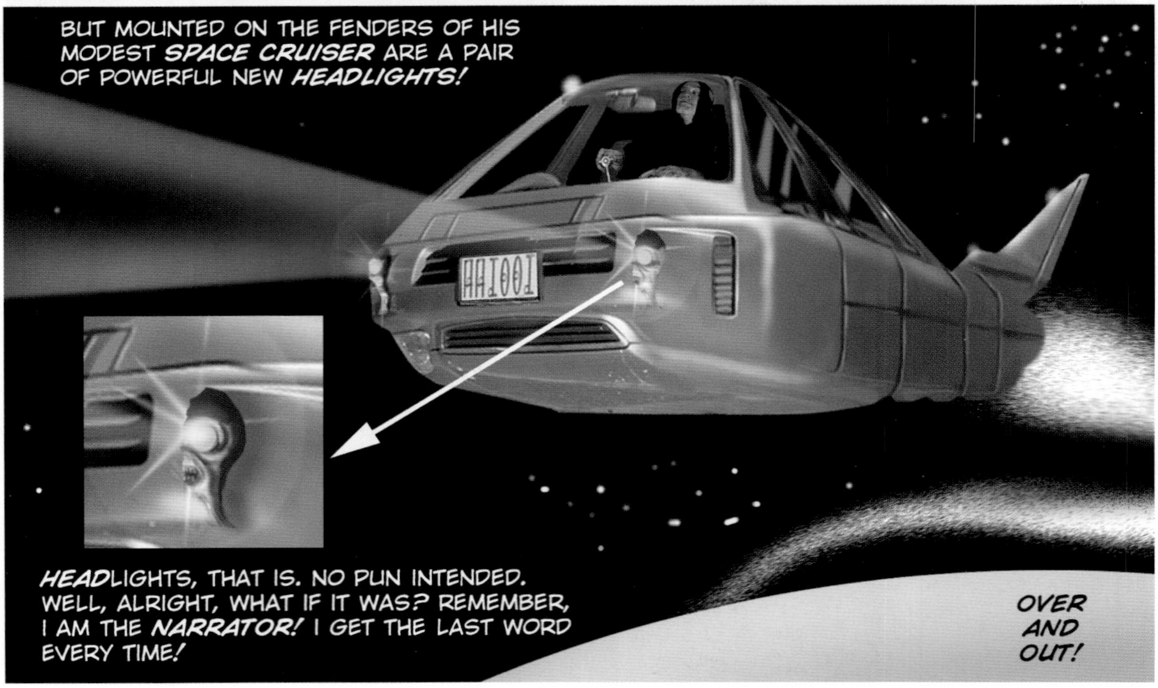
BUT MOUNTED ON THE FENDERS OF HIS MODEST SPACE CRUISER ARE A PAIR OF POWERFUL NEW HEADLIGHTS!
HEADLIGHTS, THAT IS. NO PUN INTENDED. WELL, ALRIGHT, WHAT IF IT WAS? REMEMBER, I AM THE NARRATOR! I GET THE LAST WORD EVERY TIME!
OVER AND OUT!